The Shock of the News

The Shock of the News

Media Coverage and the Making of 9/11

Brian A. Monahan

NEW YORK UNIVERSITY PRESS

New York and London

NEW YORK UNIVERSITY PRESS
New York and London
www.nyupress.org

Library of Congress Cataloging-in-Publication Data

Monahan, Brian A.
The shock of the news : media coverage and the making of 9/11 /
Brian A. Monahan.
p. cm.
Includes bibliographical references and index.
ISBN-13: 978-0-8147-9554-5 (cl : alk. paper)
ISBN-10: 0-8147-9554-4 (cl : alk. paper)
ISBN-13: 978-0-8147-9555-2 (pb : alk. paper)
ISBN-10: 0-8147-9555-2 (pb : alk. paper)
1. September 11 Terrorist Attacks, 2001—Press coverage. 2. September 11
Terrorist Attacks, 2001, in mass media. 3. Terrorism—Press coverage—
United States. 4. Terrorism in mass media—United States. I. Title.
HV6432.7.M66   2010
973.931—dc22   2009052956

New York University Press books are printed on acid-free paper,
and their binding materials are chosen for strength and durability.
We strive to use environmentally responsible suppliers and materials
to the greatest extent possible in publishing our books.

Manufactured in the United States of America

c 10 9 8 7 6 5 4 3 2 1
p 10 9 8 7 6 5 4 3 2 1

To the memories of my mother, Maureen Monahan,
and Kay and Al Ticehurst.

Contents

Acknowledgments

In the years spent researching and writing this book, I was fortunate to be able to draw on the support and encouragement of many colleagues, family members, and friends. Joel Best deserves special mention for seeing promise in this project when it was little more than an unformed collection of potentially interesting ideas and for providing invaluable feedback as the chapters began to take shape. Although the words on these pages are mine alone, I am certain that this book owes part of its existence to his valued contributions as a mentor and friend.

I am indebted to other academic colleagues who graciously made themselves available to discuss this research with me or read through drafts of the book's chapters along the way. Among them are Benigno Aguirre, Nancy Berns, Anne Bowler, David Bromley, Hank Fischer, Carol Gregory, Andrew Hochstetler, Joanne Nigg, Anastasia Prokos, David Schweingruber, Robert Stallings, Chris Steinbrecher, and Joe Trainor. My thanks also to Victor Argothy, Lauren Barsky, Rory Connell, Russell Dynes, Dana Hysock, Henry Quarantelli, Gabriel Santos, Kathleen Tierney, Manuel Torres, Tricia Wachtendorf, and the rest of the faculty and staff at the Disaster Research Center (DRC). My tenure at the center provided me with lasting friendships, taught me important lessons about the practice and politics of a life of research, and informed my initial ideas for this work. In fact, my inclusion as a member of the DRC's field research team dispatched to New York City following the September 11 attacks provided the serendipitous spark for this project and served as a reservoir of inspiration that helped me sustain my focus and passion for this research throughout the preparation of this book.

It has been a pleasure to work with New York University Press on this project. I particularly want to thank my editor, Ilene Kalish, for her guidance and continued patience, even as the manuscript remained a "work in progress" for longer than expected. This book also benefited from the insightful comments offered by the anonymous reviewers and the administrative assistance provided by Aiden Amos and the rest of the NYU Press staff.

I am also tremendously appreciative of the many friends and family members who routinely offered words of encouragement or much-needed diversions as they saw fit. Even though your good-natured probes of "how is the book going?" were often met with a terse "fine," you should know that your persistent demonstrations of interest in me and my work was a hidden source of inspiration over the years. I want to note in particular the support of my parents, Paul and Maureen Monahan, my sister, Laurie Reading-Monahan, and a collection of others who mean so much to me, including Caitlin Farrell, Megan Farrell, Melinda Fortunato, Tom Fortunato, Scott Heleniak, David Moore, Gail Moore, and Anthony Petone.

I am eternally grateful to my children, Ashlyn and Colin, for always forcing me to keep the truly important things in focus and for making sure that each day of hard work was balanced by just the right amount of hugs and kisses, laughter, and joy. Finally, my deepest appreciation is reserved for Lauren, my wife, whose keen ability to know whether I needed kindness, inspiration, critical feedback, or time alone was invaluable to me as I worked on this manuscript. I am most fortunate to have such a wonderful partner in this life.

Preface

The American news industry has undergone considerable changes in recent decades. New methods of communication have arrived on the scene, most notably in the form of twenty-four-hour television news networks and the Internet, which offer real-time access to a staggering amount of information and, in the case of the Internet, a vast and varied blogosphere and social-networking capabilities. At the same time, a number of more traditional news media, such as newspapers and magazines, face an increasing array of challenges to their continued viability. Within this "new" news marketplace, we have also seen changes in the norms of news work, especially which events, issues, and individuals are defined as "newsworthy," the manner in which selected information and images are organized for presentation to audiences, and the ways that audience members use, or consume, news. These consequential shifts offer exciting opportunities for creating and distributing information, while also challenging our ability to accurately understand the world in which we live.

This is a book about the role of the news media in social life. Specifically, I am interested in how the productions of the mainstream news media influence our perceptions of social reality. A long history of scholarship in sociology, media studies, and other academic disciplines has taught us that the news we consume influences the way we process events, assess issues, and assign meaning to our personal experiences. While there are a number of ways to judge the connection between the news media and the processes through which we make and attribute meaning, my focus is on how news is put together and communicated to news consumers. A wealth of research suggests that the manner in which news is packaged and presented is a key determinant of what people remember from their encounters with news content and how they use this information. The following chapters explore a disturbing trend in America's mainstream news media, in which media resources and audience attention are becoming more and more oriented toward news that is fashioned into long-running "serialized dramas" that bear greater resemblance to popular fiction than to journalism. I use the term *public drama* to refer to this form of news.

Public drama represents a particular style of news in which highly dramatic and emotional information and images that can be fused into a compelling story are regarded as the most newsworthy and, thus, most valuable. The list of recent mediated public dramas is much too long to be considered in full here, but I will mention a number of high-profile examples: O. J. Simpson, JonBenet Ramsey, Elián Gonzáles, Andrea Yates, Chandra Levy, Terri Schiavo, Elizabeth Smart, Laci Peterson (or Scott Peterson), Hurricane Katrina, Natalee Holloway, and Caylee Anthony. I suspect that at the mention of only a single name, most readers will readily recall these tales, underscoring the prominence of these productions in the mainstream news cycles and, by extension, the public's consciousness.

This book discusses the many factors behind the emergence and continued growth of public drama as a vehicle for packaging and presenting news. It also examines the consequences stemming from the increasing prevalence of story-driven, entertainment-oriented news content. Of the variety of public dramas that I could analyze to exemplify the features of this form of news or to articulate its effects on how we understand the world around us, I have elected to focus on a single case study of public drama: the media coverage of the September 11, 2001, terrorist attacks.

My selection of September 11 was motivated by both practical considerations and personal experiences. From a practical standpoint, the media coverage of September 11 provides an excellent window into the public drama form. The media devoted more resources to covering the attacks and their aftermath than to any other event in the media age, and audiences were riveted to that coverage for weeks and, in many instances, even months after the attacks. This attention created a context in which the dominant media narratives had an unusual influence on shaping the meanings attached to these events and the cultural and political responses to them. Ultimately, I found that the media told the story of September 11, particularly what was happening at New York City's "Ground Zero," as a public drama. Even though this was a major moment in U.S. history destined to have enormous cultural and political consequences, and therefore arguably demanding more measured and balanced coverage and discourse, the dominant narrative through which these events were communicated to the public was transformed into a dramatic tale that more closely mirrored popular fiction than detailed journalistic inquiry. September 11 was fashioned as an emotional story that, like so many popular television dramas, was stocked with stirring accounts, heartfelt moments, captivating images, harrowing encounters, and compelling characters. In this book, I examine how and why this happened and discuss its implications for how we have come to understand September 11 and act in its name in the years since that day.

In addition to the various practical considerations that guided my selection of September 11 as a public drama case study, the seeds for this book also are rooted in my personal experiences following the September 11 attacks. At the time of the attacks, I was a member of the research staff at the University of Delaware's Disaster Research Center. On Thursday, September 13, we were dispatched to New York City to generally observe the official and collective responses, collect "perishable" data, develop potential research questions that could later be explored, and, if possible, establish connections with local officials in the hopes of incorporating their insights in future research on the citywide emergency response.

The research team split into pairs and walked the streets of Manhattan. My partner and I mostly just observed the various scenes we encountered, sometimes quickly jotting down notes or speaking into the small, handheld recorder that each of us carried. Occasionally, we spoke with a volunteer, shop owner, or citizen on the street. But mostly we observed. We walked block after block for the remainder of that day and well into the evening. On Friday, September 14, we did the same thing, walking around Manhattan for about twelve hours during the day. Eventually we grew tired and decided to return to the hotel, shower, and grab a late dinner before debriefing with the rest of the team and making plans for the following day. It was shortly after 8:00 p.m. when we arrived at the block where our hotel was located. This is when I made the first of two observations that eventually became part of the foundation of this book.

Before we could walk into the lobby of our hotel, we came upon a scene that I can still vividly recall to this day. Adjacent to our hotel was a firehouse (the two were separated by a single cross street), in front of which a remarkable display of collective behavior was under way. People were placing items in front of the firehouse: candles; signs expressing grief and sympathy to the firefighters for the loss of their "brothers" or praise for their efforts; handwritten notes and pictures from children, many drawn in crayon; photographs; teddy bears and other stuffed animals; various trinkets and tokens; and flowers, lots of flowers.

I stood there, transfixed, for what felt like a very long time. I read many of the signs and letters and watched as a stream of people, many of whom were strangers to one another and to the firefighters who worked in that firehouse, entered the nearby flower shop located directly across the street from the hotel, diagonal to the firehouse, and emerged moments later with a bouquet of flowers, which they carried back to the firehouse and added to the display. I watched as more people arrived to place more items on the sidewalk and other people gathered to take in the scene. After a while, my research partner returned to the hotel. But I remained outside, where I watched as more people gathered and the makeshift memorial continued to grow. Before long, it had grown to be about ten feet wide and extend all the way across the sidewalk and to the curb, making the sidewalk in front of the firehouse all but impassable to pedestrians.

After I returned to my hotel room, showered, and had dinner, I joined the rest of the research team for a meeting. After the debriefing session, I went back to my hotel room and turned on the television. This was my first opportunity to watch the news at length since the day after the attacks (during much of this time I had been occupied with preparing for the trip, traveling to New York, and walking the streets).

As I watched the television coverage, alternating between CNN and ABC, I was struck by a second observation. The manner in which the anchors and reporters on these networks, many of whom were delivering their reports from lower Manhattan, were depicting what was happening in New York City did not seem to mesh with what I had observed. Now, I admit that I had not set out to take the pulse of the city. Nor had we gotten very close to the World Trade Center (WTC) site because of the sizable perimeter that city officials had established around that area. But I had walked down a great many of Manhattan's streets during those two days. I had spoken with many people and observed hundreds of others. I had watched as people walked their dogs, strolled around Times Square, stopped for coffee, dined in restaurants, and did other "normal," everyday things. Certainly, this was a more subdued and solemn atmosphere than usual, but it did not seem to me to be the "city in shock" that the national media headlines were suggesting.

I was then, as I am now, aware of the truism regarding media content: that is, how the media present issues and events does not tend to match the reality of those issues and events; instead, the media translate and transform their subject matter in accordance with their needs to mold news items into reportable form, to attract an audience, to entertain that audience, and so on. But I thought that these typical patterns of media refraction would be largely cast aside during the coverage of an event of such obvious sociohistorical significance. After all, this spectacle did not need to be made even more dramatic. It already was a Hollywood movie come to life. The images and facts could speak for themselves; there would be no need for news workers to ratchet up the drama, emotion, and "shock value" in an effort to "make it sell." Or so I thought.

I voraciously consumed coverage of the attacks in the following weeks, paying close attention to how my two observations—that the media coverage may have been skewed and that something extraordinary was happening with the firefighters—were playing out in that coverage. As I did, it occurred to me that these two observations were much more connected to each other than I had previously thought. I also noticed that the mainstream media coverage of the attacks and their aftermath had become disproportionately focused on New York City, as opposed to the Pentagon or Shanksville, Pennsylvania, where the two other hijacked planes had crashed. As a result, the emergency response under way at Ground Zero became a staple feature of the daily plethora of headlines, images, cover stories, articles, and editorials about the attacks and their aftermath. In response to the first observation (skewed media coverage), I tried to identify patterns in the coverage that would reveal how it was skewed and why it was taking the form(s) that it was. These patterns showed that the media were constructing a particular story about September 11. Of course, it was not just the media, as political leaders and other public figures also were desperately seeking a coherent and unifying narrative to counter the chaos of life after the attacks.

We were told over and over again that these attacks—and the "appropriate" domestic and international responses that needed to follow—should be understood simply as a matter of "good guys" (the United States) versus "bad guys" (most notably the terrorists who carried out the attacks, although this group quickly expanded to include anyone who offered financial or ideological support to the terrorists). The "good guys" were construed as the metaphorical boxer who was "down but not out" and would rise up to continue the fight, a rhetorical framing that helped fashion the story of 9/11 as a tale of a heroic victory in the face of unspeakable tragedy. The attacks, we were told, were about more than just the physical destruction of buildings or the loss of thousands of lives; rather, they were a threat to the very cultural value structure of the "American way of life" (liberty, opportunity, love of country, and so on). We were reminded again and again that we could—and would—overcome, but only by summoning the "American spirit" to face the struggle that lay ahead.

As I constructed the public drama framework outlined in this book, I began to view the September 11 coverage differently. Its form and content took on new significance and new meanings, and the reasons for the collective outpouring of emotion and adulation directed toward New York City's firefighters began to come into focus. While the initial public attention to the plight of the firefighters, such as what I witnessed that Friday night in September 2001, could be largely attributed to the staggering loss of life within their ranks (343 firefighters were killed on September 11), the death toll alone did not seem sufficient to account for their meteoric rise up the status hierarchy in the coming months. Instead, the firefighters had been positioned as stars in this mediated public drama that had been staged around the activity at Ground Zero. They were the hero-protagonists, valiantly and resolutely striving to overcome tragic loss and tremendous challenges. Their prominent role in the public drama transformed the firefighters into more than just sympathetic figures; they became "America's heroes," which gave them a new moral standing after September 11.

By packaging and presenting the attacks and their aftermath as a dramatic, emotional saga filled with tragedy, suspense, sorrow, inspiration, and heroes, the mainstream media succeeded in creating a particular reality of September 11. Once the media-fueled dramatization and personification took over, we were left with a narrow and oversimplified version of September 11. This simplistic and one-dimensional framing of "9/11" is evident in President George W. Bush's commemorative remarks on the seventh anniversary of the attacks on September 11, 2008: "On a day when buildings fell, heroes rose." This is the constructed "reality" of September 11, 2001, a deeply significant historical moment that has been reduced to sentiments that seem to have been lifted from the tagline of a Hollywood movie poster.

———————————————————— Part I ————

Introduction

Understanding Public Drama

We are in the age of the endless news cycle. At any time of any day across an ever-expanding array of print, television, and online media, news is being crafted, communicated, and accessed by millions. Much debate in recent years has centered on the merits of this environment. Some people offer a "glass-half-full" assessment of the contemporary news industry, suggesting that the benefits of the ever-present stream of news and information outweigh any negative by-products it may generate. Those in this camp may point to a number of factors to support their view: the theoretical potential of better news (i.e., more broadcast and print space *should* produce greater depth and breadth of coverage of a wider range of news), the advantages of a robust stock of readily available information, or the fact that those with the requisite motivation and news-seeking skills can select the information that they want.[1]

Others have a decidedly more pessimistic outlook on the state of news today, warning that the news industry is in the midst of a steep and prolonged decline. Those with this view often position the 24/7 news cycle—or, more to the point, the economic, technological, and cultural transitions that produce it—as the primary reason for the declining quality of mainstream news. They contend that the increasing profit orientations of news organizations, technological changes (notably, the advent and growth of the Internet and twenty-four-hour news networks), growing inter- and intramedia competition, cutbacks in newsroom resources, fragmentation of media audiences, shifting audience interests, and other forces have fundamentally altered the news industry. Many people argue that the media are now governed first and foremost by an entertainment ethos and that this new news culture has virtually usurped traditional journalistic norms, thus abandoning the investigative and educational principles on which the industry was founded. From this perspective, the efforts of the organizations and individuals who produce news are said to be increasingly favoring news that is entertaining and titillating, to the exclusion of objectivity, public interest, the pursuit of truth, and other long-standing journalistic values. These critics contend that news work is becoming more and more beholden to the "if it bleeds, it leads" standard by which greater news value is assigned to what "sells," as opposed to what could be consequential or important to society. We are said to be "entertaining ourselves to death" as we consume the productions of a mainstream media whose entertainment function has overridden its more important educational function (Postman 1985; see also Fox, Van Sickel, and Steiger 2007).

News as Public Drama

The public drama framework outlined in this book is founded on two core assumptions. The first is that news is a *social construction*, which suggests that what audiences see as "news" (i.e., the finished product that arrives in our televisions, radios, newspapers, magazines, and computer monitors) is actually the tangible manifestation of a series of decisions made by the people—editors, producers, reporters, anchors, guest bookers, news promoters, and other media figures—who determine which events, issues, and individuals will be attended to, what resources will be allocated to their coverage, what aspects of an event or issue will be the focal point, which plotlines will be followed, which characters will be promoted, and so on. From a constructionist perspective, all news is a collection of individual news elements: facts and figures, images, eyewitness accounts, expert commentary, and the like. The differences in form and content are largely in the selection of news elements and the manner in which they are presented to the audience. Information and images become part of the news not because they are inherently important or provide an accurate reflection of objective reality but because they have been defined as "newsworthy" by those whose job it is to identify potential news items and to transform them to appeal to the needs of both media officials and media audiences.[2]

We can see this in the public drama form. Public dramas are built out of those news elements that offer the most drama and emotion. Once selected, these items are then molded into an engrossing story that offers an enticing mixture of compelling characters, dynamic plot, captivating settings, and other story elements. The well-crafted public drama represents a gripping media tale that can, ideally, evolve for an extended period of time under the glare of media spotlights.

The second guiding assumption is that news matters. That is, news is the principal source of information for most of us, particularly for events and issues to which we are not directly connected. The images and information we acquire through our interactions with the media shape our perceptions of social reality. The productions of the news media, in particular, direct our attention and shape how we think and talk about what is featured as news. We use this information as a basis for activity, as a cue to how we should define the situation, and as a way to understand current events. We make sense of political and social issues and learn about our culture and social institutions through the frames and interpretations provided by the news media. Even though its forms and the media for its delivery are constantly changing, the news remains essential to both the creation and the communication of the systems of shared meanings that people use to guide their actions and interactions.

Locating Public Drama in the Media Landscape

Public drama is primarily a production of the television news media. Although other media create public dramas, it is in the television news cycle that most public dramas acquire their shape and form, attract an audience, and are generally "brought to life." Television is uniquely situated to create these kinds of stories because of its capacity to fuse images and framings in ways that, again, make their content seem more like popular fiction than news. If you were to put down this book and turn on a televised news program, you would quickly and easily find coverage of a public drama. For instance, many public dramas can be found on the networks' morning programs (e.g., NBC's *Today* and ABC's *Good Morning America*) and on the "news crawls" that show news and information in text form at the bottom of the television screen on cable news broadcasts throughout the day. The ongoing public dramas of the day also supply much of the fodder for the evening talk show news hybrids on the cable networks (e.g., CNN's *Larry King Live* and *Nancy Grace*, or the Fox News channel's *On the Record* with Greta Van Susteren). For instance, when the saga surrounding the murder of Laci Peterson and the subsequent prosecution of her husband for the crime was in full swing in 2003, it was a staple of the American news cycle. In fact, in 2003, *Larry King Live*, which has long been one of CNN's top-rated programs, devoted nearly fifty of its one-hour shows to that story (Anderson 2004, 35). More recently, CNN's *Nancy Grace* covered the story of Caylee Anthony, a two-year-old girl who disappeared and whose remains were later found, on all but six of its 117 broadcasts from July 17, 2008, to December 31, 2008.

Even though the television news media are essential to the initial development and growth of a public drama, it is important to recognize that this is not solely a television-driven phenomenon. Newspapers, general news magazines, the Internet, and talk radio all regularly consider public dramas, which help facilitate their growth and extend their reach in surprising ways. For instance, many public dramas find an unusual source of support in magazines concentrating on celebrity and human-interest stories (e.g., *People* or *US Weekly*), whose weekly editions often feature a prominent public drama on the cover or in its pages. *Newsweek*, a leading weekly news magazine, also follows some of the public dramas and has a semiregular feature that is often used to tap into older mediated dramas that have long since been removed from the news cycle. Dubbed "Closure," this section introduces its content and purpose as follows: "In the mass-media age, news stories captivate us, then vanish. We revisit those stories to bring you the next chapter." Recent editions offered brief updates of the Duke University lacrosse scandal, Jessica Lynch, Elizabeth Smart (who was kidnapped in 2002 and was discovered nine months later living with her captors twenty miles from her home), Mark Foley (the Florida congressman who was forced out of office after the discovery of his sexually charged correspondence with a teenaged boy), and—going quite a bit back in the annals of mediated drama—the story of Bernie Goetz. In 1984, Goetz, a white male, opened fire on a group of African American teens who, he assumed, were intending to rob him on a New York subway. In the media frenzy that followed, Goetz emerged as symbol of citizens' disgust with urban crime. The bigger point here is that these "next chapters" rarely contain any of the dramatic or emotional elements that initially gave life to or sustained the public drama (if they did, they would probably have become a longer news article rather than a boxed insert). Instead, this content can be seen as a mechanism for providing a brief "where-are-they-now" style retrospective on once-prominent media stories in an attempt to extract any remaining news value from them.

Much of the appeal of public drama is independent of the medium through which it is presented, although the immediacy and video footage available to television's news workers do offer certain advantages in fashioning news in this form. What makes public drama work is the manner in which it is packaged and presented. A well-crafted public drama features highly dramatic and emotional news elements, compelling characters, evocative themes, and captivating settings, all combined in an uncomplicated narrative that unfolds in a fairly linear fashion, allowing its audience to "keep up" even as the demands of everyday life necessarily preclude constant attention to the ongoing events. These features often make news fashioned as public drama seem more like entertainment than news. In fact, many public dramas explicitly exhibit the sort of entertainment ethos and narrative conventions usually reserved for those who create fictional serial dramas and soap operas. The fact that the information is being presented by a news personality, on a news program, becomes a secondary feature.

The integration of entertainment conventions into the construction of public drama often is evident in the mainstream coverage of crime, which has formed its own genre in the news industry. When stories about crime and criminal justice are packaged as public drama, the news coverage appears to be built on the reverse form of a production trick used in NBC's popular *Law and Order* series. That program, which dramatizes the detection, investigation, and prosecution functions of the criminal justice system, often contains content that is similar to real-life cases. Many episodes are promoted as having a story line "ripped from the headlines," to convey to viewers that they are watching some semblance of real life rather than just a formulaic contrivance pieced together for dramatic effect. Public drama represents the flip side of this: news workers construct news as public drama using narrative principles that have been "ripped from television" or other productions of Hollywood's fictional register.

Once firmly ensconced in the news cycle, these presentations, particularly high-profile public dramas, can remain there for quite some time, dominating the attention of media officials and the general public and permeating discourse about the issues and events at their core for years thereafter. An example is the O. J. Simpson case, which dominated the news cycle in 1994 and 1995. The death of Princess Diana, and the resultant efforts of some media to try to solve the mystery surrounding the fatal crash, remained an important item in the news cycle for the latter part of 1997 and into the following year. Following the murder of six-year-old JonBenet Ramsey in 1996, the television-like search for her killer, featuring various plot twists and unexpected developments, dominated news cycles off and on for more than a decade. Indeed, many of the most prominent public dramas take shape around criminal abductions and suspicious disappearances, especially those involving children or other vulnerable individuals.

Assuming there is enough information available to form a plot and bring the characters to life, tales like these often prove to be particularly amenable to the kind of sustained dramatic and emotional narrative that marks a public drama. This can be seen in the media sagas surrounding the disappearance of Laci Peterson (and the subsequent murder trial of her husband, Scott Peterson), the return of Elizabeth Smart (the Utah teenager who was abducted from her home), the disappearance of Natalee Holloway (the Alabama teenager who disappeared during a school-sponsored trip in Aruba), and even the rekindling of the JonBenet Ramsey story in the summer of 2007 (following John Mark Karr's admission, since proven false, that he was responsible for her murder). Moreover, the legal proceedings that often follow these cases provide a wellspring of information that can be used to advance the existing public drama or develop new directions for the narrative.

One of the more remarkable aspects of the public drama form is its longevity. The ecology of the modern news industry means that most of the news items introduced into the news cycle are discarded with astounding rapidity. But many public dramas avoid this fate, exhibiting greater "staying power" than most other kinds of news. Moreover, even after they are no longer part of the daily productions of the mainstream media, these stories rarely disappear from the news cycle altogether. Instead, they exist on its fringes, awaiting the emergence of new "newsworthy" details or developments to warrant their reintroduction.

Some public dramas become so vast and well known that their reach extends beyond the general media audience, becoming part of popular discourse and culture. When this happens, even those who do not actively follow a particular public drama in the mainstream media are still likely to overhear conversations about the mediated drama of the day among colleagues at work or see these stories on magazine covers while passing newsstands or waiting in line at the grocery store. Public dramas are, in one form or another, all around us. Clearly, they are an important device for packaging and presenting news in the contemporary news industry. The frequency with which they can be found in the news cycle and the range of media that attend to them underscore their importance to those charged with identifying and organizing content to feed the insatiable demands of a 24/7 news cycle.

Public drama, however, can be an insidious form of news. Its aura of entertainment and compelling plot structure often mask its potency as a creator and conveyor of meanings. When crafting a public drama, news workers necessarily must omit the more complex aspects of an issue or event in favor of a less complicated narrative. As a result, members of the media audience are told a dramatic tale with a fairly simple story line that unfolds in a relatively straightforward fashion and contains interesting characters or issues to which the audience can relate. This, however, requires an unfortunate trade-off: instead of a nuanced assessment of the causes or consequences of an event or the policy implications of an issue, the audience is presented with a story that has a rather narrow narrative crafted around a familiar structure, archetypal characters, and a melodramatic plot filled with notions of good versus evil.

A Case Study of Public Drama: The September 11 Attacks

The extensive media coverage characteristic of public drama, coupled with the presence of an engrossed, often large, audience, creates a context in which public drama can alter existing repertoires of meaning, create new collective definitions of issues and events, reshape the dominant culture, and affect the status of the participants (i.e., its cast). Never has the power of public drama to create and convey meanings been more evident than in the aftermath of the September 11, 2001, terrorist attacks (now popularly referred to as 9/11). This was the most widely and intensely covered event in the media age. Much of how we made sense of the attacks in those first days, weeks, and months after their occurrence and, in turn, how we have come to understand and act on "9/11" in the years since, derives from how the media first constructed and told the tale.

The way the media packaged and presented the attacks and their aftermath transformed the web of events leading up to and following the attacks into a mediated public drama. The complexities of the causes and consequences of these events were quickly stripped away as the coverage was fashioned into a story filled with spectacular moments, compelling characters, human tragedy, heroism, gripping images, and other staples of dramatic storytelling. My hope is that by examining mainstream coverage of September 11 as public drama, we can better understand some of the social, cultural, and political consequences of the attacks while also gaining greater insight into the role of mediated public drama in modern life.

I chose September 11 as a case study for this analysis because it provides an excellent window into the public drama form, illustrating not only how these mediated productions take shape, but also how their constitutive features and proffered meanings influence how we make sense of the issues, events, and individuals of our time. The huge amount of coverage generated in both the immediate and long-term wake of the attacks provides a rich source of data from which we can develop the conceptual tools needed to identify public drama, articulate its causes and characteristics, and analyze its consequences.

It is easy to forget, now that several years have passed since the attacks and the dominant 9/11 narratives have been reified through repetition, that the way these events were framed and communicated was not intrinsic to the characteristics of that day's events. Instead, what we now think of as "9/11" is a product of choices made by news workers, political officials, and others regarding what to say about those events and how to describe them. The report of the first plane crash was initially treated as a highly newsworthy accident. The working assumption at that point was that a small plane, perhaps being flown by an amateur pilot, had somehow veered off of its intended flight path. Moments later, reports of a second plane crash—along with confirmation that the crashes involved large commercial passenger planes— made it apparent that this was a significant historical moment. There was little doubt that these events would be meaningful. But the specific nature and form of those meanings required social actors to construct an interpretive framework for making sense of what had happened and communicate it to their audiences.

One of the chief arguments advanced in this book is that by packaging and presenting these events in accordance with the media logic of public drama, America's mainstream media tilted the balance in favor of certain interpretations and, by extension, determined the social and political response to the attacks. In the post-9/11 ecology of communication, the public drama narrative that emerged from Ground Zero cast an immense shadow over popular and political discourse about the attacks. Other interpretations and narratives that were allowed into the media information mix were largely confined to the furthest reaches of the Internet.

The media's efforts to present these events in the most dramatic and emotional terms severely limited the stock of frames that they and their audiences could use to make sense of the attacks. This, in turn, allowed the dramatic, emotional, theatrical, and simplistic representation of this complex and consequential historical moment to influence how political leaders, media officials, and others have constructed and used the dominant notions of 9/11 in the years since. As a result, September 11 became a story primarily about patriotism, loss, and heroes and, for the most part, *not* a story about U.S. foreign relations, U.S. military policy, poor interagency coordination, government inefficiencies, or other interpretive frames.

Ultimately, the relative stability and widespread public acceptance of these dominant framings of the attacks and their aftermath transformed September 11 into the more politically and morally charged event signifier of "9/11." This is not a small matter, as "9/11" now represents a well-stocked reservoir of images, symbols, and rhetoric from which political elites, public officials, news workers, and other social actors continue to draw in order to evoke certain sentiments or assumptions in their audiences, promote a particular version of reality, and buttress or advance agendas and ideologies.

Studying September 11 Coverage: The Data

The September 11 terrorist attacks and their aftermath generated an unprecedented level of media coverage. As word of the attacks spread on that day, people immediately turned to the news media for more information. The press and public alike remained captivated by all manner of 9/11-related issues and events through the remainder of 2001 and well into 2002. A voluminous wave of broadcast and print coverage chronicled what was happening in New York City, Washington, D.C., and elsewhere. Thousands of hours of television and radio programming and an immeasurable amount of print-based reportage and commentary in newspapers and magazines and on the Internet were devoted to the attacks. In fact, the amount and duration of the coverage devoted to 9/11 is unparalleled in the media age.[3] This period of substantially heightened media coverage presents researchers with a rich opportunity to uncover aspects of our mediated social world that have previously remained hidden from view or simply gone unexamined.

For those interested in how the media attended to an event of such magnitude, the challenge is not finding information but sifting through it to find a suitable selection for analysis. I eventually settled on a combination of television- and print-based coverage. For television, I analyzed a selection of NBC's network coverage for one week after the attacks (the full fifteen hours of coverage on September 11 and a selection of coverage from each of the following days). For print news about the attacks, I analyzed the *New York Times*'s 9/11-related content for one full year after the attacks.[4] My selection of these sources was motivated by several factors. First, I wanted to examine the media coverage in a manner consistent with *how people actually used* the media after the attacks. Second, I wanted to draw from news sources that attracted a sizable share of the post-9/11 media audience. Third, I wanted these sources to be at least somewhat representative of the broader collection of broadcast and print coverage.

Post-9/11 Media Usage Patterns

For the first of these concerns, I turned to some of the surveys and polls carried out after the attacks that asked people about their news consumption on and after September 11.[5] As news of the attacks spread on that Tuesday morning, people immediately looked to the media for more information. Studies of postattack media usage patterns reveal that most of the media audience turned to television for information on September 11 and throughout the first week thereafter (Abel, Miller, and Filak 2005; Carey 2003; Greenberg, Hofschire, and Lachlan 2002; Grusin and Utt 2005; Jones and Rainie 2002; Poindexter and Conway 2005; Rappoport and Alleman 2003; Ruggiero and Glascock 2002; Seeger et al. 2002; Stempel and Hargrove 2002, 2003). Several of these studies found that more than 80 percent of Americans used television as their primary means for gathering information about the attacks on September 11 and throughout that first week.[6]

Of course, television was not the only source of information used by the media audience in the wake of the attacks. After a few days, many people sought more detailed information than what televised news could offer, and so they increasingly turned to other sources, such as newspapers and the Internet. Television's format has a number of built-in restrictions, such as precise program length, programming conventions, and the need for commercials, which invariably limit what can be covered and how detailed that coverage can be. Newspapers and Internet news websites, in contrast, have significantly more space to devote to news, thus allowing them to provide more detailed information, reflective analysis, and contrasting viewpoints. Newspapers, particularly national newspapers with substantial operating budgets, have traditionally had larger reporting staffs than their television counterparts (PEJ 2004), more resources for research (Hamilton 2004), and greater flexibility in the kinds of stories they can produce (Klinenberg 2002), which often result in a greater diversity of content (Fischer 1998; Li and Izard 2005).

On the day of the attacks, the newspapers were relegated to a minor role, largely because the events happened hours after morning editions had been printed and delivered. Thus, even though hundreds of local and national newspapers printed special editions later in the day, most people had already settled on television as their primary information source. As the week progressed, however, many in the media audience began to look to newspapers for 9/11 coverage (Ruggiero and Glascock 2002). By late September, newspapers had emerged as an indispensable source of 9/11-related information for many news consumers, particularly after television's news holes first receded to their normal size and then gradually began to incorporate non-9/11 content (Cohen et al. 2003; Stempel and Hargrove 2002, 2003).

The post-9/11 media usage pattern, in which television took the lead and was eventually joined or supplanted by print news sources is consistent with findings from earlier studies suggesting that television use dominates during the initial "breaking news" period, after which those wanting more information turn away from television to newspapers, the Internet, and radio (cf. Stempel, Hargrove, and Bernt 2000).

Category Leaders

Given the patterns of media usage following the attacks, I decided to select one televised news source and one newspaper source that attracted a large audience for its 9/11 coverage. All the broadcast and cable television news organizations had larger audiences during that first week, with the broadcast networks (i.e., ABC, CBS, and NBC) drawing the largest audiences overall (Downey 2001a; Perse et al. 2002; Rappoport and Alleman 2003; White 2001). As Reese Schonfeld (cofounder and former president of CNN) noted, it was readily apparent after 9/11 that "most of America still looks to the 'Big Three Networks' for news." NBC, ABC, and CBS consistently outdrew each of their cable counterparts by millions of viewers per day throughout that first week (White 2001).

Among the networks, NBC was the clear favorite, attracting the most viewers on the evening of September 11 (Harper 2001) and averaging several million more viewers per day than either ABC or CBS throughout the first week after the attacks (Downey 2001b). Part of NBC's appeal in that first week can be attributed to the fact that the network's news programming already had a vast, dedicated base of regular viewers. At the time of the attacks, *Today*, its morning news program, was in the midst of a nearly six-year "winning streak," during which it had drawn more viewers than any of the competing morning news programs (e.g., on ABC, CBS, and the cable networks) every week since December 1995. (The streak has continued, with *Today* currently approaching its fourteenth consecutive year of winning every weekly ratings battle.) But NBC also made some decisions regarding its initial coverage of the attacks that arguably enhanced its appeal to potential viewers. One study found that NBC's coverage in the first eight hours after the attacks centered more on the events at Ground Zero than did that of any of the other major news networks (ABC, CBS, NBC, CNN, and Fox News).[7] This made NBC an enticing option for those interested in what was happening in New York City, which had quickly become the "main stage" of the developing media drama.

In this book, I examine NBC's coverage on September 11 in its entirety, from just before 9:00 a.m., when the first on-air report of a plane crash at the World Trade Center appeared, to the close of the day's uninterrupted coverage at 11:59 p.m. I then turn to NBC's coverage for the remainder of the first week (September 12 to 18). After preempting all regular programming to provide twenty-four-hour coverage of these events for several days after the attacks (the other news networks did this also), NBC produced nearly one hundred hours of original news programming in the first week after the attacks, making it much too difficult to code and analyze in full. Consequently, I limit my focus to *Today*-designated broadcasts in order to provide a selection of coverage that was small enough to be analytically manageable yet large enough to allow me to illustrate the processes and techniques of constructing a public drama. In all, there was a total of twenty-nine hours of *Today* programming from September 12 to 18, with almost all the reports devoted to some aspect of the attacks or their aftermath.[8]

I chose the *New York Times* to represent the newspaper category, for a number of reasons. First, the *Times* was the de facto newspaper of record after September 11, especially for the attacks on the World Trade Center (WTC) and the response and recovery at Ground Zero, largely as a result of its proximity to the WTC, its location at the head of the pantheon of print news outlets, and the generally high regard in which it is held by news consumers and other media officials. Second, the *Times* was among the most widely read print-based news sources for 9/11 coverage. It doubled its usual press run for September 12 and 13 owing to the intense audience demand and overall saw a slight upsurge in sales of its traditional print offerings and a marked increase in visitors to its online news website.[9] Third, the *Times* devoted much of its resources (i.e., reporters, photographers, print space) to the September 11 attacks and their aftermath (particularly events and activities in New York City), arguably more than any other news outlet (television or print) in the United States. The *Times* even added a special section, entitled "A Nation Challenged," devoted entirely to the attacks and their aftermath. This section first appeared on September 18 and continued daily through December 31, 2001, long after other news organizations had substantially reduced the number of 9/11-related reports and stories in their own news cycles. This meant that even as other political and social issues and events began to compete with 9/11 for headlines and page placement, the *Times* could still be counted on to provide an entire section each day containing a wide array of 9/11-related news and information. Even after the special section was discontinued, the *Times*'s coverage of the ongoing events in New York City remained extensive well into 2002.

Representativeness

The selection of NBC's *Today* broadcasts and the *New York Times* also satisfied my plan to analyze news content that would be somewhat representative of the broader collection of mainstream 9/11 coverage. *Today* has set the standard for morning news programming for more than sixty years. As a trusted and much-watched news source, *Today* still has immense influence over the form and content of morning news programming and remains a major force in the news industry. Even those who do not watch *Today* or other morning news shows are indirectly influenced by their content, as the morning programs—much as the nation's largest newspapers have long been known to do—help set the news agenda for the rest of the day's coverage.

Numerous sociologists and media scholars have noted the *New York Times*'s power in setting the agendas of other media organizations, political leaders, and the public at large (Gitlin 1980; Hester 2005; Jacobs 2000; Kadushin 1974; Sigal 1973). In addition, its "representativeness" is evident in its great reach and influence within the media industry. In the words of media scholar Ronald Jacobs, it is the "only paper which can legitimately make a claim to be the national newspaper. It is virtually mandatory reading for the political, intellectual, and journalistic elite" (Jacobs 2000, 8). As such, the *Times* greatly influences the content of network and cable television news, other newspapers, wire service copy, and news magazines. Even those people who do not actually read the *Times* no doubt feel its influence in the news sources that they do consult.

This book explores how the productions of the mainstream news media influence the way we understand the events, issues, and individuals of our time. My central argument is that the form of news—how it is packaged and presented—plays a crucial role in what people take from their encounters with news content. I use a public drama framework to articulate this connection between how news is fashioned and the broader processes in meaning-making and attribution. The project is guided by two interrelated goals. First, I want to develop a framework of public drama, which is an increasingly common, yet largely unexamined, form in which the mainstream media package and present information, issues, and events as "news." The second goal is to use this public drama framework to analyze the mainstream media coverage of the September 11, 2001, terrorist attacks to understand why that coverage took the shape that it did and what consequences it had for how the dominant notion of "9/11" has been constructed and used since.

The book is divided into three sections. The first sets the parameters for the public drama form and provides a language for thinking about and exploring news that is packaged and presented in this way. Public drama is more than just a vehicle for presenting news; it also has become an essential part of the framework, or media logic that news workers use to guide their efforts in identifying, selecting, and organizing news items that will appeal to their audiences. Chapter 2 locates public drama within the broader media industry, positioning its emergence and growth as a response to a series of economic, technological, and cultural shifts that have fundamentally altered how news is produced and consumed. This is followed by a discussion of the consequences of the trend toward public drama, not only what our news looks like, but also how these productions influence the way we encounter and understand the world around us.

Chapter 3 examines how something becomes a public drama. I explore its constitutive features, describe the elements that must be in place for a public drama to take shape and endure, and discuss the various strategies that news workers use to create news in the form of public drama.

In the second section of the book, the focus shifts to the media coverage of the September 11 attacks. Here, I examine how and why these events were fashioned into public drama. Chapter 4 provides an overview of how the media and their audiences responded to and processed these events in the ensuing weeks and months. The patterns of coverage revealed in this chapter offer insights into how and why certain frames for understanding September 11 were cultivated and communicated by the mainstream media and, more important, why other frames were not advanced.

Chapter 5 analyzes the full fifteen hours of NBC's network news coverage starting on the day of the attacks. This chapter demonstrates that this first day of coverage, even though it was highly emergent and unstructured, provided the foundation for the broader patterns of representation that emerged after the attacks, marking this as a crucial period in the development of the dominant framings and story lines of 9/11.[10] The in-depth analysis of NBC's network coverage continues in chapters 6 and 7, in which I look at all twenty-nine hours of NBC's *Today*-designated coverage from the remainder of that first week after the attacks (September 12 to 18). These chapters demonstrate how the journalistic strategies and routines on which news workers rely to cover breaking news and crisis events merged with the increasingly pervasive media logic of public drama to produce the highly dramatic and emotional tale of September 11.

The third section of the book moves the analysis beyond the etiology of the mediated public drama crafted around Ground Zero to examine one of its most prominent framings: the positioning of the firefighters as heroic icons vested with moral prestige. Chapter 8 offers a detailed look at the primary factors behind the firefighters' ascent up the status hierarchy. The central argument in this chapter is that the emergence of the firefighters as "America's heroes" was not an inherent feature of the attacks or the response-and-recovery operation. Instead, media officials, political leaders, and cultural elites recognized the value of this story line and used it to achieve their own aims in the months after the attacks. In addition to shedding light on the specific case of the firefighters, this chapter shows how social actors can gain certain status rewards by participating in high-profile mediated representations.

Chapter 9 builds on the notion that those who are cast as characters in a public drama (the firefighters in this case) often find themselves thrust fully into the news cycle and, hence, the view of the mainstream media audience. The resultant public identity can be a valued symbolic marker, giving its holder a measure of newsworthiness and affording access to previously unavailable political and cultural realms. This chapter examines how the firefighters, once imbued with substantial moral prestige (discussed as moral currency), effectively "spent" that status to benefit themselves, their organization (FDNY), the widows and surviving family members of firefighters killed in the attacks, political figures, and a host of other social actors.

2

News as Public Drama

The Era of the Endless News Cycle

Members of the mainstream media audience have been witness to and, as news consumers, partially complicit in, an important shift in the media landscape over the last two decades: the increasing trend toward news that is fashioned into dramatic and emotional stories. This form of news, what I refer to as *public drama*, is now regularly found in the foreground of the media landscape, taking up residence in some of the most valued news real estate, such as lead stories on the morning news programs, discussion points for prime-time news programs, front-page or section leads in newspapers, and the covers of news and entertainment magazines. How did this happen? And how does this affect ways that members of the media audience process and use the news?

This chapter explores how public drama came to hold such a prominent place in today's mainstream news cycles. The emergence of public drama as a vehicle for organizing and delivering news is located in the context of broader shifts in the economic, technological, and cultural foundations of the news industry, shifts that affect what news producers and their audiences believe the news should look like and how it should be made. As media officials, news workers, and media audiences have adjusted to the complexities and constraints brought about by these shifts, public drama has emerged as an increasingly viable framework for organizing, presenting, and receiving news.

The prominence and pervasiveness of public drama in mainstream news cycles, coupled with its characteristic emphasis on news items that can be molded into a compelling and sustainable story populated with interesting and identifiable characters, renders public drama a potent creator and conveyor of meanings. News fashioned as public drama provides a stylized window into contemporary social life and, in many instances, holds tremendous sway over how news consumers come to understand the world around them.

The Role of News

News is, in the most general terms, a mechanism for bringing the world "out there" into view, giving audiences information that they do not encounter directly. People look to news sources to find out "what's happening" in the world, to appraise local and national events, and to learn about and develop a perspective on contemporary issues. Virtually everyone relies on news in some capacity just about every day. As Deni Elliot, a noted media scholar, remarked, "Even the most cynical of consumers of news get most of their information about the world from the media" (Elliott 1989, 162).

While media scholars have long argued that news serves a number of important functions in modern society, two in particular often receive special attention. First and foremost, the mainstream news media are able to bring attention to issues, events, and individuals that otherwise might not attract the general public. This capacity to attract and direct attention is referred to as the news media's *agenda-setting function*. The general premise of agenda setting is that the amount and the nature of media coverage afforded a particular issue determine how the public will view that issue, that is, whether they will see it as being of consequence for society, salient to their lives, and so on. Media researchers contend that by allotting broadcast or print space to some issues but not others, the media have a profound impact on what is deemed important to social and political life.[1] This agenda-setting capacity enables the news media to direct public discourse and concern which, in turn, can affect how resources are allocated and policies are developed around those issues featured in the mainstream news media.

In addition to orienting their audiences' attentions, a second prominent function of the news media is their influence on people's assessment of the information they provide in their news coverage. This is referred as the *framing function* of the news media. *Frames* are visual and verbal communication devices that are used to ascribe meanings to actions, events, and issues and to guide interpretations of social life. If agenda setting is the capacity to influence *what* issues will come to the attention of the media audience, framing is the role of the news media in shaping *how* the audience thinks and talks about those issues brought to its attention.[2]

Frames are essential to all communications and social interactions. We use frames every day to organize our experiences, make sense of complex events and issues, and construct our interactions with others. For example, imagine that a child is injured while riding her bike on the street in front of my house. When I arrive at the scene, the only information known to me and my neighbors is that the child was struck by a car while crossing the street on her bicycle. Soon thereafter, we are told by the responding paramedics that the child's injuries are not considered serious. Relieved that the harm is minimal, I might remain on the sidewalk with my neighbors. During this time, I can talk about—or frame—this issue in many ways in my conversations with the other bystanders. I can talk about it as an issue of driver competence and care ("I've always noticed that people drive too fast on this street"). I can position it as an issue of parental negligence ("Why was that little girl riding her bike without a parent watching?") or suggest that it was a result of the bicyclist's inattention to personal safety protocols ("Too many of these kids are riding their bikes while listening to their iPods or without stopping to look before crossing"). I can talk about it as a municipal issue ("I've always thought the city should place a stop sign at some of these intersections") or a law enforcement issue ("We need more speed traps and routine patrol in this neighborhood"). Each of these examples constitutes a different frame that will not only take the conversation in a certain direction but will also position the accident as a particular kind of issue (e.g., the dangers of unsafe drivers, bicycle safety, the need for parental vigilance, municipal growth, and the maintenance of order). Thus frames help us more easily make sense of new information or occurrences by attributing meanings to them that can be readily assimilated into our existing structures of meaning that we use to think and talk about the world around us.

Frames also are important to the world of news work, in which a vast stream of information, images, and complex issues must be molded to meet the challenges inherent in making news. News workers must identify newsworthy material, gather information, and organize it for presentation to an audience, all of which is challenging enough before considering the pressures created by deadlines, limits on broadcast time and print space, the profit goals of the company's executives and shareholders, and the expectations of the audience. In this context, news workers must rely heavily on frames as a means to quickly give shape and form to complex and unexpected events and to create a shared understanding between them and their audience. A media frame can be understood, according to Gamson and Modigliani, as an "organizing idea or story line that provides meaning to an unfolding strip of events" and suggests what is happening and why (Gamson and Modigliani 1987, 143. For more on how news workers select and use frames, see Gamson and Modigliani 1989; Iyengar 1991; Lester 1980; Shoemaker and Reese 1991; Scheufele 1999; Snow and Benford 1992).

At the same time, news frames provide the foundation for how people will begin to assess and talk about the issues and events that are depicted. Remember that how something is framed greatly influences how people think about it and respond to it. This means that the media's audience is rarely left to its own devices to decipher this array of information and images. Instead, news workers incorporate certain "frames" into the packaging and presentation of the news, and these frames promote particular interpretations or ways of thinking about the issues. As Robert Entman noted, "To frame is to select some aspects of a perceived reality and make them more salient," often as a means to "promote a particular problem definition, causal interpretation, moral evaluation, and/or treatment recommendation" (1993, 53).

The media audience comes to rely on the media's frames to understand and organize the information and images presented to them each day.[3] The accounts of the news media, in the words of Murray Edelman, "construct social worlds, histories, and eschatologies, evoking grounds for concern and for hope and assumptions about what should be noticed and what ignored, who are respectable or heroic, and who are not respectable" (1988, 28). People routinely refer to media frames to define everyday social life and to make sense of complex political and social issues or develop a better understanding of ambiguous occurrences and events. Media frames often prove remarkably resilient, with many members of the mainstream media audience more or less accepting the accounts offered by their "trusted" news sources. Even those who remain critical of what they read and hear in the news are unlikely to fully reject a media account, instead modifying it in subtle ways that bring it more closely into alignment with their own ideology and experience. As sociologist Robert Stallings pointed out, "Whether rejected, accepted, or modified . . . news accounts serve as points of departure for personal conversations" (1990, 81).

The capacity of the news media to direct the attention of their audiences and provide cues to how to think about the news content makes their productions essential to the creation and communication of a shared social reality. This, in turn, gives the news media tremendous power in shaping public discourse and setting the parameters of public debate.

Making News

All news begins with certain core elements. That is, all news is built on a collection of basic ingredients, what we might call the "building blocks" of news. These include factual information, still photographs and video, official statements, eyewitness accounts, statistics and figures, expert opinions, pundit commentary, and so on. How these elements are pieced together is what distinguishes one form of news from another. Implicit in the notion that news can be pieced together in a variety of different ways is the assumption that news is a social construction.

Social construction refers to a particular way of looking at social action and social order. Constructionists look at how society, culture, and the participating institutions and individuals contribute to the creation, or "construction," of social reality. At the heart of the social constructionist perspective is the idea that the meanings attached to the things that make up social life—symbols, language, objects, and so on—do not merely exist "out there" waiting for people to discover them. Rather, they argue that meaning is created through social interaction and then attached to social phenomena and cultural objects. The challenge for constructionist sociology is to determine *how* we organize experience and action in ways that create and ascribe meaning to individuals, issues, objects, and events. To explain this, constructionists look to social interaction and other social processes, along with the broader cultural and institutional contexts in which those interactions and processes transpire.

From the perspective of social construction, something becomes news not because it is inherently important or deserving of attention but because it has been defined as "newsworthy" by those whose job is to identify news items and shape them into the kind of news that will appeal to the target audience. Viewing news in this way sees news work as about choices; that is, it directs our attention to the fact that there are people (reporters, anchors, editors, producers, guest bookers, and so on) whose job requires them to choose what should be included in the news and how it should be covered. The actions of these individuals—referred to as *news workers*—determine not only what will become news but how that news will be organized and presented to the public. Thus, a constructionist view of news suggests that the products delivered to audiences as "news" are a tangible reflection of the media's decisions about how to frame and present the *who, what, when, where, why,* and *how* of a particular issue or event.[4]

A constructionist view of news also underscores the connection between mediated representations and the processes of news work (i.e., the strategies and techniques that news workers employ), as well as the broader organizational and cultural contexts in which this work occurs. This perspective reveals that news workers' choices do not take shape in a vacuum. Rather, their work is highly contextualized, with their efforts inextricably embedded in a context of constraints (budgets, deadlines, time and space limitations), complexities (intense inter- and intramedia competition), and goals (attracting and sustaining a sizable audience in hopes of maximizing profits). In deciding what to cover and how to cover it, news workers must consider the organizational structure of contemporary media organizations, the demands of today's media marketplace, the norms and conventions that govern how mainstream news workers gather and disseminate news, the audience's shifting interests, political leaders' ideologies and agendas, and various other factors.

The Rise of Public Drama

These twin notions—that news is a social construction produced by people who must operate in a broader cultural and institutional context, and that news must be created in a way that will satisfy a complex collection of goals and constraints—are essential to understanding why and how news is packaged as public drama. A public drama is a social construction. That is, it is a type of media story, not a type of issue or event; a public drama reflects the nature of media coverage rather than any inherent features of its source material. With this in mind, I turn next to the reasons for the emergence of public drama as an increasingly popular form of news. The rise of public drama as a vehicle for organizing and presenting news is based on a series of changes in the economic, technological, and cultural foundations of modern news work. Public drama thus has created a context in which media officials, news workers, and media audiences have come to favor news that features an abundance of drama and emotion that can be presented in a form more similar to popular scripted serial dramas than to news.

Structural Shifts in the News Industry

The news industry has undergone a number of seismic shifts in recent decades. Perhaps the most significant is the transition to a for-profit model, which began in the last quarter of the twentieth century and has accelerated considerably in the last fifteen years.[5] In the past, the production of news was viewed primarily as a public service; it was generally understood that news divisions would lose money, which was simply seen as the cost of making news. According to this model, news divisions were distinct from the profit calculations of the larger corporations in which they were housed. In today's media marketplace, however, particularly in the mainstream news organizations, the news-as-public-service model is virtually extinct, having been replaced by a bottom-line ethos of profitability. News divisions are increasingly being counted on to operate at a large profit for their shareholders and executives. Profit has now also become a chief calculation in determining what is to be considered newsworthy and how it is to be organized and presented to audiences.[6]

The second important shift that has fundamentally altered the structure of the news industry is advancements in technology, which have resulted in the development and widespread diffusion of more outlets for the presentation of news. Most notable of these advances are the advent and explosive growth of the Internet and the twenty-four-hour news channels, which have produced an unending news cycle that permits—and even encourages—the around-the-clock creation and consumption of news.[7] What this means, of course, is that the "news holes" of mainstream news organizations are substantially larger than they were even two decades ago. News hole is a term that journalists use to refer to all nonadvertising content in a news medium.[8] Having an expanded news hole enables the news media to provide extensive and sustained coverage of a vast range of subject matter whenever and as often as they wish.

Fortunately (or unfortunately, depending on one's views regarding the condition of news today), those whose job is making news now have greater access to potential news items than ever before, thanks to a number of advances in communication technology. Recent decades not only have brought the advent and growth of the Internet and cable/satellite television, but they also have seen major innovations in the production and distribution of newspapers and magazines (particularly e-versions of the products), advances in communication speeds (e.g., broadband and wireless technology), and the mass diffusion of cellular phones and other modern conveniences (e.g., video cameras, digital photography equipment, cell phones equipped with cameras). These innovations have changed the manner and speed in which information and images can be identified, gathered, processed, and packaged for mass audiences and, in turn, altered the way we share information and communicate. No longer do we have to wait for a scheduled news broadcast (e.g., the nightly news on network television) or the morning edition of a newspaper to learn about the latest developments in the news stories that interest us. Instead, at any time on any day, we can tune in or log on and get the most current information. Through the ever-increasing web of news outlets on cable television and the Internet, we have twenty-four-hour access to a seemingly infinite array of images, facts, figures, warnings, breaking news, live look-ins, news crawls, and dramatizations. The news industry now operates against a cultural and technological backdrop in which virtually any information or image can be rapidly accessed, organized, and disseminated for mass consumption.

The interrelated technological and economic transitions discussed to this point also are connected to another significant structural shift in the news industry: the evolution of how audiences seek news. Today's news consumers can choose from a huge collection of news—on the Internet, from cable and satellite programming, and from more traditional sources (network television, newspapers, news magazines, and radio broadcasts)—and the evidence suggests that they obtain news from several of these media throughout the day. A recent study by the Project for Excellence in Journalism (PEJ) found that more than one-third of Americans are regular consumers of four or more different kinds of news outlets (e.g., network news, cable, local television, newspapers, Internet, radio, and magazines) (PEJ 2005).[9] Furthermore, people are increasingly using the various media forms in combination with one another to construct their views of the world around them or to make sense of ambiguous historical moments.[10] This means that the mainstream news organizations must put more emphasis on creating a brand of news that is likely to attract and retain audiences at a time when audience members are no longer as committed to a single news source as they were in the past. Indeed, as the authors of a recent study on the state of the contemporary news media discovered, "Americans are now news grazers sampling, through the course of the day, a varied media buffet" (PEJ 2005). This shift in audience interest, coupled with the various economic and technological shifts in the modern media industry, affects how news personnel identify, gather, organize, and present the news.

Cultural Shifts in the News Industry

Making news is a highly contextualized process for news workers, as they must identify, package, and present news in a way that is in line with the demands of news work, aligned with the preferences of targeted audiences, and above all else, consistent with the profit-driven business model of the news industry. Over time, news organizations develop an internal culture in response to these broader economic and cultural conditions and the focal concerns of the news environment in which they operate. In other words, those in this culture of news work (reporters, editors, anchors, producers, photojournalists, graphic artists, video technicians, and so on) cultivate a shared understanding of how news can and should be made and communicated. Sociologists David Altheide and Robert Snow (1979) studied this shared understanding, which they termed *media logic*, to better understand how it takes shape and how it influences the processes of making news.[11] *Media logic* refers to the various habits, strategies, informal routines, and journalistic norms that affect how news is collected, shaped, and presented to the audience. This is an important part of making news, as news workers come to rely on the dominant media logic for guidance regarding the potential news value of a news item and their efforts in gathering, interpreting, and disseminating the selected news items to their audience.

Media logic is not static but changes in response to structural shifts in the news industry and in the broader sociopolitical environment. In the twenty-first century, the media logic associated with mainstream news work has evolved along with the changing economic and technological conditions. Two relatively recent shifts in the media logic of mainstream news work are important to understanding the emergence and increasing use of public drama as a vehicle for packaging and presenting news. The first of these shifts is the waning distinction between "hard" and "soft" news. *Hard news* is generally defined as stories pertaining to politics, the economy, war, disasters, science and medicine, international relations, and other "significant" topics that involve reporting basic facts. *Soft news* refers to things like scandal, gossip, human-interest and atrocity tales, popular culture content, and other diversions from "more important" matters.

For much of the twentieth century, news workers used this difference between hard and soft news to categorize various news items and organize them for their audiences. Hard news was expected to be presented in serious fashion, with little color or commentary and most emphasis placed on facts. Soft news, in contrast, afforded news workers more creativity in their presentation, allowing them to put together news to entertain and editorialize. Indeed, those producing soft news often built the news content around human interest, emotion, humor, and other such elements in an effort to tell the stories of "regular" people. Now, however, this distinction between "hard" and "soft" news has become increasingly—and, many argue, irreparably—blurred, beginning with the spread of 24/7 cable news channels in the 1980s and 1990s and then the explosive growth of the Internet in the last ten years. The emphasis on creating news that is an attractive product rather than a vehicle for public enrichment and substantive discourse has helped dampen the normative expectations of the traditional categorizations (i.e., genres and beats). Today's news producers can blend the elements of "hard" and "soft" as they see fit, borrow from any news genre, and use almost any technique in the media arsenal. No tactic of news work is off limits, no format is too rigid, and few if any topics, issues, or events are too sacred.

A second shift in the media logic of modern news work is a greater emphasis on fashioning news into story form. Although short-lived, exciting events (e.g., a high-speed police chase on a freeway) and sensational occurrences (e.g., a worker dangling precariously from a tall building after his scaffolding gave way) are still considered valuable for filling available space in the twenty-four-hour news hole, news workers are now told to identify and cultivate news items that can remain in the news cycle for a longer period of time. Reporters, anchors, producers, guest bookers, and other news personnel try to ascertain the potential news value of an issue or event by how easily it can be related as a story. Both news workers and their audiences favor material that is "evocative, encapsulated, highly thematic, familiar to audiences, and easy to use" (Altheide 2004, 292). As a recent study by the Project for Excellence in Journalism found, "a growing pattern has news outlets, programs and journalists offering up solutions, crusades, certainty and the impression of putting all the blur of information in clear order for people" (PEJ 2004, 10). If a story can be made compelling, dramatic, visually appealing, and emotionally charged—and if it is given enough time and prominence in the news cycle—audience members are more likely to discover it and become involved in the plot and its characters.

For news workers, molding news into a story is invaluable. As Pamela Shoemaker and Stephen Reese noted, "The story represents a routine way of processing 'what happened' and guides the reporter in deciding which facts to include in transforming events into a news commodity" (1991, 93). Story-driven news appeals to the media audience because it is generally entertaining and easy to follow; it appeals also to the news organization's corporate executives and shareholders because it is popular and usually relatively inexpensive to produce.

Even though the story form may be good for those who make and consume news (and those who profit from it), its informational value can be problematical. First, an emphasis on the story may shift news workers away from traditional journalistic standards, which are designed to focus on what is most "important" or what will yield the most complete picture of an issue or event. Accordingly, such an emphasis means that "newsworthiness" is determined largely by the presence of interesting and relatable characters, settings, and events that can be made into a captivating narrative. A second problem is crafting a highly dramatic and emotional narrative without strictly following the traditional principles of news work (i.e., objective news gathering, careful fact checking, measured reporting) and particularly without basing it on the facts of the issues or events being covered.[12] Finally, when the processes of news work (i.e., identifying news items, gathering information, and framing that information for presentation) are guided principally by the need to tell a good story, the more complex features of the original issues and events are likely to be ignored in favor of a more appealing story and more simplistic portrayals that better lend themselves to dramatic treatment.

The Emergence of Public Drama

We have arrived at an interesting media conundrum: From a technological standpoint, the media are now capable of providing immediate, in-depth, and virtually unlimited coverage of just about anything, almost anywhere around the globe. But from an economic standpoint, there are strict limitations on what the media can attend to (in regard to the number and kinds of issues and events they can focus on) and still turn a profit. Immersed in the broader context of profit goals and intense competition for increasingly diversified and fragmented audiences, today's news organizations are always looking for ways to reduce the cost of providing news.

Constructing and presenting events and information as public drama offer a way to satisfy these competing demands and constraints. A well-crafted public drama should appeal to all the parties with a vested interest in either the production or the consumption of news (i.e., media officials, news workers, and the media audience). Media officials can appreciate public drama because it is a cost-effective form of news, is relatively easy to produce, can captivate and hold a large audience, and can be sustained within the news cycle longer than most news items.

Some public dramas become ensconced in news cycles for so long that they can become a "news franchise," and these kinds of news stories are particularly valued commodities in today's resource-strained news industry. The Project for Excellence in Journalism (PEJ) showed that faced with the challenges of a fragmented audience, fewer resources for producing news, and increasing evidence that journalism is less central to the public's overall "information mix," news organizations are trying to redefine their appeal while becoming more cost-effective (PEJ 2007). As a result, many news organizations are looking for "brand" or "franchise" areas around which they can build their coverage.[13] The recent steady stream of high-profile criminal justice proceedings that have become embedded in mainstream news cycles provides an excellent illustration of the propensity of the news media to focus on content that is likely to yield long-running stories and news franchises. Examples are the investigation into the murder of six-year-old JonBenet Ramsey in the mid-1990s, the disappearance and murder of Chandra Levy in 2001, the "Beltway Sniper" saga in 2002, the abduction of Elizabeth Smart in Utah in 2002, the disappearance and murder of Laci Peterson in 2003, the abduction and suspected murder of Natalee Holloway during a school trip in Aruba in 2006, and the mystery surrounding the disappearance of two-year-old Caylee Anthony in 2008. The appeal of many of these sagas is heightened by the possibility of subsequent criminal trials, which can provide a "second act" for a public drama and indefinitely extend its viability within the news cycle.

Once developed, a public drama (assuming it features sufficiently compelling dramatic and emotional appeal and possesses the requisite story elements that will attract and sustain an audience) can provide material for the news cycle for an extended period of time. Moreover, these ongoing stories offer the prospect of becoming "big" stories that can be tapped into as needed to fill future news holes. And if they do become "big" stories, they can cast an immense shadow over the entire media landscape. This was noted by a *Boston Globe* reporter as the saga of Laci and Scott Peterson was winding down in 2004:

> It's probably not an exaggeration to say that hundreds of broadcast hours have been devoted to her disappearance; Peterson's mistress, Amber Frey; the retrieval of the bodies of Laci and Conner; every twist of Peterson's murder trial; his conviction; and the death sentence the jury handed down yesterday. For months, the case has been featured at or near the top of newscasts, especially on all the morning network and cable news shows, sometimes taking priority over even the war in Iraq. (Graham 2004, B7)

An additional benefit of drawing on news stories that are already in place and fairly well established in the news cycle is that they tend to be cost-effective. This is an important consideration in a news industry that is continually cutting its resources for original reporting, especially in television news. Ongoing news stories usually do not require much boots-on-the-ground reporting. Instead, news workers can advance or sustain an ongoing public drama by relying on wire services, stock footage, and other information sources.[14] Much of the appeal of this form of news for news workers is that it generally satisfies their two main constituencies: their bosses (media officials) and their customers (the media audience). But news workers also benefit from the flexibility afforded by the range of events and issues and the array of journalistic techniques that can be used to construct such a drama. As an amalgam of various types of news and entertainment that refuses to adhere to traditional news categories and formats, a public drama gives news workers tremendous latitude in constructing the news.

Social and Cultural Consequences of Public Drama

The productions of the mainstream media play a pivotal role in modern society. The images and information we acquire through our interactions with media shape our perceptions of social reality. We use the information media provide as a basis for activity, for our definition of the situation, and for our understanding of current events. This is particularly true for news content, which offers more than just information about what is happening from day to day. That is, we also make sense of political and social issues and learn about our culture and social institutions through the news media, and, perhaps a bit too often, through the entertainment media as well.[15] The messages we receive from the news media inform our views of the world around us, affect how we appraise issues and events, and shape how we make sense of our personal experiences.

Making Meanings

The strategies and framing devices used to construct a public drama can make it appear more like popular fiction than news, which gives it a subtle potency. Viewers receive the story as a sort of serialized drama made all the more compelling because it stems from real events. Unfortunately, the greater emphasis on creating entertaining news often means less emphasis on providing news that can educate and enlighten. As a result, the more complex aspects of an issue or event tend to be cast aside in favor of story lines, memorable moments, and characters more amenable to dramatic and emotional portrayal. Considered cumulatively—over time and across a range of news media and productions—this is a significant development for how audiences interact with and use the news. When news seems like a benign form of entertainment, audiences are more likely to become less interested in or less capable of critically evaluating the news content. Most important, making and presenting news in an entertaining format may diminish the agenda-setting and framing effects of the media content, thereby masking their power and influence over how the audience ascribes meaning to events, issues, and individuals and interprets their social worlds.

In constructing a public drama and its story, news workers often identify and promote a single narrative (e.g., 9/11 as a melodramatic morality tale built on the struggle between good and evil and populated with villains, heroes, and victims), which, because it is emphasized over and over, tends to obscure possible alternative lines of reasoning or ways of making sense of an issue or event. Furthermore, this single narrative is crafted to be as simple as possible. Indeed, public drama is simplistic, its plot based on a clear, linear narrative arc, its characters molded to fit familiar archetypes, and its complexities abandoned in favor of more easily followed aspects. The few meanings and interpretations that are conveyed are repeated ad nauseam as the public drama unfolds, making them appear to audience members to be objective conditions of the issue or event. Ultimately, such meanings can become reified and resistant to alterations or counterinterpretations.

Making Culture

Culture, which refers to the shared systems of meanings that we use to structure social life and guide our social interactions, is not a static entity; as is the case with meanings. Instead, it is constantly being shaped and reshaped through the complex interplay of social interactions and structural forces. The productions of the news and entertainment media are by any measure essential to communicating, revising, and reinforcing culture in modern society. "One of the most distinctive features of modern society is the extent to which our knowledge and experience of the world is mediated. We conceive of, and act in, this world via television, movies, radio, newspapers, and computers" (Desfor Edles 2002, 56). News content is vital to how we fill and use our "cultural tool kit" and to how we form meanings, set the terms of public debate, shape social reality, and construct culture (Swidler 1986).

This capacity to shape and reshape meanings gives public drama great power in the broader culture. A well-crafted public drama can reinforce or alter existing systems of meaning, help maintain existing societal power arrangements, shape public opinion, influence the development or implementation of social policy, and mold collective memory. By directing "the attitudes of an audience toward a version of cognitive reality and moral order," public drama can fundamentally change how we view our past, present, and future and how we think about various events and topics.[16]

In constructing a public drama, the chief goal of news workers is to create a story in which audiences will become interested enough to follow. Part of that comes from creating a story that is full of drama and emotion. But some public dramas offer more than that, providing a narrative that is linked to broader cultural themes (e.g., 9/11 and patriotism, Katrina and the racial divide, Natalee Holloway and widespread concern about threats to children).[17] Among the most potent public dramas are those built around core cultural values and morality. A public drama of this kind represents the kind of media coverage that can, in the words of Ronald Jacobs, "encourage a break from the quotidian, the instrumental, the self-focused and, instead, orient public attention to questions of society and morality" (2000, 9).[18] We saw this in the public drama that formed around the arrest and trial of O. J. Simpson in 1994 and 1995. The incidents, moments, and issues that combined to make up that public drama might have been treated as rather ordinary events and occurrences (unfortunately, spousal homicides take place more frequently than we would like to think, vehicular police chases are not uncommon in the United States, and much print and programming has emerged around the misdeeds of celebrities), but the way that the media packaged these events and linked them into a broader narrative about such topics as domestic violence, race and the justice system, violence among athletes, and celebrity culture rendered them more than just ordinary news and, ultimately, gave rise to a long-running media saga, a public drama.

The Simpson case underscores the capacity of public drama to create and disseminate meanings that influence how we understand the events and issues at the heart of that particular public drama, as well as how we understand the broader culture and our place within it. Often what we see or read in the news is our only exposure to those institutions, social spheres, and cultural figures with which we do not have direct experience. For instance, many people do not have firsthand experience with the criminal justice system, meaning that what most of us know about the police, the courts, or prisons we learn from various news and entertainment programs. Research has repeatedly revealed that when the news media extensively cover issues of crime and criminal justice, this coverage can greatly influence how people view the criminal justice system and its actors. A study by Brown, Duane, and Fraser (1997) regarding the media effects stemming from the O. J. Simpson trial found that many in the media audience attributed much of what they knew about the workings of the criminal justice system to what they learned from the extensive coverage of that trial. Similarly, several studies have found an increase in negative views of police during or immediately after extended news coverage of alleged or actual police brutality, corruption, or other scandal (Kaminski and Jefferis 1998; Sigelman et al. 1997; Tuch and Weitzer 1997; Weitzer 2002; Weitzer and Tuch 2004).

A high-profile public drama can fundamentally alter social institutions by focusing official and public attention and discourse on how those institutions are organized or on the activities of institutional representatives who are ordinarily shielded from public view. For example, a public drama that forms around a high-profile criminal case and the legal proceedings that follow can expose the inner workings of the justice system to the audience and invite scrutiny and further investigation.[19] Similarly, when a public drama forms around an alleged or actual incident of bureaucratic ineptitude (e.g., recent allegations made against the Federal Emergency Management Administration [FEMA] regarding Hurricane Katrina) or police misconduct (e.g., the alleged assault of Abner Louima, a suspect in custody, by New York City police officers in 1997; the shooting of Amadou Diallo by New York City police officers in 1999), the resulting media coverage and audience attention can uncover wider processes of disorganization or individual or collective malfeasance.[20]

Making Characters

The plot of a public drama is crucial but not sufficient to sustain it. Equally important to the longevity of a public drama is its characters. The audience must be made to care about the people who are dealing with the particular tragedy or predicament, and the story must contain people with whom the audience can identify, or at least take an interest in.

News workers go to great lengths to identify potential characters and "bring them to life" for the audience. Consequently, they spend a great deal of time detailing and discussing the individuals' connections to the story, exploring their backgrounds and biographies, and incorporating them into the ongoing coverage. Recently, I discovered a link on CNN's website that connected to a page on that site devoted entirely to the "cast" from the O. J. Simpson trial. Even though that trial concluded nearly fifteen years ago, the main page immediately takes the reader back to a time when this case was front and center in the national consciousness. The page offers a brief biographical overview of all the individuals featured in the story in some way, referring to them as "the players." Although much of the text is devoted to those who held "starring" or prominent "supporting" roles in this drama— O. J. Simpson, Marcia Clark (a prosecuting attorney), Johnnie Cochran (a defense attorney), "Kato" Kaelin (a friend of O. J.'s), and Lance Ito (the judge)—even the most minor characters receive mention, such as jurors who were dismissed along the way and people who had attended Simpson's daughter's dance recital the evening of the murder. Even the parents of the presiding Judge (Ito) are included, because "they sat in court on January 23, 1995" (CNN.com 1995).

The importance of characters in the initial construction and continued development of a public drama gives rise to one of the more unusual features of this form of news: the ability to substantially alter the status of the individuals depicted in its stories. Because a public drama can remain in the news cycle for an extended period of time and because so much emphasis is placed on identifying the characters and bringing them to life for the audience, those who become part of a public drama's cast often find themselves, sometimes unwittingly, as public figures with public identities.[21] Indeed, being cast as a character in a high-profile media story can change the status of those portrayed, as Ronald Jacobs pointed out: "Depending on how they are defined, linked together in story or plot, and the things that determine what is or is not in the narrative, events can have important consequences for social identities and social actions" (2000, 8).

By participating in a public drama or other mediated representation, an individual can become famous or emerge as a dominant symbol and widely known image, a public figure with a public identity, which can itself become a resource available for use in a variety of social realms.[22] Thus participants in public drama, particularly those whose involvement is most prominently displayed in the glare of media spotlights, may receive certain status rewards.[23] Some become celebrated public figures (e.g., Rudy Giuliani after September 11), but others become infamous targets of public scorn (e.g., Kato Kaelin or Tanya Harding). Such public derision need not be entirely negative, however, as it can also bring the individual to the attention of news workers and, increasingly, those who produce certain entertainment content, such as reality television programming. Some enjoy greater rewards, perhaps becoming a spokesperson for the issues related to the source of the public drama, such as when a parent whose child was abducted and murdered becomes a spokesperson for issues regarding threats to children or, after 9/11, when the mother of a New York City firefighter became an advocate for skyscraper safety.

Status Rewards from Mediated Representation

Visibility

Given the fact that a public drama is, by definition, presented to a large audience through the media for an extended period of time, it is not surprising that the most common reward for playing a role in a public drama is increased visibility. *Visibility* is essentially a measure of how well or widely someone is known and can take several forms, including recognition, fame, infamy, celebrity, financial gain, and political advancement (Boorstin 1978; J. Gamson 1994; Klapp 1964; Monaco 1978). Visibility can beget more visibility; "after a point, celebrity can be parlayed—by celebrity and by media—into more celebrity: it is like money or a credit rating" (Gitlin 1980, 147). One way that this visibility can be enhanced is when the "visible" comes to the attention of those media personnel who identify and organize content for news and entertainment programming.[24] This gives those who hold even minimal visibility an opportunity to enhance their public appeal, which can be leveraged to gain placement in future media presentations.

Visibility derived from participation in public drama can transform an unknown individual into a public figure with a public identity, or it can enhance the public persona of those who already have a measure of visibility. This is important because a public persona is a symbolic commodity in the media marketplace, and if robust enough, it can become a resource available for use in a variety of social realms. For instance, several of the characters from the O. J. Simpson trial became somewhat famous following the trial and were able to parlay that status into other opportunities beyond the courtroom. Of course, the ability to gain media-driven visibility is by no means unique to public drama; we see it every day in a variety of realms ranging from politics, to sports, to entertainment and even weather—it is all part of what Maureen Orth termed the *celebrity-industrial complex* (2004). More recently, the emergence of "Joe the Plumber" as a celebrity figure in the final months of John McCain's campaign for U.S. president in 2008 (which is certainly not a public drama) hints at the ways that visibility via mediated representation can greatly expand one's access to media presentation cycles and the various channels through which media organizations construct news.

The value of visibility as a social resource is somewhat limited by its ready availability and the fact that it is often not terribly difficult to attain, a point underscored long ago by the media scholar Daniel Boorstin: "Anyone can become a celebrity, if only he can get into the news and stay there" (1978, 60).

Given the seemingly infinite array of available media outlets and the ever-shifting standards of who and what is to be considered worthy of placement in these outlets, we find ourselves in a period in which visibility is more easily attained than ever before.[25]

Ownership

Another status reward that can be derived through participation in public drama is a measure of authority that permits one to become a spokesperson for a particular issue. In his research on how social problems are constructed and communicated, Joseph Gusfield referred to this as *ownership* (1981, 1996). The owner of an issue becomes, in a sense, certified as newsworthy with regard to that issue and may become empowered to participate in news and policy discussions about that issue.[26] When news workers are charged with covering a particular issue, they are likely to seek out those who have both a link to that issue and the authority to speak about that issue. Moreover, ownership may, according to Gusfield, afford one the "power to influence the marshalling of public facilities—laws, enforcement abilities, opinion, goods and services"—in dealing with the issues to which it is related (1996, 21).

Where does the issue-owners' authority come from? In many instances, the owner of an issue derives authority from his or her official capacity, and for this reason, government officials and scientists often become issue-owners. But ownership need not stem solely from professional expertise; having firsthand experience with the issue in question can also enable one to become an issue-owner. This is quite common, as we often ascribe a measure of legitimacy to those who have emerged from personal encounters with that issue (e.g., the victim of child abuse who, as an adult, becomes a spokesperson against child abuse, or the parent of a child who was injured or killed who becomes a regular spokesperson regarding the issue involved in the child's injury/fatality). News workers seek out and value the comments of those who can draw on their professional expertise or personal experience to provide an authoritative voice.[27]

Although ownership is not as widely available or as easily attained as visibility, it is by no means exclusive, as there can be multiple "owners" of an issue. For example, although John Walsh is clearly the most visible, longest tenured, and influential of today's child-safety advocates, other "owners" of this issue are frequently invited into news coverage and help shape the way we think about and deal with issues of child safety.[28] Similarly, in recent years, the former vice-president Al Gore has become closely associated with the issue of global warming and enjoys a great deal of newsworthiness and political influence with regard to that issue, but he does not have exclusive control over the various policies and initiatives created to deal with global warming.

Ownership of an issue clearly can be a powerful symbolic commodity, as it permits someone to speak as a person of authority about that issue and on related matters. Becoming an owner of a public drama may be especially valuable, given the longevity of many public dramas in the news cycle. The owner of a public drama operates as a consultant on the issues or events associated with the particular public drama. Owning at least part of a public drama creates the perception of an indelible link between that person and the issue, condition, or event at the heart of that drama.

Moral Currency

The third reward that may be derived from participation in a public drama or other mediated representation is what I refer to as *moral currency*. This concept is similar to John Kane's notion of *moral capital* (2001), with a subtle but important distinction regarding my use of the term *currency* rather than *capital*. Kane's discussion of moral capital largely focuses on the nature of this moral resource and how it is accumulated and invested. In contrast, I use *currency* to underscore my interest in how this symbolic commodity, once acquired, can be used, or "spent," in the "symbolic marketplaces" of social and political life.

Moral currency is not simply a mark of distinction or a "status badge"; it is a viable political resource that can affect social interaction and political processes in a variety of ways.[29] Having moral currency means being known to a wide audience (like visibility) and having a measure of legitimacy to speak or act on issues (like ownership), but more than that, it signifies that its holder has a measure of moral prestige, an "aura of moral authority" (Kane 2001). Moral currency derived from public drama is a symbolic resource that gives its holder broad authority over the issues related to that particular public drama, and to issues beyond that public drama as well.

I view moral currency as having the greatest symbolic worth of the three types of rewards for participation in public drama discussed here, although the exact value of any such reward varies according to the recipient's own needs and aspirations. The morally grounded legitimacy that characterizes moral currency gives its holder an authority to weigh in on a range of issues, even those that may be only marginally related to the public drama. Furthermore, although the possession of moral currency may be fleeting, it can provide access to previously unavailable areas of social and political life and allow its holder to bypass the usual political power structure to contribute to various agenda-setting processes.[30] Ownership, in contrast, is much more restricted, as its holder's authority is typically limited to a particular issue or set of issues, and visibility carries with it no such authority.[31]

Making Public Drama

Telling a Good Story

Public drama has become an effective framework for packaging and presenting news amid the clutter of the modern media, particularly television. Audiences find news in this format to be appealing because of its entertainment-like quality; that is, it is simplistic and story driven and offers a collection of compelling images and characters. Media officials and news workers enjoy packaging news as public drama because it is relatively easy to put together and inexpensive to produce. Once the story is established, it can often be communicated with a mixture of anchor/reporter commentary, interviews, stock footage, and wire reports. Moreover, the fact that a public drama can provide a sustainable source of news content for an extended period of time adds to its appeal as well.

Examples of this form of news coverage can be found in recent news cycles of the mainstream media: the O. J. Simpson trial; the investigation into the disappearance of six-year-old JonBenet Ramsey; the disappearance of Chandra Levy; the right-to-life saga of Terri Schiavo; the search for the missing Laci Peterson and the subsequent trial of her husband, Scott, for her murder; the "Runaway Bride"; Hurricane Katrina; and the abduction and suspected murder of Natalee Holloway while on a graduation trip in Aruba. Even more recently, regular viewers of television news programs have been inundated with stories and reports about the disappearance of Caylee Anthony.

In many ways, the Caylee Anthony case was the quintessential public drama. It featured many of the news elements that attract news producers and appeal to the media's audience. It offered a sustainable story arc, filled with the suspense of criminal activity and an ongoing investigation, as well as the tragedy of a child victim and the horror of a mother's potential culpability in the death of her child. The story of Caylee Anthony enjoyed a great deal of institutional support across the entire spectrum of network and cable news programs.[1] On any given night (or morning) in the summer and fall of 2008, viewers could tune in to a fictional serial drama masquerading as news, a "real-life" version of *Law and Order* or *CSI: Crime Scene Investigation*. The plot was both titillating and shocking. New details and developments arrived so quickly that there never seemed to be a break in the action. As the saga unfolded, its cast grew to include a number of people with connections to the story or its characters, many of whom (the grandparents, the uncle, and family friends) had been deemed "suspicious" by news personalities and other media observers (which only added to the case's overall intrigue).

Caylee's story first came to national attention on the Thursday, July 17, 2008, broadcast of CNN's *Nancy Grace*.[2] Caylee was a Florida toddler who had been missing for more than a month, although law enforcement officials had only recently been made aware of her disappearance.[3] Nancy Grace, the program's host, ushered in what became a deluge of Caylee coverage:

> Nancy Grace (host): A beautiful 2-year-old little girl is missing. Right now we have a live shot. Breaking news, there in the backyard of the home that was shared by the family, we have learned that police are gathering, they are converging in the backyard around an apparently a plastic playhouse. They have lifted it up. Also there in the backyard, we see German shepherd dogs. We don't know at this juncture whether they are cadaver dogs or search dogs. We do know that little Caylee has been gone now for several weeks. Weeks had passed without the mother reporting her missing.

Grace and her production staff quickly worked to interject the small and scattered collection of known details in an attempt to bring this story to life. Viewers saw live shots of the home where Caylee had lived, and an on-site reporter stationed outside the home provided additional information ("investigators say that Casey, the mother in this case, has told them lie after lie"; "neighbors . . . told investigators that they saw Casey . . . here recently alone when . . . the grandparents in this case were not here"; "Casey might have buried Caylee . . . here in the backyard"). Then viewers were introduced to Cindy Anthony, the victim's grandmother (and the mother of Casey), who became a main character in this public drama and who also lived in the home where the reporters and investigators were currently at work. The broadcast closed with a plea from Grace for the viewers' involvement: "Everyone . . . please help us. There is a desperate search going on right now in the Orlando area for a beautiful 2-year-old little girl Caylee. The tip line is 800-423-8477."

In short order, coverage of Caylee's disappearance and the eventual discovery of her remains became a staple of national television news cycles. This story turned into the most prominent public drama in all of 2008 and perhaps 2009, as the investigation into these events and the trial of Caylee's mother, who has been charged with the child's murder, continue to unfold.

On July 18, the morning after it was first discussed on *Nancy Grace*, the Caylee Anthony story was picked up by NBC's *Today*. Its coverage included a brief live report delivered by an NBC reporter who was stationed "outside the little girl's Orlando home," along with a taped interview that the same reporter had conducted with Caylee's grandparents (Cindy Anthony and her husband, George) in Florida. This marked the beginning of a string of twelve consecutive *Today* broadcasts that included at least one feature report devoted to the Caylee Anthony story, excluding Sundays, when the program is devoted almost entirely to politics and lifestyle content.[4]

While the attention to this story on *Today* was considerable in the latter part of July, it paled in comparison to the time and resources that CNN's *Nancy Grace* spent on it.[5] Indeed, the Caylee Anthony story was a featured segment on every single broadcast of *Nancy Grace* from July 17 to 31. Furthermore, this story was discussed, often at great length, on all twenty-one original broadcasts in August, all twenty-two original broadcasts in September, and the first nineteen broadcasts in October.[6] Although not featured on every broadcast of *Nancy Grace* in November and December 2008, the Caylee case was discussed on seventeen broadcasts in November and twenty in December. Even when the new year began, the coverage of Caylee Anthony did not subside; in fact, it gained momentum following a series of new developments in the case: a child's remains had been found and were positively identified as Caylee, video footage of the home where Caylee lived was made available, legal motions were filed by defense attorneys, reports surfaced that Caylee's grandfather had gone to a remote Florida hotel and was threatening to commit suicide, and a memorial ceremony was held for Caylee. In all, CNN's *Nancy Grace* discussed the Caylee Anthony case on 149 broadcasts from mid-July 2008, when it broke the story, through the end of February 2009.

Members of the media audience proved to be increasingly willing to follow along as surprising twists were encountered and new details were uncovered.[7] The strong connection that audience members formed with the Caylee coverage is evident in the following responses to Internet blog postings and online news items devoted to this story:

This is the first time I've ever been "glued" to a case like this. I think because I have a 20 month old granddaughter.

I haven't missed one night of Nancy Grace, she has breaking new's about the story every night.

I am not only listening to Nancy Grace, I am also listening to every channel that brings up this story . . . and I did my share of research. It kills me, I see that little girl's photos, and I cannot imagine how anyone can possible hurt the girl.

I am sick to my stomach about this poor innocent little girl. How can anyone hurt a child? I have two nieces and two nephews all under the age of ten and I love them like my own kids and I can't see how anyone on earth can hurt a child.

Along the way, many audience members seemingly went beyond mere viewership and became fully engaged in the stories, sending droves of e-mail to Nancy Grace and other program hosts and posting highly detailed messages on Internet news sites and blogs, many of which indicate that a great deal of time and attention had been spent following the case and working to resolve its mysteries.

I have been following this tragedy since it first aired. At times I have had to turn off the TV b/c it troubled me so much. I have read some of the posts here and I do believe that there is more to this than anyone knows. Shame on the grandparents of Caylee. They knew that their daughter is sick and obviously mentally disturbed. We all know that Casey is a murderer. A selfish, self-centered, maliscious, evil, immature, lying, non-human, sick individual. Casey will pay for her crimes.

She killed caylee on may 16th, put her in the pink play house in the Anthonys back yard, then on the 17th backed her car up which she never did, borrowed a shovel from a neighbor. And put her body in the trunk. Then drove around with her trying to figure out what to do. Then drove out to the airport in a swampy wooded area, around 5.23 pm and drove away from that area at 8.23 pm. As she drove away she called her best friend Amy and said "i got rid of the smell" I scraped the squirrels off the car. . . . I just hope and pray they find her body, just so she can finally be at peace. . . . She is so guilty.

The Caylee Anthony case is typical of many high-profile public dramas in that it formed around issues of crime and criminal justice. It is important to remember, however, that a public drama is still a social construction, that it can take shape around anything: a missing child (JonBenet Ramsey); a custody battle (Elián Gonzáles); a terrorist attack (September 11); a celebrity trial (O. J. Simpson); an accident (Minneapolis bridge collapse); a crime spree (the "Beltway Snipers"), and so on. There is nothing inherent in those events, issues, or individuals that automatically transforms them into public drama. Whether or not an event becomes a public drama is a reflection of the media's coverage, not the event's features. In the remainder of this chapter, I describe the elements that a public drama must contain in order to take shape and endure.

The Core Elements of Public Drama

Media Attention

If information, issues, images, individuals, or events are to become part of the news, they must be deemed newsworthy and selected for attention. The emergence of a public drama signifies that its core issues or events have become more than a single news item or a brief collection of related reports. For this to happen, the media must pay a lot of attention to it—in the form of broadcast time or print space, personnel, and other resources—for as long as it takes for the story to develop and its audience to take note. Only after the plot and the characters are given shape and communicated to the audience can a public drama emerge.

The introduction of a *potential* news item into the news cycle, of course, depends on more than the desire or willingness of news workers to attend to it. Today, only a minuscule proportion of the events and issues unfolding at a given time are identified as "potential news items," and only a small fraction of these actually become the news that we watch, read, or hear. Despite the expansion of cable and the broadcast media and the explosive growth of the Internet, a limited amount of space is available for the seemingly infinite array of things that might be considered worthy of broadcast time or print space.[8] Quite simply, there are many more issues and events that could be considered newsworthy than the media can realistically attend to.

The social organization of news work creates a number of constraints and challenges that media officials must take into account when making news. These include the need to create a diverse collection of news content (e.g., politics, crime, lifestyle, entertainment, weather, regional/local content) to broaden appeal, a predetermined number of limits on broadcast time and print space, a fairly small and shrinking stable of reporters and production personnel, budgetary constraints, and so on. Consequently, it is impossible for the news media to cover everything.

These structural limits are compounded by the demands of an unending news cycle, which leaves reporters little time to wait for a story to develop, and the drastic decline in resources allocated to gathering news, which restricts the range of possible story angles that can be covered. Confronted with the complexities of profit calculations, inter- and intra-media competition, expansion, technological advancement, and shifting audience preferences, news producers try to identify possible items of interest and potential news stories that can be produced quickly and efficiently while also being able to attract and sustain the interest and attention of an audience.

Media Treatment

Mass media attention is obviously vital to the emergence and growth of public drama. But media attention alone is not sufficient for a public drama to take shape and endure. News producers can train their cameras on something for days on end or write about something for as long as they wish, but for something to become a public drama, it requires that the media organize and present their material in a particular manner.

Sensational facts and figures, novel moments, stunning images, and the like may be able to capture an initial burst of media and audience attention, but if they are not molded into a particular form, they will remain merely a collection of isolated news items and be unlikely to attract the prolonged media attention and audience interest necessary for a public drama. To create a public drama, therefore, the media must construct narratives and frames that link the various news elements and transform them from individual news *items* into a coherent, dramatic news *story*.

The first step in crafting a public drama is finding a suitable plot, which provides the backbone for the public drama. Without a plot to tie the various news elements together, it will remain merely a collection of dramatic images and emotional moments. Furthermore, only those public dramas based on a compelling story line will endure in the news cycle. Those elements most amenable to this story format can serve as a foundation for the plot or story line, and those that are deemed too complex or not sufficiently compelling or dramatic are dropped.[9]

Another important component of a public drama is its characters, those individuals associated with the events or issues around which a public drama is formed (e.g., victims, offenders, friends and relatives, spokespersons, witnesses, lawyers) and selected by media for inclusion in the "cast." Because public dramas are designed to resemble scripted serial dramas, news producers often include characters that can be manipulated into familiar archetypes with which the audience can easily identify.

Finally, the setting in which the public drama unfolds must also be brought to life. The setting is particularly important for connecting the public drama to its audience because it is the "stage" on which the actors in the public drama perform. As Gary Alan Fine and Ryan White suggested, the setting of a news story "provides an interpretive space in which the audience can place themselves," thereby increasing the likelihood that the audience will continue to follow it as it unfolds (Fine and White 2002, 67). News workers use evocative language and captivating images to convey the scene, particularly on television, which regularly uses live video, stock footage, and reenactments to further enliven the story. Visual images (which can also include still photographs) are invaluable for enhancing the dramatic or emotional appeal of their presentation, as they help connect otherwise disconnected strands of a narrative, set the scene in ways that words cannot, and make the audience feel that they are a part of the unfolding story.

The Audience's Investment

The third element that must be present for a public drama to remain in the news cycle is an audience willing to accept what is being presented and follow the story as it develops.[10] The news workers are the "gatekeepers" deciding what will and will not become news, with the audience functioning as a kind of "silent partner" in the news-making process. Their interest helps determine what enters and remains in the news cycle, for if not enough people respond to the presentation, it will be abandoned. Thus, when crafting a public drama, news workers look for news elements that are likely to elicit a psychological or emotional connection from the audience.

A primary goal of today's news producers is, in the words of Danny Schechter, a former producer of CNN and ABC's 20/20, to "get an audience hooked, breathlessly awaiting every fresh disclosure." One way to do this is to choose a story that features "a recognizable cast of characters they can either love or hate, with a dramatic arc" that viewers will want to see resolved (Scott 1998, 1).[11] The underlying assumption is that if the audience can find significance in the plot or the characters and their actions, they may come to believe that what is being presented is of great significance to them or, at the very least, entertaining and worthy of their attention.

The desire to create a strong and lasting connection from the audience to the story explains why public dramas are often constructed like scripted serials or soap operas. The plot is simplified and often linked to long-standing moral values or contemporary social concerns. Characters are presented as one-dimensional figures, portrayed as archetypal villains or victims or other roles that fit the plot. All this helps make the public drama seem less like news and more familiar and entertaining and, therefore, more appealing to a larger audience.

A Closer Look at Media Treatment

Technology now offers a window into virtually all aspects of social life. Thus, almost anything can be rendered "public" in modern society; all it requires is a motivated media organization with sufficient resources and a willing audience. But for news to become "public drama," the media and audience must be more than conduits of information and images and their recipient. The media must create and sustain the public drama by presenting the material in ways that will accentuate or increase the dramatic and emotional aspects of the story. The audience must do more than simply watch, listen, read, or talk about the media presentations; they must be willing to invest in these presentations and make an emotional connection between themselves and the story or its characters.

To take shape and endure in the news cycle, a public drama must contain three elements: the media's attention, a certain treatment of the news, and an invested audience. The first and third elements are not, of course, unique to public drama but are key components of all news. The media's attention is needed for an event to become news. It is the second element—the media's treatment of the event—that characterizes public drama and distinguishes it from other forms in which news is presented. The success of a public drama depends on how media *treat*, or process, package, and present the subject matter.

Although how a story is told and which news elements are emphasized may vary, news workers rely on two techniques to effectively package and present news as public drama. First, they must identify and emphasize the dramatic elements of an issue or event; I refer to this as *dramatic amplification*. Second, they must portray the story and its characters in a way that is likely to establish an emotional connection between the public drama and the audience; I refer to this as *cultivating emotionality*. Selecting suitable news elements and accentuating their dramatic and emotional features is not sufficient to create a public drama, however. These elements also must be combined into a story with a compelling plot and a relatively clear narrative.

Dramatic Amplification

The ability of a public drama to sustain the interest of the media and their audience hinges on its dramatic appeal. This appeal is not intrinsic to an issue or event; instead, news workers must amplify the drama. That is, news workers must identify potentially dramatic news elements and remove them from the realm of the mundane and play up their dramatic appeal. Drama is neither new nor unique to the public drama form: it has long been a key criterion in assigning news value. Accordingly, news workers routinely favor news elements that will help persuade the audience that what they are seeing or reading is exciting, "now!" and "not before seen."[12]

The media use a variety of techniques, both visual and narrative, to accentuate the dramatic elements of an event or episode or to create those elements if they are not present. Dramatic narratives often feature highly evocative words, statistics, images, or other sensationalizing agents. They are frequently organized and presented in a "this-just-in" format, which makes the audience feel that they are participating in an unpredictable, still-unfolding, and particularly dramatic moment.

The easiest form of drama to amplify is live drama. This is usually "breaking news" (e.g., car crashes, explosions, white Ford Broncos being chased by police on a California freeway). This kind of drama more or less works on its own; that is, news workers do not need to do much to convey the drama other than to highlight the facts and provide basic information. Live drama is a crucial part of news, as it can quickly attract viewers and is a valued asset for those trying to fill a 24/7 news hole. But live drama can be sustained for only so long. Eventually, the car chase ends, the fires are extinguished, or the young girl is rescued from the well.

When an event or issue is no longer at the dramatic apex of its "breaking" phase, news workers often have to do more to communicate its dramatic appeal to the audience. Perhaps the most common technique for boosting dramatic appeal is to "set the scene," to draw audience members into the story, and to give them a sense of how it *feels*, *looks*, and *sounds* to those involved. Television's capacity to provide live or recorded video footage of key locations and moments can be particularly effective in setting the scene.[13] The on-location report, for which a reporter is sent to the scene to deliver commentary on the air is perhaps the most common and effective scene-setting mechanism.[14] When images are not available or not as viable, as in print media, news workers use other techniques to describe the setting to the audience. Eyewitness accounts are often used for this purpose. If delivered effectively, these can provide a measure of experiential authority to the presentation and convey the on-the-ground reality in ways that a news report may not. Accounts from those connected to the event in some official capacity (e.g., government employees, public officials, lawyers) are often used to help set the scene.

Another technique for amplifying drama is to recount harrowing moments from earlier stages of the drama or replay footage of those moments. This is particularly common when footage of the unfolding drama exists, such as the September 11 attacks or the destruction wrought by Hurricane Katrina. Dramatic amplification is also apparent in news workers' efforts to identify ongoing dangers and speculate about the form and extent of the problems that these dangers might cause. This technique is used when the drama is still being played out, such as in the first few days of the September 11 coverage, when there was much fear regarding the instability of other buildings at the World Trade Center complex.[15]

Cultivating Emotionality

The second way that the media refashion the raw materials of news into a public drama is by highlighting news elements that are likely to produce a strong and lasting emotional connection between the audience and who or what is being presented. I refer to this as *cultivating emotionality*. Although most public dramas are constructed first and foremost with the aim of enhancing their narrative and visual appeal through an emphasis on or introduction of certain dramatic elements, a story cannot survive on drama alone. The captivating images or "this just in" drama of breaking news may capture the attention of the media and their audience, but for that initial drama to become a long-running story (i.e., for it to have "legs"), it must have something more: a compelling plot and characters that resonate emotionally with the audience.[16]

The increasingly profit-oriented requirements of contemporary news work dictate that a public drama or other news form cannot endure for long without an audience that will become involved in the story and the ordeals of its principal characters. Researchers have shown that the salience of media presentations is largely determined by whether the individual feels personally involved in what is happening or directly influenced by what is being presented (Cantor 2002; Grabe et al. 2000; Hoffner et al. 2002; Rogers 2003). If public dramas are packaged and presented appropriately, they can lead their audiences to believe that the unfolding events are relevant to them, that they *should* care about the issues and events and participate directly or vicariously by reading about or viewing the public drama. If the viewers perceive an affiliation or identification with the participants of a public drama or with certain aspects of the plot, they may become caught up in aspects of the drama, thus creating an emotional link between themselves and the unfolding story.[17]

The idea that there can be an emotional connection between mass media and their audiences is supported by research. Some researchers argue that the mass media contribute to social cohesion by giving people "a sense of connection to the collective whole that few other institutions today can rival."[18] This was a central theme in Daniel Dayan and Elihu Katz's study of media events, in which they contend that the establishment of a connection between the audience and the performance through the mass media allows the audience to "share in the ceremony and unfolding of big events" and can create an "upsurge of fellow feeling" (Dayan and Katz 1992, 22, 5). Other researchers have found that interactions with the media, particularly television, can have psychological benefits. Some audience members identify with the media personalities they most often encounter, such as news anchors or weather persons, even coming to view them as friends.[19] Still others, such as sociologist Orrin Klapp, have explored how audience members connect to the characters in news stories. Klapp found that audiences often use public performances, such as news stories, psychologically, as a way to be transported vicariously out of their everyday lives (Klapp 1964, 24).

Cultivating emotionality means emphasizing certain elements that help the audience identify with the story and its characters. Audiences seem to readily identify with stories about ordinary people who find themselves in extraordinary circumstances. Even though they may not have faced a similar predicament, they can easily see similarities between themselves and the characters and can speculate as to how they would handle the situation. "For a story to have 'legs,' it requires individuals whom the audience feels they know because they can place themselves in the situation or because they have compelling cultural images of the otherness of the figures" (Fine and White 2002, 68).[20]

Giving news coverage an emotional appeal is neither new nor unique to public drama. The human-interest story has long been a staple of print and television media, particularly in today's morning news programs on network television and infotainment style magazines like *People*. What makes public drama different from other news forms is the extent to which the content is organized around this emotional appeal. It is not just a part of the coverage, it is a pillar of the coverage. In fact, after the drama inevitably wanes, it is the emotional connection that has to sustain the story over the long term. The successful cultivation of emotionality increases the likelihood that the audience will continue to follow the story.

How is this emotionality cultivated or constructed? Some of the emotionality in a public drama stems from dramatic amplification. When the story contains tension, conflict, melodrama, suspense, and other dramatic elements, as well as real people with whom the audience can identify, they are likely to take an interest in how the tension is resolved. If a public drama narrative is crafted properly, it will lead its audience to find significance in the plot, the characters, and/or their actions. News workers also can use a variety of strategies and techniques to cultivate emotionality beyond that generated by the narrative's inherent dramatic structure.

One strategy is to flesh out the "characters" in the public drama, perhaps through relevant details of their biography, to increase their resonance with members of the audience. Revealing the tragedy and sorrow faced by the protagonists—the mother whose young child has disappeared, the husband who lost his wife in a plane crash, the family of a slain police officer—gives viewers a way to symbolically immerse themselves in the story. One need not be a parent or a spouse or have a family member in law enforcement to empathize or sympathize with those involved, and few can remain unmoved when confronted with the human face of tragedy and loss.

A common means of bringing the characters to the forefront of the media narrative is to personalize the story. This involves providing details about those involved, such as their ages, social status, marital or parental status, occupations, and aspirations. This helps show them as real people rather than as one of some amorphous categorization (e.g., victim, rescuer, soldier). By framing it this way, those involved become people with a back story and set of experiences to share. Characters can be "personalized" in a variety of ways. If the victim is available and able, she can be asked to provide a first-hand account of her experiences. If the victim is not available, his family or friends may be asked to provide biographical or experiential details about him. Using the accounts of those involved to personalize the story has much symbolic value. For instance, when a television audience sees and hears a family member or friend discuss how he or she feels in the wake of a tragic loss, it becomes more like a conversation than a newscast and allows them to imagine themselves in this position, thereby giving the story greater emotional resonance and perhaps making a stronger and more lasting emotional connection with the audience.

Other strategies for cultivating emotionality include highlighting the emotionally resonant features of the events rather than the characters. News workers often frame an event in ways that not only will make the audience take note but also convince them that what is happening is relevant to their own lives. One way to do this is to promote a sense of arbitrariness regarding when, where, and against whom unexpected occurrences and tragedies happen. This is a staple of crime-related news coverage, where viewers are routinely given the impression that they are at great risk of falling victim to an array of crimes and criminals. We also saw this in the September 11 coverage, in the stories of people who were supposed to be among the passengers on a plane that crashed but arrived late to the airport and missed the flight. It works the other way, as well, with accounts of those who were affected by the tragedy when they varied their routines in a way that inadvertently brought them into harm's way, such as the World Trade Center employee who arrived extra early for work on September 11 or the local citizen who, on a whim, decided to visit the World Trade Center's rooftop observation deck on that fateful morning.

Part II

Framing September 11

*Overview of the Media and
the Audience's Response*

It is difficult to imagine that an event could receive more media attention or produce a more attentive audience than did the September 11, 2001, terrorist attacks. The sheer volume of media coverage devoted to the attacks and their aftermath was staggering, as was the fervor with which the public sought and consumed coverage of these events. In the words of media scholar Bernhard Debatin, "The whole world was watching the events in real time or very shortly after the events occurred" (Debatin 2002, 165). Although this statement may be construed as more hyperbole than fact, to do so is to miss the larger point, as it captures the essence of the "9/11 experience" for so many. This chapter looks at the patterns of how the media covered September 11 and how their audiences reacted to that coverage, in order to better understand some of the ways that the media and their audiences processed these events.

Initial Media Response

On the morning of September 11, the media dropped everything to cover the attacks. Television, as the medium best able to quickly capture and disseminate information about and images of the attacks, set the standard early for what the overall media coverage would be (i.e., extensive and, eventually, excessive). The three major broadcast networks (ABC, CBS, and NBC) preempted their entire programming schedules, including commercials, to cover the attacks from the morning of the eleventh until Saturday, September 15, transforming themselves into twenty-four-hour news channels, like those of the cable news networks, all of which also focused exclusively on the attacks. One of the most remarkable aspects of this coverage was that the competition among news organizations was forgotten as rival networks shared coverage with one another. In addition, the media's usually hidden vertical integration was made visible as parent companies simulcast the feeds from their news channels to other channels unable to cover the live events.

Although television took the lead, the Internet also was important to the media response on September 11. Many people who were at work when the attacks began did not have access to the television coverage, so they turned to the Web to learn more about what was happening. Initially, the attacks were covered on each network's home page, but these quickly became overtaxed, leading many people to turn to other media sources, such as radio or television. These technological difficulties, coupled with news consumers' long-standing preference for traditional news sources, especially television, during a crisis, made the Internet mainly a supplement to television. People thus principally used the Internet on September 11 to communicate with friends and family rather than as a source of information.[1]

Several researchers have concluded that the failure of news organizations to streamline and/or frequently update the content of their websites ultimately limited the role of the Internet in the immediate aftermath of the attacks. As Steve Jones and Lee Rainie observed, "For all of the online activity that focused on the terror assaults, this was not a breakthrough moment for use of the Internet compared to other technologies" (2002, 28). The Internet became a more widely used source for 9/11 coverage after the networks and other operators of news-oriented websites rectified the problems by first streamlining the content on their institutional home pages (e.g., removing non-9/11 items and reducing the amount of photos, graphics, and other items requiring more memory) and later by creating new websites devoted exclusively to coverage of September 11 (Brown et al. 2003).

Newspapers also responded, though not as quickly as television or the Internet could, owing to structural limitations of production and delivery, by blanketing the nation with coverage of the attacks beginning on the morning of the twelfth. Some markets had special late editions of newspapers on the eleventh that were produced specifically in response to the attacks, but most merely repeated much of the same content already available on television and the Internet. The attacks were, quite literally, the only front-page news in virtually all the nation's leading newspapers in the next few days, with each providing extensive daily reports accompanied by vast photo spreads. Other print news media also responded to the attacks as quickly as their forms would allow. Three of the major weekly news magazines (*Newsweek, Time,*

U.S. News & World Report) produced special editions devoted solely to the terrorist attacks, and several other magazines that had already gone to press were stopped in order to revise them to focus more on the attacks (Jones 2001).

Initial Audience Responses

Just as the media had dropped everything to cover these events, the public also quickly dropped the usual demands of work and life to follow the coverage. The fact that the attacks began just before 9:00 a.m. EDT permitted the coverage to reach "the largest live audience possible because most people around the globe were awake. Instantaneously, the shocking events profoundly interrupted the normal flow of time . . . and created a worldwide synchronization of attention" (Debatin 2002, 164–65). On September 11, news of the attacks spread rapidly, with most East Coast residents learning about them within two hours of their occurrence and the rest of the country finding out as the morning progressed.[2] Modern technologies played a vital role in this rapid diffusion, with people drawing on all kinds of media and communication technology to get as much information about the attacks as quickly as possible.

Several studies of postattack media usage patterns were conducted in the wake of 9/11, and while the numbers vary, all point to the same conclusion: television was the source to which most members of the media audience turned for information.[3] The Internet also proved to be a valued information source for many, both on September 11 and in the following weeks.[4] MSNBC. com experienced a nearly 500 percent increase in traffic at its site between 9:00 and 10:00 a.m. on the eleventh, and CNN.com enjoyed an equally robust (nearly 450%) boost in the number of visitors to its site during that same period.[5] Twenty-nine percent of Internet users (30 million) reported seeking news online, which was 33 percent higher than usual (Rappoport and Alleman 2003). Of course, with the Internet (especially the websites of major U.S. media organizations) overtaxed by the unprecedented demand, many would-be users found it difficult to access mainstream-news webpages and eventually turned to other news sources for information, including local-news websites (Jones and Rainie 2002; Randle, Davenport, and Bossen 2005). Regardless of whether they continued to look to the Internet for news of the attacks on September 11, many people still used it for e-mail and instant messaging and to discuss the events and share their feelings in various chat rooms and discussion forums. In sum, virtually everyone turned to some form of media on September 11 to gather information and follow the unfolding events.

9/11 as Moral Shock

To understand what kind of event the terrorist attacks were and why they elicited this kind of media coverage and audience attention, we look to the notion of "moral shock," which was originally offered by James Jasper and Jane Poulsen to explain how, in the absence of traditional recruiting opportunities (i.e., preexisting social networks) social movement leaders could recruit new members to participate in movement activity, in essence, how they might persuade strangers to care about an issue and take political action in its name. A *moral shock* is an event that takes place in public, occurs unexpectedly, receives a great deal of publicity, and "raises such a sense of outrage in a person that she becomes inclined toward political action, with or without the network of personal contacts emphasized in mobilization and process theories" (Jasper 1997, 106; for more on moral shock, see Jasper and Poulsen 1995).

The concept of moral shock takes on a slightly different meaning when applied to public drama and the media. Jasper and Poulsen's definition of moral shock has three components: (1) the event, (2) the sense of indignation and moral outrage that it produces in some people, and (3) the political action that those so outraged might undertake. Although Jasper and Poulsen linked these three components, they are in fact quite different. I see the September 11, 2001, attacks as a moral shock, with the anger they produced followed by heightened political awareness or action as possible consequences. I do not believe that a highly publicized event needs to produce indignation or lead an individual to political action in order to be considered a moral shock. Another consequence of moral shock is that it can quickly attract widespread public attention to the source of the event. In fact, in relation to public drama, collective orientation becomes the most important function of moral shock.[6] Moral shocks demand immediate media coverage and compel people to join the media audience.

Prior research indicates that people generally rely on the media in their daily lives and that this reliance is substantially heightened during periods of ambiguity, emergency, or crisis (Ball-Rokeach 1985; Cohen et al. 2003; Hannigan 1995; Mogenson et al. 2002; Seeger et al. 2002). When we feel compelled to follow a particular event, the media become our link to it, giving us details and images and explaining what they all mean. As Robert Stallings found in his research on risk: "The reality of risk for most of us exists mainly in images created by others" (1990, 81). That is, we use the media's depictions and analyses of such events to make sense of them.

When packaged and presented appropriately by news workers, the media attention and audience interest engendered by a moral shock can give rise to a public drama, such as the assassinations of President John F. Kennedy and Martin Luther King Jr. in 1963 and 1968, respectively, and the Three Mile Island (TMI) nuclear disaster in 1979. Admittedly, the form and content of the coverage for these events were quite different from what we would likely see today, given the much less complex media infrastructure of those times. We can also see media events derived from moral shock following the 1985 explosion of the space shuttle *Challenger* and the 1995 Oklahoma City bombing. Moral shocks that produce extensive media coverage often are "Where were you when . . .?" moments that are collectively experienced and shared and often demarcate social time and space. Public dramas produced by moral shocks capture the nation's collective consciousness, dominate national newspapers, and preempt scheduled programming for days or, in the case of 9/11, weeks.

Moral shocks do more than just capture attention; they challenge collectively held meanings of a particular issue or the world at large. A basic component of everyday social action is our ability to construct a definition of the situation (Ball-Rokeach 1973; Thomas 1923). Because moral shocks are unusual, unexpected, and ambiguous, they invalidate many of these collectively held meanings.[7]

In response to a moral shock, people seek ways to make sense of their suddenly ambiguous and uncertain surroundings, often resulting in a collective rush to the mass media. Given the kind of media attention and audience interest that a moral shock elicits and how it challenges existing meanings, it is not surprising that the public drama of a moral shock can be a potent creator and conveyor of meaning.

Clearly, the September 11 attacks were a moral shock. They immediately captivated a vast audience, with most people finding it immensely difficult to make sense of what was happening. They had no readily available point of comparison; everything that was happening was new. This meant that the public had to rely on the media for information and sense-making frames, especially in the first hours after the attacks. The majority of the media audience thus turned to television to follow the unfolding horror in real time. Several studies of how and how much people used the media on and after

September 11 indicate their intense demand for information on September 11 (Abel, Miller, and Filak 2005; Carey 2003; Cohen et al. 2003; Greenberg, Hofschire, and Lachlan 2002; Jones and Rainie 2002; Mogenson et al. 2002; Perse et al. 2002; Rappoport and Alleman 2003; Rogers 2003; Rogers and Seidel 2002; Seeger et al. 2002; Stempel and Hargrove 2002). A study of public perceptions of news media after the attacks found that "for some people, the information gleaned from the media about the events surrounding September 11 was extremely influential in their initial appraisals of the terrorist attacks and their longer term implications" (Perse et al. 2002, 51). Similarly, Tom Ruggiero and Jack Glascock noted that "on September 11, and thereafter, as the mass media began disseminating 'news,' government agencies and individuals relied on different media for information vital to comprehending this national crisis event" (2002, 66).

The reservoir of meanings from which we ordinarily draw to make sense of various personal, social, and political happenings was suddenly inadequate. All the tools we usually employ to define a situation, like past experience and cultural vocabulary, were unable to explain the scenes of calamity and destruction on our television screens. As Bernhard Debatin noted in his assessment of the media officials' immediate postattack discourse, "The sheer magnitude of the events was incomprehensible. There were no words and no signifiers that would have been adequate to describe the events" (2002, 166).

For many people, Hollywood seemed to be the only viable frame of reference. Numerous eyewitnesses remarked that "it was like a movie," and reporters borrowed from Hollywood's fictional register to describe the events, as evident in the comments of NBC's on-air personnel in the hours immediately following the attacks:

> I have to say, I've never, ever . . . witnessed anything quite as horrific. I hate to keep saying it because we have seen these types of things play out in movies and, you know, in worst-case scenarios and in dramatic renditions of this kind of incident, but certainly no one has ever seen this kind of thing unfold, and it is really shocking. (Couric, NBC [10 a.m.], September 11)
>
> The building began to disintegrate. And we heard it and looked up and started to see elements of the building coming down and we ran. And honestly, it was like a scene out of *Independence Day*. Everything began to rain down. . . . It was a very deep gray smoke. It was, in honesty, looked like a bit of a nuclear winter, the type of thing you see in the movies with ash all over the ground, on top of cars, on police cars, on windows. (Insana, NBC [11:00 a.m.], September 11)

[I]f you can envision again that scene in *Independence Day*—that terrifying alien movie—that showed New York City exploding in a horrific fireball. Without the fire, that is exactly what the corridors in lower Manhattan looked like. (Insana, NBC [2:00 p.m.], September 11)

And then I walked down Broadway to Canal Street. And it was like walking through something that looked like out of a movie set of a nuclear holocaust. (Thompson, NBC [12 noon], September 11)

Certainly I can tell you that when we were standing just about . . . six, seven, eight blocks north of the World Trade Center this morning when that tower went down and the smoke literally billowed the dust up the avenue. It was precisely like the movies that we have seen. Much of this is like the movies. It is very, very hard. As a reporter, you know that the first thing to do is reach for something to make a comparison to and, frankly, through much of this it is almost impossible to find things that are a satisfactory comparison. (Dawson, NBC [3:00 p.m.], September 11)

For many people who saw it, the image of a commercial airliner loaded with passengers and veering sharply before deliberately slamming into the WTC's south tower proved extremely difficult to process cognitively.[8] Similarly, the live shots of the towers—with the upper reaches of each engulfed in flame and billowing thick black smoke—which provided nearly all the on-screen imagery for the first hour after the attacks, was very hard to comprehend, as were the eyewitness accounts of people falling or jumping, often in pairs, hand in hand, from the upper floors of those towers. I, for one, will never forget the images of each of the towers teetering oh-so-slowly and then swaying more violently before crashing down in a cloud of dust and debris just after 10:00 a.m. (south tower) and just before 10:30 a.m. (north tower).[9]

Later, the live images of the search and rescue activity at the WTC site proved no more amenable to cognitive or affective processing; nor did the rapidly rising casualty figures. The most common estimate bandied about on September 11 was about 20,000, although some speculated it could be as high as 50,000.[10] All in all, the suddenness, scope, and nature of the attacks (i.e., the deliberate targeting of civilians within the borders of the United States, using hijacked commercial aircraft filled with civilians) induced extraordinary sense-making difficulties for many Americans in those first hours and days (and, for many, much longer). Most people thus turned to the media to alleviate this ambiguity and give some semblance of meaning to what they were witnessing.

Minutes after the first plane crashed into the World Trade Center's north tower, the press quickly recognized the palpable drama and sociohistorical significance of these events and swiftly reallocated its resources to cover them. The attacks immediately supplanted all ongoing and planned news content. The leading cable and broadcast news networks immediately cleared their news holes in order to cover the attacks. Things that had seemingly been of great importance just moments earlier could no longer claim newsworthiness.

In addition to forgoing all non-9/11 news content and all commercials and non-news programming, the three broadcast networks (ABC, CBS, NBC) expanded their news holes in order to provide around-the-clock coverage of the attacks and their aftermath. This immediate switch to an "all-9/11-all-the-time" format created an interesting dilemma for the television news media. None of the planned news content and the news items held in reserve to supplement the planned content could be used any longer. But at the same time, these events had not yet crystallized into "reportable" news. The initial on-air coverage on all the broadcast and cable news programs was consequently marked by uncertainty about just what was happening. As a result, much of what was presented on-air throughout the morning and into the afternoon hours was speculation, conjecture, or unsubstantiated reports.

The juxtaposition of these elements—a fully expanded and suddenly emptied news hole, an unfolding event with an uncertain framework, a lack of coherent story lines, and new information that was revealed only in incremental bits—created a complex context for news producers, which was compounded by the public's demand for information. Media officials realized they could not afford to be patient and wait for the stories to develop. Instead, they had to search for a framework for these events and for narratives through which to convey the drama.

Because they were a moral shock, the terrorist attacks immediately captivated a vast audience, with many turning to television to follow the unfolding horror in real time. But most people found it immensely difficult to make sense of what was happening. There was no readily available point of comparison; everything that was happening was new and had never before been seen or experienced by most every member of the media audience. This meant that the public had to rely on the media for information and sense-making frames, especially in the first hours after the attacks.

These events were highly ambiguous and intensely dramatic. Media attention was sudden and expansive, and audience interest was extremely high.[11] People continued to turn to the media in record numbers throughout the week. The demand for television news was so high in the first week after the attacks that all broadcast and cable television news organizations had larger audiences (Carey 2003; Perse et al. 2002; Rappoport and Alleman 2003; White 2001). Each of the cable networks saw at least fivefold increases in the size of their audience during the first week after the attacks, with CNN having the largest, nearly ten times its normal audience (Downey 2001b).[12]

Despite being largely shut out of the immediate information seeking on September 11, the newspapers began to find their place in the coverage by September 12. The September 12 edition of the *New York Times* sold 1.65 million copies (nearly half a million copies more than on a usual weekday), and a reissue of that edition (on September 13) sold another 100,000 copies. The *New York Daily News* also outsold its usual weekday total, with more than 1.1 million copies sold on the morning of September 12 (Jones 2001). Notwithstanding their robust sales, the role of the newspapers as an information source in the first week after the attacks was rather minor relative to that of television. In fact, one could speculate that much of the increased circulation of newspapers on September 12 was attributable to souvenir and commemorative purposes, which is supported by the return to more proportionate sales figures on September 13.

After the first week, however, the newspapers became an increasingly valuable information source for many news consumers, especially after television's news holes first returned to their normal size and then gradually began to incorporate non-9/11 content (Cohen et al. 2003; Stempel and Hargrove 2002, 2003). Thirty-eight percent of the respondents in one study reported spending more time reading newspapers after 9/11 than before, and about two-thirds of those responding to a national phone survey in October 2001 cited newspapers as a useful source for news about the attacks.[13] A key factor in the increased centrality of newspapers as an information source is that newspapers had the advantage of being able to continue to provide extensive coverage of the attacks even as they, too, gradually incorporated more and more non-9/11 news content over time. For instance, the *New York Times* ran a special section, entitled "A Nation Challenged," for more than three months after the attacks, beginning about a week after the attacks and concluding on December 31, 2001, that was devoted entirely to the attacks.

As the days, and then weeks and months, passed, the U.S. print and broadcast media continued to cover the stories of 9/11, and their audiences kept listening to, watching, and reading that coverage. Surveys conducted after the attacks underscored the heightened interest in news engendered by the attacks. Two-thirds of the respondents reported being more interested in news after September 11 than before, with a twofold increase in the number of people who said they paid very close attention to typical news stories before 9/11, from 23 percent before to 48 percent after the attacks.[14]

Framing 9/11

There were plenty of raw materials available for the media to use in depicting these events and telling the stories of 9/11. With this in mind, we might expect that the media coverage was broad and far reaching. After all, most news organizations had expanded their news holes and there was no competing content, so they had an opportunity to explore the events and their aftermath in detail and to provide nuanced analysis. Yet the mainstream television news workers did not seize this opportunity. In fact, they ignored the more complex aspects of both before and after 9/11 to wedge the event into a few narrative frameworks. My analysis of NBC's *Today* from the first week after the attacks reveals that it covered an extremely narrow range of topics. All but a few of NBC's news reports from that initial seven-day period came from one of two categories, which I refer to as *responsibility and retaliation* and *dealing and healing*.

The Responsibility and Retaliation Frame

The *responsibility and retaliation frame* contains those stories that ask or answer questions like "Who did this?" "How did this happen?" "How should the United States respond to these attacks?"[15] This frame was prominent in the media coverage following the attacks. Several studies have examined the media coverage from the day of the attacks to see how it took shape and to determine its influence on the advancement and acceptance of a frame centered on military action (Anker 2005; Breithaupt 2003; Debatin 2002; Reynolds and Barnett 2003). All found that the initial mainstream media coverage, principally television, evoked a dominant frame that advanced the twin notions of American victimization and the need for a militaristic hunt for justice.[16]

In a general statement about the network and cable news content on September 11, Bernhard Debatin, a noted media scholar, argued that the efforts of television media personnel to understand and frame these chaotic and highly ambiguous events as rapidly as possible contributed to the production of a "simplifying and mainstreaming narrative centered on a desire for retaliation" that contributed to advancing the military response frame (Debatin 2002, 172). This is evident in the Fox News channel's programming from the afternoon of September 11 which, according to Elizabeth Anker, who analyzed the network's coverage from 5:00 p.m. to 6:00 p.m. EDT, revealed "a narrative trajectory of injury, pathos, and moral retribution" (Anker 2005, 22) running through its coverage that arguably helped determine how viewers experienced and understood the attacks. Portraying America as the innocent victim of an unwarranted attack created a context in which retribution was necessary to complete the melodramatic transformation from victimhood, giving the Bush administration a moral ground to respond militarily.[17] These melodramatic narratives were not limited to Fox News. CNN's coverage on September 11 also helped further the responsibility and retaliation frame by promoting war as a response while substantially limiting public discourse regarding other possible responses. CNN, according to Amy Reynolds and Brooke Barnett, who analyzed the networks' initial coverage, "created a powerful visual and verbal frame with its coverage by arguing to viewers that the events of September 11 comprised an act of war so horrific that immediate military retaliation was not only justified but necessary" (2003, 86).

The responsibility and retaliation frame also found support in other media forms, such as the Internet. An examination of all major U.S. news websites that covered the attacks found a similar justification for war. Not only was the responsibility and retaliation frame evident in their content, but it also was embedded in the sites' formats, with several navigational links promoting military action as the only viable response to the attacks. This led the researchers to conclude that the coverage (i.e., headlines, top stories, images) on the leading U.S. news agencies' websites "gradually hardens into a kind of 'total' narrative that, regardless of the order of its pathways in browsing, moves naturally, without contestation, toward a justification for war" (Brown et al. 2003, 109).

Given the abundance of evidence supporting the centrality of the responsibility and retaliation frame, we might surmise that this frame provided the de facto lens through which these events were understood. But even though this frame was clearly a powerful shaper of how we came to view 9/11, it was by no means the only coverage frame. In fact, I argue that a closer look at NBC's coverage beginning in the first week after the attacks reveals that responsibility and retaliation was not even the principal frame during that period.

The Dealing and Healing Frame

Many of the stories and reports offered by mainstream media in that first week were outside the responsibility and retaliation frame, pertaining instead to how the United States was handling the attacks within its own borders. This coverage often focused on the instrumental (e.g., emergency response, policies implemented, actions taken) or affective (e.g., how people were psychologically, emotionally, or cognitively processing the trauma) components of the aftermath. I refer to this as the *dealing and healing frame*. The "dealing" component refers to stories about the physical response at the three crash sites (the WTC, the Pentagon, and the field in Shanksville, Pennsylvania) or the policies implemented in response to the attacks (e.g., the grounding of all flights after the attacks or changes in airport security once the flights resumed). The "healing" component involves stories about the emotional or cognitive processing of these events (e.g., coping with the loss of a loved one or talking to kids about the attacks).

Table 4.1 provides an overview of the content of NBC's *Today*-designated coverage from the first week after the attacks and indicates that reports pertaining directly to some aspect of the dealing and healing category were more than twice as common as those in the responsibility and retaliation category (210 to 92). Moreover, more than 50 percent (110 of 210) of the reports in the dealing and healing category focused on New York City or Ground Zero. In fact, there were more reports about New York City and/ or the World Trade Center site in the first week of NBC's *Today* coverage (110) than there were in the entire responsibility and retaliation category (92) during that same period. The preponderance of New York City– / Ground Zero–focused reports in NBC's coverage was consistent with the coverage across all the mainstream media. According to one observer, "The terrorist attack on the World Trade Center was the most documented event in history" (HBO 2002).

The amount of coverage focused on New York City strongly suggests that the media's portrayals and framings of what was happening, along with other reports reflecting the dealing and healing frame, played a significant role in shaping individual appraisals of the attacks and the construction of collective meanings about 9/11.

In all, NBC's *Today* had more than three hundred reports during the first week after the attacks, all but four of which were related to 9/11.[18] Three of the exceptions stemmed from, ultimately false, reports of two hijacking attempts on September 13 at New York's Kennedy and La Guardia

TABLE 4.1. *NBC's Today-Designated Coverage, September 12 to 18*

Date: September	12	13	14	15	16	17	18	Total
RESPONSIBILITY AND RETALIATION								
Who did this? How did this happen?	15	13	4	3	1	4	2	42
How should the U.S. respond?	9	11	7	3	1	16	3	50
DEALING AND HEALING								
New York City / Ground Zero	28	20	23	9	4	17	9	110
Pentagon	5	4	0	1	2	0	0	12
Shanksville, PA	2	0	1	0	0	0	1	4
General National	2	4	1	0	1	16	11	35
Airports / Air Travel	6	9	3	2	1	2	3	26
Coping	3	7	8	3	1	0	1	23
OTHER								
Story Overview / Recap	1	0	0	0	1	0	0	2
International	3	0	4	1	1	1	4	14
Non-9/11	0	0	3	0	0	0	1	4
Coded Items per Broadcast	74	68	54	22	13	56	35	322
Reports per Broadcast	70	65	52	18	12	54	31	302

airports, which were featured on the September 14 broadcast because of a presumed connection to the September 11 attacks. The fourth non-9/11 report, entitled "News Headlines That Have Gone Unnoticed in the Past Week," appeared midway through the September 18 broadcast, probably to facilitate the reintroduction of future non-9/11 content. Only sixteen of these reports during that first week did not fit in either the responsibility and retaliation or dealing and healing frames. These include stories with an international focus and those recapping the attacks or the key moments from that first week.

New York: A City like No Other

The funneling of media attention toward New York City began shortly after the coverage commenced. During just the second hour of coverage on September 11, NBC coanchor Tom Brokaw promoted the World Trade Center as the main site of this massive drama:

Let's go back and show you the pictures of lower Manhattan where the situation only gets worse, not better. That is the financial district of the world; it's also a residential area and a great commercial area. Both twin Trade Tower buildings now have collapsed onto the ground. There is an untold loss of life. The ripple effect goes on with all the smoke and dust that has spread out across that very densely populated area. It goes down below ground as well as in the high-rise buildings there. There are many residential structures in that area as well. Some heroic rescue workers were down there trying to get people out of the building when the first building came down, and then the second building did as well. Without any sound, I'm looking at this. There is a kind of a surreal quality, but that is the epicenter of a great, great national tragedy and a great loss of life, no question about it this morning. (Brokaw, NBC [10:00 a.m.], September 11)

The fact that media disproportionately focused on New York City is certainly understandable given the spectacle that was under way in lower Manhattan. What was happening in New York City was equal to anything Hollywood's script writers could dream up. This was clearly a monumental event whose newsworthiness was heightened by the fact that it had been captured on film. These events contained plenty of human interest and human drama and offered a wide array of compelling images, many of which were as captivating and powerful as anything on film.

One of the most important factors in how quickly the media focused on New York City and in how long their collective gaze remained on what was happening there was the location of the WTC complex. Media researchers know that the proximity of a news organization to an event is a key determinant of if, as well how quickly, news organizations will turn to that event. In this case, lower Manhattan was home to the WTC complex as well as the headquarters for the news divisions of many of the nation's largest media organizations, which ensured that plenty of resources were available immediately to provide comprehensive coverage that could be sustained indefinitely.

Another factor was the WTC site's visibility and relative accessibility. Even though the other, non–New York City locations associated with these attacks had great news value, they did not possess nearly the same amount or offer the same mixture of news elements that New York City did. For instance, the attack on the Pentagon contained many potential dramatic story lines, but as a government building to which entry was limited and about which information was often classified, it had strict security protocols that impeded the flow of information about the event to the media and the public. In addition, in the first hours and days, the crash of United Airlines flight 93 in western Pennsylvania did not have the dramatic story lines and stunning visuals as did the WTC, or even the Pentagon.

The first on-site report from the scene of the crash in Shanksville, Pennsylvania, was not delivered until well into the evening on September 11.[19] Matt Lauer, a coanchor of NBC's *Today*, even admitted during an on-air discussion that the availability of video footage was a factor in the disproportionate coverage of the World Trade Center relative to other aspects of the attacks: "We've forgotten somewhat to remind people that there was the crash of another plane, a fourth plane outside Pittsburgh about 80 miles from Pittsburgh. And we don't have video of that story at the moment. That's one of the reasons we haven't been talking about it as much" (Lauer, NBC [12 noon], September 11). Although the Pennsylvania crash eventually was given a more prominent place in the 9/11 story when the media learned of and promoted the heroic actions of the passengers, it was more of a footnote to the overall drama in New York City in the first few days, when most of what became the dominant media frames were being constructed.

As the coverage of the September 11 began to take shape, it was clear that a hierarchy of 9/11 sites had emerged, with New York City being the focal point of America's mainstream media and their audiences. This was evident in the lead-in to the report by Katie Couric, a coanchor of NBC's *Today*, on the September 12 broadcast of *Today* about the scenes in New York City's streets during the attacks: "Twenty-four hours ago, this city was attacked while there was also death and destruction in Washington and Pennsylvania. New York is a place like no other."

Seeking Sense amid the Shock

The Coverage on September 11

When word that a plane had crashed into one of the World Trade Center towers first broke on the morning of September 11, the cable and broadcast networks' on-air personnel knew little about what they should say about the scene unfolding before them. The suddenness with which these events began and the way that the drama and calamity built in those first frantic morning hours presented extraordinary difficulties for the anchors, reporters, and other news workers who were trying to fashion what was happening into reportable news. The events were clearly newsworthy, even if what they were witnessing was not entirely clear.

The initial television coverage on the day of the attacks deserves special analytical attention, for it was during this period that many of the dominant framings and story lines began to take shape. The way the media attended to these events on the morning of September 11 and the information and images introduced throughout that first day were crucial to the transformation of September 11 into "9/11." This chapter examines NBC's coverage on the day of the attacks. I selected NBC for two reasons. First, the media's audience overwhelmingly turned to television throughout the day on September 11 and for several days thereafter. Second, NBC's network news coverage attracted more viewers than any of the other leading broadcast or cable news channels (for more information on postattack patterns of media use, see Abel, Miller, and Filak 2005; Carey 2003; Downey 2001b; Poindexter and Conway 2005; Ruggiero and Glascock 2002; Seeger et al. 2002).

NBC's News Division

In the fall of 2001, NBC's news programs were among the most popular of all television news. MSNBC, NBC's twenty-four-hour cable news network, was steadily gaining viewers, although, at that time, it still lagged far behind the Fox News channel in the cable news ratings. The network was increasing its web presence with the continued growth of MSNBC.com, and *Dateline*, its long-running television news magazine, continued to draw a significant number of viewers, although this was a period of marked decline in the ratings for television news magazine programs on all network and cable channels. The two flagship programs in NBC's news division were *Today*, its three-hour morning news program, and *NBC Nightly News*, its half-hour evening news program, each of which aired on network television.

NBC Nightly News is fairly standard evening network news. Like its counterparts on ABC and CBS, NBC's evening news runs thirty minutes in length, features mostly political and international news, and contains very little human interest or entertainment content. Much of the news on these programs is delivered as taped story packages, rather than the live interviews and lifestyle segments usually found on the morning programs. In addition to their familiar and well-worn structure, network evening news broadcasts are distinguishable from other television news programs in their general approach, which was described in one recent study as "a seriousness of purpose, a sense of responsibility and a confidence that the significant can be made interesting" (PEJ 2009).

Perhaps the most notable feature of the *NBC Nightly News* in 2001 was its anchor, Tom Brokaw. Brokaw's tenure as anchor since 1982 coincided with the news industry's move toward a profit-oriented model. In their efforts to make news programming more commercially viable, media officials often made their network's on-air news personnel the centerpiece of their promotional campaigns. This transformed many television personalities, especially the anchors, into celebrities, and helped make Brokaw one of the best-known and most trusted news anchors. In addition to his clout in the media industry, Brokaw had become an amateur historian with his book *The Greatest Generation*, chronicling the experiences of Americans who fought in World War II or lived through that tumultuous period. Accordingly, Brokaw's standing as a venerated newsman and chronicler of history enabled him to shape NBC's developing postattack narrative in a number of important ways.

Even though Brokaw was in many ways the journalistic face of NBC news in 2001, he was not necessarily the news division's biggest celebrity. Instead, that distinction was shared by Katie Couric and Matt Lauer, the coanchors of *Today*, the network's immensely popular morning news program. Since its inception in the early 1950s, *Today* has become one of the most watched, influential, and profitable news programs of all time. *Today* pioneered the now-familiar morning news format and provided a model for news production that could effectively meld "hard" and "soft" news content in ways that could be both informative and entertaining.[1] *Today* still remains a driving force in America's mainstream news industry. The program has been a ratings leader for more than a decade, drawing more viewers than any of its morning news competitors every week since December 1995. Furthermore, *Today* is by far the most profitable of all news programs on network or cable television; in fact, it is the most profitable show in NBC's entire stable of news or entertainment programming.[2]

When it began, on January 14, 1952, *Today* ran for two hours each morning from Monday through Friday. A one-hour Sunday edition began airing in 1987, followed by a two-hour Saturday edition in 1992. The weekday version eventually expanded to three hours in 2000, and a fourth hour was added in 2007. The typical *Today* broadcast is structured in thirty-minute segments, with the last five minutes of every half hour devoted to local news and weather. National and world news are concentrated at the front of the program, generally the first hour, with much of it in the first thirty minutes.

The program usually begins with the anchors providing an overview of the main news stories that will be featured on that broadcast. After a brief run through some of the other leading news headlines of the day (these are given not by the general anchors but by a designated "news anchor" at the "news desk"), the show features in-depth, usually on-scene, reporting for the leading stories. This continues for much of the first hour and, depending on the amount of suitable material for that day, may extend into the second hour as well. The remainder of the content is oriented more toward entertainment and human-interest stories, such as celebrity interviews, lifestyle stories, viewer involvement segments (e.g., weddings and contests), and musical performances (the fourth hour is spent almost entirely on this lighter fare).

While the program's overall structure and content are essential to its longstanding popularity, the key to *Today*'s success may be the manner in which it is packaged and presented. Much of the broadcast seems less like a formal news program and more like a group of friends enjoying one another's company while casually discussing the topics of the day. Interviews with guests are often very informal, with the anchor and interviewee sitting across from each other in comfortable chairs. When they are not interviewing guests, the anchors often sit side by side at the anchor desk or on a comfortable sofa and share their thoughts on a preceding or upcoming story. When seated on the sofa, the anchors often are joined by other on-air personnel, such as the weatherperson, news anchor, or visiting reporter, where they all engage in playful banter around the lighter stories.

NBC's Coverage on September 11

This was very much the scene on the morning of September 11, 2001. At the time of the first plane crash at 8:46 a.m. EDT on that Tuesday morning, *Today* had already been on the air for nearly two of its scheduled three hours. Up to that point, the day's broadcast had been geared mostly toward lighter content. Although the first full segment, following the general introduction, is usually reserved for the leading "hard" news about politics or crime or the economy, on this day the first in-depth item was a lengthy feature on the possible return of Michael Jordan to play professional basketball. After a brief overview of the day's headlines from the news desk (which included updates on the travails of Gary Condit and Andrea Yates, two of the most prominent public dramas of the summer of 2001), there was an eerily prescient preview for that evening's scheduled *NBC Nightly News* broadcast: "Tonight, three numbers that could save your life, 911. One hundred and ninety million calls each year, but you won't believe the problems we found. Why some wait for hours for help. Information you need when seconds count. That and much more ahead tonight." The first half hour of the program closed with a discussion about the economy with Donald Evans, the Bush administration's secretary of commerce.

Beginning with the 7:30 a.m. block, the morning's broadcast featured a series of lifestyle segments (e.g., "Living Better after 50"), updates from the news desk, and interviews with authors, celebrities, and others: Jack Welch, retired chairman of General Electric (NBC's parent company); Senator Edward Kennedy, who was invited to speak about the thirtieth anniversary of the Kennedy Center for the Performing Arts; comedian Tracy Ullman, promoting her new television show; musician Harry Belafonte, interviewed about an upcoming music project; and Richard Hack, discussing his book about the reclusive billionaire Howard Hughes. It was during this last interview with Richard Hack that the first plane struck the WTC's north tower, prompting Lauer, who was conducting the interview, to bring the interview to an abrupt end:

RICHARD HACK: The man [Hughes] was a bit compulsive, let's face it. But on the other hand, he was absolutely the most amazing man that America has ever created.

MATT LAUER: OK. I have got to interrupt you right now. . . . Richard Hack, thank you very much. We appreciate it. The book is called *Hughes*. We're going to go live right now and show you a picture of the World Trade Center, where I understand—do we have it? [asking producers if the live shot of the WTC is available] We have a breaking story, though. We're going to come back with that in just a moment. First, this is *Today* on NBC.

When the live broadcast resumed after the brief, unplanned commercial break, NBC still was uncertain about what had happened. In particular, the anchors and other on-air personnel had great difficulty orienting the discussion and framing these events. In their efforts to bring a measure of coherence to the coverage, NBC's news workers immediately began to draw on their stock of conventions and guidelines for organizing and presenting news.[3] Thus, even as information accumulated clearly indicating this was anything but a routine news story—particularly after the crash of a second plane and the reported hijacking of additional planes—the news workers resorted to the familiar strategies and techniques for making news. With this, the seeds for fashioning the attacks and their aftermath into a public drama were inadvertently planted.

Initially, what had caused the explosion was unknown; some reports suggested a plane, and others speculated that a bomb had been detonated on the tower's upper floors. Eventually, eyewitness reports determined that the explosion was the result of a plane crash, which led the *Today* anchors (Katie Couric and Matt Lauer) to apply a tentative accident frame: "We have a breaking news story to tell you about. Apparently, a plane has just crashed into the World Trade Center here in New York City. It just happened a few moments ago, apparently. We have very little information available at this point in time" (Couric, NBC [8:00 a.m.], September 11). A few moments later NBC's Al Roker implicitly supported the accident frame by recounting various accidents involving aircraft and high-rise buildings in New York City's history: "Tall buildings have had a real problem here in New York. Back in the [19]40s, a plane hit the Empire State Building. In the [19]60s, a helicopter crashed . . . on the top of what was the PanAm Building, now the MetLife Building."

Couric followed this a few moments later with a statement that lent further plausibility to the accident frame: "Right now, we are getting information . . . that it was a small commuter plane."

Following this initial flurry of reports and speculation, which lasted for less than ten minutes, the network elected to go to another brief commercial break. This respite was an attempt to adhere to the standard programming format (it was customary to have an end-of-the-hour commercial break, and the scope and magnitude of what had happened were not yet established) and, presumably, to give the anchors a few minutes off the air to try to gather information and find out just what was happening. Unbeknown to both them and the behind-the-scenes production staff, this would be its last commercial break for more than ninety hours.[4]

The Morning Hours, 9:00 a.m. to 12:00 Noon

Live coverage resumed at 9:00 a.m., with Lauer offering a brief introduction to viewers to explain what they were seeing, accompanied by live images of the upper floors of the tower engulfed in flames and billowing smoke.[5] After the brief update, Lauer provided the first on-air speculation that these events might be something other than an accident: "Immediately, there is speculation or cause for concern. This is the World Trade Center that was the center of a terrorist bombing some years ago. So the questions have to be asked, was this purely an accident or could this have been an intentional act" (Lauer, NBC [9:00 a.m.], September 11).

The anchors then welcomed Elliott Walker (a producer on the *Today* show who lived a few blocks north of the WTC), who joined the coverage via telephone to offer an eyewitness account. Walker described the sound of the plane flying low and fast overhead and its collision into the WTC tower as she saw it from several blocks away while walking her daughter to school. It was during this interview that a second plane struck the WTC's south tower at 9:03 a.m. Although the terrorism frame gained traction after the crash of the second plane, the accident frame proved remarkably resilient, with Walker invoking it again just after the second crash: "I wonder if there are air traffic control problems."

After the first plane crash, hundreds of media personnel and civilians descended on lower Manhattan to take in the unbelievable spectacle, many with video cameras in hand. Thus, hundreds of cameras were trained on the north tower when a second plane roared low over the city and slammed into the south tower. NBC's reporters on the scene immediately sent the captured images back to the studio, and within seconds of impact, the first of what became hundreds of replays of the footage of the second crash was aired. As the images of the impact appeared on the screen, Lauer advanced the terrorism frame a little further: "And now you have to move from talking about a possible accident to talk about something deliberate that has happened here."

When the live coverage began, NBC News had dispatched its reporting staff in New York City to lower Manhattan and requested information from its correspondents in Washington, D.C. to try and get some sense of how top U.S. officials were interpreting and responding to these events, but these moves had yet to pay dividends. Reporters were still making their way to lower Manhattan and gathering information to send back to the studio, and correspondents were still reaching out to contacts. Thus, NBC's on-air anchors were left to gather information through live phone interviews with various eyewitnesses. Most of the interviews were very brief and designed to have the eyewitnesses "set the scene" and describe those things that could not be conveyed by the horrific video footage of the crash (which was being continually replayed at this point) or the live images of the tower engulfed in flames. As the coverage shifted back to the anchors in the studio after a series of eyewitness interviews, the accident frame somehow remained in play:

> Well, of course, this is, as we've said, completely shocking video and a shocking turn of events. And we've been talking here that the first incident, one might surmise that it was some kind of accident. And then to have a second, what appeared to be a 727 jet. Of course, the question of terrorist activity has to surface. (Couric, NBC [9:00 a.m.], September 11)

Couric continued to breathe life into the accident frame, noting after another interview of an eyewitness at the scene:

> You know, some wires [wire reports] just came out and said in 1945, an Army Air Corp B-25, a twin engine bomber, crashed into the seventy-ninth floor of the Empire State Building. That occurred in dense fog. This was a crystal clear day in Manhattan. So it is completely unclear how there would be any kind of problems with visibility. (Couric, NBC [9:00 a.m.], September 11)

The terrorism frame gained greater footing a few minutes later during a conversation between the in-studio anchors and Jim Miklaszewski, NBC's Pentagon correspondent, who reported that "there are some officials here at the Pentagon who are calling this an obvious terrorist attack based on very preliminary information." This was confirmed minutes later by comments by NBC's national correspondent, Jamie Gangel: "I've just spoken to top U.S. officials with access to the latest intelligence. And they said, quote, that 'This was clearly terrorist-related, no question about it.'" At 9:30 a.m., President George W. Bush briefly addressed the nation from an elementary school in Florida and all but confirmed the terrorism frame, calling the events "an apparent terrorist attack on our country."[6] Shortly after Bush's statement, NBC correspondents advanced the terrorism frame by reporting that information gathered from intelligence officials suggested that the planes that had crashed had earlier been hijacked. The terrorism frame then became cemented when it was learned that a third hijacked plane had struck the Pentagon in Washington, D.C., at 9:43 a.m.

As the 9:00 a.m. hour came to a close, Tom Brokaw joined NBC's broadcast, coanchoring the coverage alongside Katie Couric and Matt Lauer for much of the day. Brokaw's arrival on the set was significant and gave the developing 9/11 narrative a moralistic and instructive tone.

Coverage in the 10:00 a.m. hour opened on a live shot of the scene in lower Manhattan (just as the previous hour had and much like nearly every hour of NBC's coverage of these events in the following days would) while the news staff tried to transform the chaos unfolding before them into reportable news. The mandate in this second hour of coverage seemed to be twofold: (1) seeking more information and (2) setting the various scenes of this unfolding drama, with a focus on the crash sites in New York City and Washington, D.C.

NBC's New York City–based news reporters were making their way to the WTC complex to gather information and provide on-scene coverage of these events. By this time, the network of eyewitnesses sharing their stories with news outlets had grown, with many recounting what it was like to see and hear a plane fly low overhead and then watch as it made an abrupt turn toward the WTC towers. It is here that we heard for the first time about people jumping to their death, often in pairs and holding hands, from the upper floors of the tower to escape the intense heat from the flames. By that point, the coverage had expanded from New York City to include Washington, D.C., following the attack on the Pentagon. Images of the damage caused by that attack and reports from the NBC News correspondent stationed there and reporters in the field throughout Washington, D.C., were featured along with the coverage of the events in lower Manhattan. The exclusive focus on New York City that marked the coverage before the attack on the Pentagon was abruptly reinstituted at 10:05 a.m. when the south tower collapsed, sending plumes of dust, debris, and smoke through the streets of lower Manhattan.

In the immediate wake of the south tower's collapse, NBC's reporters who had been near the scene were forced to flee, along with everyone else in the immediate area, and so they were unable to correspond with the in-studio anchors (Brokaw, Couric, and Lauer). The only NBC reporter in lower Manhattan with whom the anchors were able to establish contact was Bob Bazell, who was stationed at St. Vincent's Hospital, located some blocks north of the

WTC complex. The anchors immediately tried to incorporate his accounts into the broadcast, but it quickly became apparent that the hospital—despite its relative proximity to the WTC site—was simply too far from the scene to yield the in-person information being sought for the coverage. With that, the coverage shifted back to the anchors in the studio.

By this point, producers had made contact with a *Today* show employee who had witnessed the collapse of the first tower, and she joined the discussion by phone. She discussed what she saw ("clouds of smoke everywhere. People running towards me . . . I've never seen a scene like it") and tried to describe the reactions of others who were also at the scene ("everyone in tears . . . wondering if people that they know in the buildings next door . . . are OK."). After a brief exchange with Jamie Gangel, an NBC correspondent stationed in Washington, D.C., about whether air traffic controllers at that city's airports had offered more information about the planes' origins or flight paths (they had not), Brokaw offered the first of what became one of the signature elements of his coverage of the terrorist attacks: the invocation of historical parallels as a means for sense making:

> You know, it goes without saying, this is the most serious attack on the United States in more than one hundred years. Not since the War of 1812 and certainly the damage that we did to ourselves during the Civil War, has this country suffered this kind of damage within its interior. Obviously, Pearl Harbor, which triggered World War II, was a horrific event as well, but there has never been an event to match the magnitude of this one in which everything has been shut down in terms of air traffic, the national capital has been immobilized, the White House, State Department, Pentagon has been attacked, the financial markets have been shut down, there is an untold loss of life here in Manhattan, the nerve center of America, to say nothing of what's going on at the Pentagon. (Brokaw, NBC [10:00 a.m.], September 11)

Couric followed Brokaw's lead in trying to conjure up some aspect of our historical memory that could make these events somehow familiar: "It combines the horror of the TWA Flight 800 bombing and the Murrah Federal Building, because it's both of these incidents, of course, coming together in the most horrific way" (Couric, NBC [10:00 a.m.], September 11).[7]

The focus then returned to lower Manhattan where a reporter depicted the initial foray of rescue workers toward the WTC and the difficult task before them as they coped with the intense fires and the smoke, ash, and debris unleashed by the collapse of the south tower. This report was interrupted as the nationwide drama was ratcheted up further, first by Couric's relaying a report of a car bomb exploding outside the State Department and then by Brokaw's relaying a report from an NBC correspondent that a plane that was still airborne had been hijacked and was reportedly headed for Washington. As these two stories were being followed, at 10:28 a.m., the coverage yet again abruptly shifted back to lower Manhattan, with the collapse of the north tower.

Obviously, it took several minutes to reestablish contact with the reporters in lower Manhattan after the second collapse, and the in-studio anchors used that time to (1) alternate between live images of the WTC's smoldering remains and the Pentagon's severely damaged outer wall; (2) repeatedly show footage of key moments to that point (e.g., the plane crashing into the south tower, the collapse of each tower); (3) provide summaries; and (4) offer editorializing narratives.

When contact with field reporters at the scene was eventually reestablished, they began to describe what was happening in the immediate aftermath of the collapse of the second tower. Then came a report that another hijacked plane had crashed about eighty miles southeast of Pittsburgh, followed by a succession of dramatic developments that, at that time, seemed to strongly suggest that more attacks were imminent: (1) reports of other hijacked planes that remained airborne and were headed for the nation's capital; (2) word that potential targets of additional attacks, like government agencies, key facilities (e.g. nuclear plants), tourist destinations (e.g., Disney resorts, Philadelphia's Liberty Bell, Seattle's Space Needle), and tall buildings in large U.S. cities (e.g. Chicago's Sears Tower), were being closed and evacuated; and (3) reports of bombs being detonated in Washington, D.C. and New York City.[8] The fear of imminent attack became even more pronounced as NBC's Jim Miklaszewski reported that security forces in Washington, D.C., continued to fear that a still-airborne plane was heading for that city:

There was a very telling dramatic moment just a second ago when a U.S. Air Force F16 flew very low level, did a wide, sweeping turn around the Pentagon and back over Washington. And as one air force officer standing near me said, "My God, they're now flying air cover over Washington." A very dramatic moment, a milestone in what Tom has already described as a declaration of war. (Miklaszewski, NBC [10:00 a.m.], September 11)

As the suspense from these reports lingered, the coverage shifted back to the WTC site, where Brokaw briefly recounted what had happened thus far and offered the first of what became another signature element in his coverage of 9/11—the use of melodramatic narratives to depict these events—by referring to lower Manhattan as "the epicenter of a great, great national tragedy and a great loss of life" and offered the first description in NBC's coverage of the rescue workers as heroic. This was followed by one of many didactic messages he imparted on this day, suggesting that the events marked an epochal shift in American history:

> It is hard to overstate the consequences of all this, and this is just the beginning. We'll be living with this story and dealing with the consequences of it for some time. The United States will change as a result of all of this . . . this is going to change this country profoundly in not just the coming days but the coming months. . . . America has changed today. This is a dark day in this country. It will be in bold print in future history books about how America was attacked within its continental borders with devastating effect by terrorists' coordinated assault using hijacked civilian airliners to do just that. (Brokaw, NBC [10:00 a.m.], September 11)

By the time the third full hour of coverage began at 11:00 a.m., subtle shifts in the form and content of the coverage had begun to emerge. For instance, more eyewitness accounts had become available to incorporate into the coverage. In fact, because the headquarters of NBC News is in Manhattan, many of its staff members had witnessed or heard the first plane crashing into the north tower or had mobilized in response to that crash and were at or en route to the WTC when the second crash and/or collapses occurred. They were able to relay their experiences of that morning either from the field or by making their way back to the studio to deliver their accounts on the air.

Another change in this hour of coverage is that NBC's reporters—having emerged safely (albeit disheveled and traumatized) from the dust and debris—were finally able to report from various locations throughout lower Manhattan. Their accounts, which were not available in the previous hour, brought an important semblance of familiarity to the overall coverage in the next hours.

The 11:00 a.m. hour also provided the first sustained on-air discussion of what became two of the more closely followed stories of the first week of coverage: (1) the potential death toll and (2) the possibility of survivors in the WTC rubble. The potential for survivors and the possibility of a tremendous loss of life had been mentioned in passing throughout the first two hours of coverage (NBC's anchors had even speculated at one point that there might have been more than fifty thousand people in the two towers during the attacks), but in this hour the anchors, reporters, and other staff members began to spend more on-air time and off-air resources to gauge the totals of each. Although Mayor Rudy Giuliani and other public officials steadfastly refused to offer hard estimates of the death toll, conceding only that it was likely to be "in the thousands" and "more than any of us can bear," the anchors and reporters began to actively try to piece together estimates of the possible death toll during the on-air coverage. Each reporter was asked for estimates from the aspect of the attacks that they were covering (e.g., casualty figures from the hospital, number of casualties from the hijacked planes, and losses among the rescue workers).

The possible death toll was a central focus of an on-air interview conducted jointly with the chief of the Port Authority police and the director of the World Trade Center. During this interview the chief and the director suggested that it would be fair to assume that there were about ten thousand people in each tower on a normal business day, and since these interviewees had official connections to the WTC, this number, twenty thousand, became the first working estimate of the death toll in the WTC component of the attacks (its viability as an estimate was corroborated later in the day when the manager of the World Trade Center Club offered a similar figure during an on-air interview). This interview also featured speculation about potential survivors under the massive piles of debris and rubble, with the chief and the director noting that there were several possible air pockets and cavities in the underground parts of the WTC in which people could survive for days. Again, since these sources had intimate, official knowledge of the entire WTC complex, the idea that there could be people alive in the mountain of debris became an assumptive feature of the coverage.

In addition to these new elements, several features from the first two hours of coverage had carried through into the 11:00 a.m. hour: (1) the search for information and efforts to convey the "being there" aspects of the various scenes of this unfolding drama; (2) summaries and time lines of the day's events; (3) footage of the second plane slamming into the south tower and live images of the WTC towers' smoldering remains; and (4) dramatic reports of "ongoing threats."[9] In fact, the fear of further attack from still-airborne hijacked aircraft reached its apex during the 11:00 a.m. hour when Bob Hager, an NBC correspondent, reported on the air that the Federal Aviation Administration (FAA) had confirmed that there were still several planes in flight that were unaccounted for and were believed to have been hijacked. Hager appeared again on the air late in this hour to try to downplay the level of threat portrayed by his earlier report, but this did not succeed in mitigating the perceived threat, as evidenced by a comment from Brokaw just moments after Hager's amended report:

> The big story, obviously, that's still to be resolved is how many planes were hijacked. We now have a report that there could have been as many as four of them . . . there still could be planes in the air under control of the hijackers. We don't know for sure what flights they are or where they're headed. (Brokaw, NBC [11:00 a.m.], September 11)

The Early-Afternoon Hours, 12:00 Noon to 3:00 p.m.

As the coverage shifted into the early afternoon hours (discussed here as noon to 3:00 p.m.), many facets of the morning's coverage were carried over. The suspenseful, "What's next?" element of the day was prolonged by a variety of continuing subplots and new developments. For instance, the saga of airborne commercial airliners feared hijacked continued, although it finally ended just after 2:00 p.m., when Hager reported on the air that

> the FAA has just been able to confirm that the last of any scheduled domestic flights, last of the domestic flights that were in the air are now known to have reached their airports. So there is no other domestic flight that is unaccounted for. The implication is there's no other hijacked flight up there, that this is over as an event. (Hager, NBC [2:00 p.m.], September 11)

The on-air reporting of bombs detonating in Washington, D.C., New York City, and elsewhere, which was so prevalent in the first hours, also had subsided by this point. But even as these stories were closed, new developments were presented on air that prolonged the drama. As reports of F-16 fighter jets flying over Washington, D.C., and New York City continued, NBC's Jim Miklaszewski stated that military warships had been dispatched to the waters outside those two cities:

> We just learned a few moments ago that the U.S. Navy is dispatching a couple of aircraft carriers from Norfolk, the *JFK* and the *George Washington*. One will be stationed off of New York. The other will be stationed in the Atlantic as close to Washington, D.C., as [it] can get. They'll be there to provide any possible military support that may be needed, including flying any kind of air cover should there be any additional warnings of any further terrorist-

attempted attacks. . . . [T]o see two air craft carriers moved into locations off the United States to provide air cover . . . I mean that's the kind of thing you normally see in a war zone. (Miklaszewski, NBC [12 noon], September 11)

Perhaps the most significant new contributor to the suspense and tension of this period of coverage was President Bush's unavailability. After first learning of the attacks and delivering brief remarks to the nation while at a Florida elementary school, the president had been whisked away by his security team with no word of his intended destination. As the morning gave way to afternoon, on-air discussion about the length of time since the president had addressed the nation (or even been heard from outside his closest advisers) began in earnest. While the lack of information about the president's whereabouts was certainly understandable given the level of threat at that point, it was discussed by NBC personnel in ways that made it a dramatic story line on a par with the others that day. This histrionic portrayal of the president's clandestine movements was best exemplified in a report from Campbell Brown, an NBC reporter stationed outside the White House:

We're not actually sure at the moment where exactly the president is right now. He was in Florida this morning. We understand that he was told about the situation while he was in a holding room at the Booker Elementary School where he was scheduled to do a reading event. . . . One of the key questions . . . that we're asking right now, given that no one's been informed where the president is—and this is, of course, deliberate—is whether or not the White House will decide to put him on the so-called Doomsday Plane. This is a special plane designed for the president in the event of a nuclear attack. And it's far more sophisticated than Air Force One. It has the absolute most advanced electronics equipment on board. He's able to communicate with anyone at any time and able to command the armed forces from this plane. They're able to refuel it mid-air, and they could essentially keep the president on this plane for an extended period of time. We don't know if that's an option that has been considered or something that they are looking at trying to do right now or whether or not his plan is to come back here to the White House. (Brown, NBC [12 noon], September 11)

Coverage in the early afternoon hours also saw continued efforts to gauge the death toll of these attacks, discussion of the possibility of survivors beneath the rubble at the WTC site, frequent summaries of the day's events, and more of Brokaw's moralistic, historically instructive narratives.

Although these continuing threads and ongoing subplots remained, the early afternoon coverage departed from the morning's coverage in a number of important ways. First, various public officials and "experts" were increasingly incorporated into the on-air presentation. Second, the terrorism frame was now firmly in place, and it guided a good deal of the overall discussion and helped determine some of the story lines to be followed and the sources to be incorporated into the coverage. In fact, the selection of sources is one of the chief ways that we can see the influence of the terrorism frame at work, as the collection of those invited on air for comment was dominated by "terrorism experts," military leaders, and public officials who oversaw terrorism-related committees or programs.[10]

A third way in which the early afternoon coverage was noticeably different was that by this time, NBC's news staff had gathered literally hundreds of accounts from eyewitnesses (including several from the network's field reporters and other staff members throughout lower Manhattan) who had witnessed some of or all the key moments of the day (e.g., the crash of one of the planes, the collapse of one of the towers, the massive egress out of lower Manhattan). As I noted earlier, in the initial hour or two of coverage, NBC's anchors had to rely almost entirely on eyewitness accounts to supplement their in-studio narratives because reporters were not yet at the scene or were not available to report, and local, state, and federal officials were still assessing the situation and not available for comment, and these initial accounts varied greatly regarding how much new information they provided or how well they "set the scene" and conveyed the drama of the day. But now, with hundreds of accounts to choose from—and the luxury of more time for the news staff to sift through them—NBC's producers and anchors could be more selective as to which got on the air, choosing only the most dramatic, emotionally gripping accounts.

A fourth new element in the early-afternoon coverage was an intensified focus on the overall search and rescue effort at the WTC and those involved in it. Early in the coverage, NBC reporter Pat Dawson had positioned himself at the staging area for the rescue effort, where he remained throughout the day. His reports served to highlight some of the rescue units as principal figures in that response (representatives of the FDNY, NYPD, or Port Authority were often interviewed on the air). It was during these reports that we first heard detailed discussions of the difficulties of this search-and-rescue effort: massive and unstable piles of debris, intense heat from the burning jet fuel and underground fires, deleterious air quality, and the instability of some of the other buildings in and around the WTC complex. These accounts led Dawson to describe the rescue effort multiple times as nothing short of a

"Herculean task." It was also from these early afternoon reports that we first heard hard estimates of the calamitous losses suffered by the FDNY. At the time, it was estimated by FDNY officials that a staggering 200 to 225 firefighters had been killed during the initial emergency response and the collapse of the towers. Hard as it would be to believe, this turned out to be a conservative estimate. We eventually learned that a total of 343 New York City firefighters perished in the early stages of the rescue effort. While it was not apparent at the time to most in the news media or their audiences, this early-afternoon coverage provided the first hints that the firefighters were emerging as leading characters in this public drama and, by extension, becoming an increasingly prominent part of the 9/11 narrative.

A fifth shift that first became apparent during this period of coverage was that the presentation was becoming increasingly redundant, which became even more pronounced as the around-the-clock coverage continued. In this way, the afternoon of September 11 was a turning point in the life of the 9/11 coverage: no longer did it have a rapid succession of fresh developments, occurrences, and rumors to be followed and reported on. At the same time, many of the events, symbolic moments, story lines, and characters that sustained the coverage in the ensuing months had not yet become apparent. Among the ways that these redundancies revealed themselves were (1) numerous summaries by Brokaw and by field reporters each hour, including particularly glaring redundancies on several occasions, such as when a Brokaw summary was immediately followed by a similar summary from a reporter in the field; (2) on-air guests (i.e., experts, public officials, and eyewitnesses) being recycled into the coverage, which meant that several of those who had appeared earlier in the day were again invited to discuss the day's events, often with little new information or insights; (3) reporters regularly delivering live updates from the field, regardless of whether they had new information; and (4) NBC reporters and staff members who had experienced the trauma of the day firsthand recounting their tales multiple times throughout the afternoon and evening.

The Late-Afternoon Hours, 3:00 to 6:30 p.m.

The late-afternoon period (defined here as the period from 3:00 until 6:30, when NBC's *Nightly News* began) did not signal any major shifts in the coverage. It featured continued redundancies in the form of summaries, time lines, "new" interviews with some of the individuals who had previously been interviewed, saying more or less the same things; and an increasingly familiar rotation through the collection of official sources, field reporters, and correspondents.

There were, of course, some new elements introduced into the coverage during the late-afternoon period. It was here that the first substantial discussions of the economic impact of these attacks (which had largely gone unmentioned throughout the morning and early-afternoon coverage) were held, as well as a brief dialogue about the need to place these attacks—and their causes and consequences—into a broader international context. In addition, the late-afternoon coverage first featured edited montages filled with images and quotations from earlier coverage that day.

Viewers also learned during this part of the coverage where the president was. At the outset of the 3:00 hour, reports surfaced that the president had earlier arrived safely at an air force base in Nebraska. While this would seem to most people to be a satisfactory resolution to the question of the president's whereabouts, NBC's on-air personalities continued to discuss his location in dramatic terms, as evident in Tim Russert's suggestion that the decision to send the president to a secure military facility might indicate that the threat of imminent attack was not over, as we had earlier been led to believe:

> The fact that he has chosen to go there, a place which is the nerve center of all our military activity, is an indication that perhaps this threat has not ended. There was some thought that he may be coming back to Washington, and the fact that he has not underscores the concern that there still may be a continuing threat. (Russert, NBC [3:00 p.m.], September 11)

The notion that that the attacks might still be under way was further reinforced by Brokaw's comments following Russert's report: "That, it does appear, is where the president is going to be for the time being, at least, until they sort out whether this wave of attacks is over" (Brokaw, NBC [3:00 p.m.], September 11). Shortly before 5:00 p.m., much of the tension surrounding the president's whereabouts dissipated when word went out that President Bush had left Nebraska and was aboard Air Force One en route to Washington, D.C., and that he would address the nation later that evening.

The late-afternoon hours also continued to focus on the search-and-rescue effort at the WTC site, with the anchors or reporters often describing the rescuers as "heroic" (an adjective that Brokaw had first used about an hour into the coverage but had not been used again until now) and referred to members of the FDNY as "New York's finest."[11]

If the late-afternoon coverage had a trademark characteristic, it was the much-intensified focus on calculating the number of casualties resulting from these attacks and the number of people who might be trapped in the rubble (and where in the rubble they might be). This focus was neatly summarized by Brokaw's statement early in the 3:00 hour, as live images from the WTC site appeared on screen:

> As we continue to look, with a sense of disbelief at the magnitude of the destruction in lower Manhattan, the physical destruction, to repeat, as we have throughout the day, we still don't know how many people remain trapped in the rubble, what the exact numbers are. But as you look at that scene, I'll leave it to you to determine in your own mind just how widespread the human loss will be in New York City alone. (Brokaw, NBC [3:00 p.m.], September 11)

Much of the on-air discussion among anchors and many of the updates from correspondents and field reporters concentrated wholly or partly on the possible loss of life in the WTC attacks and the potential for people to be alive beneath the rubble:

> Tom, breathtaking, by the way, what that man from the World Trade Center said about 20,000 people supposed to be in there at that hour of the morning. So goodness knows where this toll is going. What we do know in terms of hard numbers are those killed on the various flights of these airplanes that were turned into weapons. And that total is 266 in the four planes that were hijacked. (Hager, NBC [3:00 p.m.], September 11)

Brokaw went off the air at 5:00 p.m., replaced by Katie Couric and Matt Lauer, who coanchored the coverage from 5:00 to 6:00 p.m., after which Brian Williams carried the coverage for thirty minutes until Brokaw returned to the anchor chair. Upon her return as coanchor, Couric continued to emphasize the possible death toll as she opened the 5:00 hour:

> It's been more than eight hours since the first plane hit the World Trade Center Tower this morning. We do know the devastation is unfathomable, but at this hour, there is much we still do not know. For example, it is unclear how many people have died here in New York or at the Pentagon, where another jet crashed this morning as well. In Manhattan, it's believed that thousands of people may have been killed or injured, but a definitive

number may not be known for days or even weeks. We do know 266 people died on board this—on board four airliners, hijacked and turned into deadly weapons this morning. (Couric, NBC [5:00 p.m.], September 11)

Shortly after Couric's remarks, David Bloom promoted the number of casualties as a central element of this story in his report from lower Manhattan:

There are two questions at this hour that people still don't know the answers to. Number one, how many people were killed or injured in these series of attacks? Number two, who's responsible? We know, as you mentioned, that 266 people aboard the four hijacked planes are dead. The New York City officials estimate that, most likely, the casualties here in New York City alone will number into the thousands, that dozens, if not hundreds, of New York City police and firefighters are missing and presumed dead, those who went into the buildings that used to stand behind me, trying to rescue people inside. (Bloom, NBC [5:00 p.m.], September 11)

This quotation is significant not only because it illustrates the renewed focus on the casualty figures but also because it places the firefighters and police squarely in that focus, which made them principal figures in two of the dominant ongoing story lines (the death toll and the search and rescue activity at the WTC). The casualties in the ranks of the NYPD and FDNY were again pushed to the forefront during an update from Bob Bazell, a reporter who had been monitoring activity at area hospitals throughout the day:

Right now, we know of about one thousand casualties in all the New York area hospitals that have been taking them in. The one where I was, St. Vincent's Hospital, has about 250. . . . In addition to that, about one in five of the people who were brought in seriously injured or dead were either firefighters, policemen or EMS workers. An enormous number of the people who were injured today were rescue crews because of the timing between the crash and the explosion in the first World Trade Center tower. And the second one, a lot of people were going in to put out that emergency and then the building— the second building—exploded, and then there was the collapse. So we were seeing a lot of heroic firefighters and police and emergency service workers who were injured as well. (Bazell, NBC [5:00 p.m.], September 11)

As the late-afternoon period of coverage drew to a close, NBC's production staff decided to briefly replace the images of horror and destruction from

Ground Zero and the Pentagon with the patriotic image of an American flag fluttering in the breeze. As this image played on the screen, Couric and Lauer somberly noted some of the more alarming facts and figures from the day.

The Evening Hours, 6:30 p.m. to 12:00 Midnight

The evening coverage (defined here as 6:30 p.m. until 12:00 midnight) commenced with a ninety-minute block of programming that was designated as NBC's *Nightly News*. While this new designation might seem unnecessary, given that this period featured the same on-air personnel who had provided coverage throughout the day, it actually marked an important shift in the overall form of the coverage and in the way that information was presented.

Although relatively little new information was provided during this broadcast, the fact that it was delivered under the *Nightly News* banner and anchored by Tom Brokaw helped reinstate some semblance of normalcy by offering a familiar tone, style, and form of presentation (e.g., introductory music, edited collections of images, carefully selected sound bites from earlier interviews and reports, reporters' prerecorded narratives played over the edited collections of images and footage). Implied in all this is perhaps the most important distinction between all the earlier coverage and this *Nightly News* broadcast, which was that the latter offered the first opportunity that day for news personnel to take a proactive approach to covering the attacks. Since just before 9:00 a.m., anchors and reporters had been forced to react to the succession of events, developments, and rumors. But the *Nightly News* broadcast allowed news personnel to plan ahead and provide a script for what they would cover and how they would cover it.

The program opened with the standard dramatic music that ushers in every evening's broadcast. As this introductory music played, a rapid succession of images from the day flashed on the screen—a still shot of the second plane crashing into the south tower, images taken from various vantage points of the WTC towers on fire, and footage of the north tower collapsing—against a background image of an American flag blowing in the breeze. As the series of images closed with the footage of the crumbling tower, the words *Attack on America* were superimposed on the on-screen images, and a voice announced this was "an NBC News Special Report" and introduced Tom Brokaw. As soon as he appeared on screen, with video footage of the smoke-filled lower Manhattan skyline appearing over his shoulder, Brokaw immediately offered the sort of historically contextualized framing of the events that had become his trademark throughout the day's coverage:

September 11, the year 2001, a day unlike any other in the long course of American history. A terrorist act of war against this country. President Bush saying today that "freedom had been attacked by a faceless coward and freedom will be defended." Not since Pearl Harbor was attacked on December 7, 1941, has this country undergone such a devastating and damaging attack. And it may not yet be over.

The introductory montage and Brokaw's opening statement inadvertently underscored one of the most prominent features of the developing September 11 narrative: the increasingly disproportionate focus on New York City (the montage contained images only of the events and destruction there, and Brokaw's entire opening statement was accompanied by footage of the attacks and the aftermath in New York City, save for about twenty seconds of Pentagon footage).

The return to a more organized format and orchestrated presentation style was evident for all the designated *Nightly News* programming. The primary aim of those who contributed to the program was to depict the day from the various perspectives of those who experienced it. Hence, a correspondent at the Pentagon discussed how the day proceeded for the government and military communities in the nation's capital; a reporter at the White House recounted the day as the president might have experienced it; a reporter in lower Manhattan provided a comprehensive synopsis of the day's key events there; another reporter in lower Manhattan described the day from the perspective of the rescue workers; and various NBC staffers who were near the WTC site when the towers collapsed shared their dramatic and harrowing accounts. Stories also became more singularly focused during this *Nightly News* broadcast (as opposed to the earlier, understandably more scattered reports), with a speculative report exploring how the hijackers may have succeeded and what the scenes on the hijacked planes might have been, as well as a report about the rescuers and the overall search-and-rescue effort.

This *Nightly News* was not, however, a complete departure from earlier presentations that day, as many of the staple features of the earlier coverage remained, including frequent summaries and time lines from the day, replays of key footage (e.g., the second plane crash, the towers' collapse, the damaged Pentagon, the postcollapse scene in lower Manhattan), more depictions of the rescuers as "heroic," continued efforts to estimate the death toll, and further speculation about the possibility of survivors in the rubble.

After the formally designated *Nightly News* portion of the broadcast concluded at 8:00 p.m., NBC's coverage continued to become more routinized as the evening progressed, eventually becoming a familiar flow of summaries, time lines, images, editorials, and accounts. Anchors repeatedly solicited comments from the various correspondents and reporters in the field in an increasingly familiar rotation (i.e., to Campbell Brown at the White House, Jim Miklaszewski at the Pentagon, Pat Dawson monitoring the rescue effort, and David Bloom or other reporters throughout lower Manhattan) and offered more and more edited pieces. In fact, the events of 9/11 underwent what we might refer to as their first *Datelining* at the hands of Stone Phillips, Jane Pauley, and other *Dateline* personnel during the 8:00 p.m. hour. *Dateline* is NBC's televised "news magazine" program, known for packaging news in a way that is designed to shock and entertain. Most *Dateline* broadcasts feature some combination of investigative pieces and carefully edited interviews focusing on sensational crimes and other tabloid-worthy topics and emphasizing traumatic events, deplorable acts, and matters of human interest. That evening, the *Dateline*-oriented segments were edited pieces carefully crafted to present the events in as dramatic and emotional a manner as possible, with only the most gripping sound bites from eyewitness accounts, the most horrifying and dramatic images, the most memorable statements from President Bush and other officials, and the most evocative language to piece it all together, as evidenced by Stone Phillips's report: "Live cameras, trained on the first stricken tower, captured another huge explosion, this one on the south tower. Only this time, the attack was documented. This indelible image to be replayed again and again, seared into the American memory" (Phillips, NBC [8:00 p.m.], September 11).

Jane Pauley presented a similarly evocative story package during the 9:00 hour:

> The mighty World Trade Center tumbling down. Everyday New Yorkers had to run for their lives. How fragile the city seemed today. We deployed a team of *Dateline* staffers to bring us images of a city under siege on handheld digital cameras. . . . They brought us a startling glimpse of what it was like to be at ground zero of a major terrorist attack. (Pauley, NBC [9:00 p.m.], September 11)

The evening coverage also featured President Bush's address to the nation, as well as a renewed focus on the Pentagon (after federal officials in charge of that operation released estimates that as many as eight hundred people had died in that attack) and the first live report and footage from the field in Shanksville, Pennsylvania, where the fourth hijacked plane had crashed.

Discussion of survivors beneath the rubble at the WTC site continued throughout the evening, especially after information surfaced that victims had been pulled out alive. This first was reported by Brokaw, who remarked that a high-ranking NYPD official had made that claim at a press conference earlier that evening, then in a discussion between Brokaw and New York Governor George Pataki, and again in a press conference held by Mayor Rudy Giuliani, at which he announced:

> We have been able to rescue two people, two Port Authority employees who are alive. We don't know what condition they are in. But we're hopeful that we'll be able to rescue some more people. I have no idea how many others, but at least there's hope that we may be able to get some people out. We have been able to get two people out who have been identified as Port Authority police officers. (NBC [11:00 p.m.], September 11)

The most notable feature of the evening coverage was the focus on the emergency response at the WTC and those involved, particularly the FDNY and the NYPD. The search-and-rescue effort at the WTC had become a regular feature of the day's coverage since the early afternoon when NBC's Pat Dawson took up a position at the staging area of the rescue effort and delivered a series of on-air reports from that location throughout the day. Dawson's reports continued in the evening coverage, and the focus on the search-and-rescue effort intensified as three more NBC reporters began to describe various aspects of the emergency response or tell the tales of those involved. NBC reporter Rehema Ellis described how she and her camera crew "managed to make our way past the security guards and the police officers and get right down into ground zero" and provided footage of what was happening within the restricted areas of the WTC site:

> I've just come back from Ground Zero. It's like going inside a disaster. We have some pictures we want you to take a look at. There's an eerie light that's cast over the entire area. Fire crews are hosing—hosing down the smoldering remains. There are firefighters everywhere. They are literally sifting through the rubble trying to see what there is—who they might be able to find. I asked one firefighter—it is hard to imagine that anyone could survive this kind of devastation. But one firefighter said to me, "We never give up. We will continue to search through this area until the very last word is given that we shouldn't search anymore." They are hoping against all hope they can—they can find someone out of this rubble. . . . Tom, it

is almost unbelievable. It takes your breath away to stand in what was the center of America's financial area, and now it doesn't exist anymore. There is still dust, choking dust. The air is so thick. It's very hard to breathe. It's very difficult to see. The firefighters however, as I say, they refuse to give up. We went one block away from ground zero. It is the staging area where all the firefighters are. We talked with one of the chiefs who told us that they felt that they were able to bring someone out alive. He couldn't tell me what the condition of the person was at this moment. (Ellis, NBC [10:00 p.m.], September 11)

This footage provided the foundation for three extended reports from Ellis between 10:00 p.m., when the footage first was shown, and midnight. In addition to providing an inside glimpse of the rescue efforts under way, this report and footage also affirmed the impression that firefighters were principal figures in this response, from their distinctive uniforms visible in Ellis's footage from Ground Zero and in her interviews with several of them. Firefighters were also interviewed in most of the other reports from those assigned to cover the search and rescue, and they figured in several of Brokaw's comments from the anchor desk.

This is the scene in New York tonight. This is a city that is still hurting very deeply. The New York City Firefighters Union says tonight, these are unconfirmed numbers, but it is from the Firefighters Union, that it has lost and the city has lost 200 of its finest, 200 firemen killed today in the World Trade Center attack. The buildings came down, of course, many of those firemen were at the base of those buildings involved in fire fighting and rescue efforts at the time. That's the first number that we have had from reliable source, it comes from the Firefighters Union tonight. (Brokaw, NBC [8:00 p.m.], September 11)

A real brotherhood, obviously, in these big city fire departments and rescue operations. . . . They don't call them New York's finest for nothing. Those are really heroic efforts that are underway tonight in the lower end of Manhattan. (Brokaw, NBC [11:00 p.m.], September 11)

The September 11 coverage closed with a focus on the firefighters, providing a hint of what was to come:

There are reports that between 200 and 300 firemen are missing who were in there at the time trying to rescue personnel. We heard earlier in a report from Dawn Fratangelo about a woman who was coming out of the building. She said the firemen were going up. She just knows that they were lost. (Brokaw, NBC [11:00 p.m.], September 11)

"9/11" Taking Shape

The mainstream coverage on September 11 was a reflection of news workers' collective efforts to impose form and meaning on these emerging, chaotic events. Several factors identified in this chapter—the decision to expand and empty the news hole, adherence to an overall media logic favoring dramatic and emotional stories, the premium placed on visual images and official accounts—influenced the form and content of the coverage on the day of the attacks.

As the initial day of coverage ended, much of the mainstream media's attention had been directed to New York City, largely because it offered the best mixture of dramatic developments, emotional accounts, and compelling images. The World Trade Center, which came to be known as "Ground Zero," emerged as the epicenter of these tragic events, with several of the central figures in that emergency response (e.g., Mayor Giuliani, the NYPD, the FDNY) pushed to center stage as the stars of this public drama. Although the significance of these emerging patterns of coverage might not have been evident at the time, they proved to be crucial determinants of both media and popular discourse about the attacks and what should be done in response.

The Drama Is in the Details

Dramatic Amplification at Ground Zero

NBC's September 12, 2001 edition of *Today* opened with what had already become a familiar collection of video footage and still photos: the flames and smoke billowing out of the upper reaches of the WTC's north tower, a plane flying into the south tower of the WTC, the two towers on fire after the impact, the explosion at the Pentagon, the crumbling of each of the WTC towers, the chaos of the emergency response, devastated rescue workers covered in soot and ash, and wide shots of the smoldering debris and ruins at Ground Zero. While these images were showing on the screen, Katie Couric, the *Today* coanchor, ushered in the new day of coverage.

> Good morning. America may never be the same, and this is why. A beautiful Tuesday turned tragic when American Airlines Flight 11 crashed into the north tower of the World Trade Center, and that is just the beginning. This morning, less than twenty-four hours later, the heart of commerce and the signature of the New York skyline is no more. Meanwhile, the nerve center of the U.S. military has been deliberately and viciously attacked, leaving a nation and the rest of the world stunned today, Wednesday, September the twelfth, 2001.

This was still very much a developing story on that morning, but the broadcast was no longer characterized by the frantic collection of information and warnings that marked the earliest hours of coverage on September 11. This much slower pace, coupled with the added processing time (it had now been almost twenty-four hours since the story broke), gave NBC's news personnel time to better shape the form and content of their coverage.

Amplifying Drama on Today

With the start of the September 12 edition of *Today*, it became clear that the coverage had acquired a certain narrative form. In particular, news workers spent a great deal of attention and resources on identifying and describing the most dramatic elements of the attacks and their aftermath. This is significant because even though these events were routinely being labeled by journalists and political leaders as a major moment in U.S. history destined to have tremendous cultural and political consequences, television's news workers attended to these events in much the same manner, albeit much more extensively, as they would other high-profile issues or events. That is, news workers fashioned these events into a dramatic and emotional story (i.e., a public drama) that was likely to resonate with their audiences.

The media logic of public drama places a premium on dramatic elements (e.g., suspense, surprise, conflict, melodrama) and the need to mold selected news items into a captivating and compelling story built around an interesting but not overly complicated plot. This chapter examines NBC's *Today* programming for seven days after the attacks and explores the extent to which the media logic of public drama guided NBC's coverage of the response and recovery operation at the World Trade Center site. My analysis illustrates the strategies and tactics that NBC's news workers used in their efforts at "dramatic amplification" during their coverage of what was happening at Ground Zero and also underscores the importance of these efforts to the emergence and content of the mediated public drama surrounding those events.

Setting the Scene

One of the most common ways that news workers evoke the drama of an event or episode is to "set the scene," to give the audience a vivid image of the who, what, when, and where of it all. As discussed in chapter 3, the setting is as valuable for crafting a good story as are the characters and plot. The scene must be set in a way that captivates audience members and gives them a sense of how it *feels*, *looks*, *sounds*, and *smells* to those involved. NBC's anchors and reporters did this in numerous ways. For instance, the video footage showing the second plane slamming into the WTC's south tower was replayed hundreds of times that week. Efforts to set the scene also were evident in the incorporation of live video of the WTC site and the emergency response under way there, which often filled the screen while Couric and Lauer talked with each other or with guests. However, the two most common means of scene setting in NBC's coverage of the response and recovery at Ground Zero were the live, on-location reports and the eyewitness interviews.

Reporters frequently delivered their reports at Ground Zero, and many went to great lengths to position themselves so that the smoldering ruins and/or rescue workers would be visible over their shoulder, as is apparent in the following report from NBC reporter David Bloom on September 13:

> Day three of the rescue efforts here in lower Manhattan, and I think you can see from the shot we're showing the thick acrid smoke that the rescue workers have been breathing in. Much more dense, filled with particulate matter, including asbestos, just the latest complication in this rescue effort. I want to take you inside showing you the latest videotape of the rescue effort, of the recovery process going on right now.

Immediately after the attacks, an expansive perimeter had been put in place around the WTC site to help keep reporters and other nonessential personnel (i.e., convergers and information seekers) at a safe distance and to prevent them from slowing the rescuers. An unintended consequence of these restrictions was that they enhanced the value of images and information related to the activity at Ground Zero, thereby increasing the incentive for reporters to try to bypass the restrictions. As I discussed in chapter 5, a particularly compelling moment in NBC's coverage on September 11 was when an NBC reporter, Rehema Ellis, was able to circumvent the restrictions against media access and report from "inside" Ground Zero. Throughout the ensuing week, her colleagues at NBC repeatedly sought to do the same in an effort to give their depictions of the scene at the WTC site as much drama and excitement as possible. For instance, Soledad O'Brien's entire report from Ground Zero on September 13 was an "insider's" view of the activity inside the WTC perimeter.

> Right now, we're just about six blocks away from what's being called Ground Zero, and there's a series of checkpoints that have been set up to keep everybody out except for essential personnel. Obviously, if you get closer to the building, the smoke is thicker, the air is more difficult to breathe. As you mentioned, we went in to talk to some of the rescuers. Some of them had been on the job now for forty-six-plus hours. They are exhausted, but they're not giving up. Escorted by paramedics, we carry just a digital video camera and a small disposable camera. The first thing we see, what remains of the north tower. It's where firefighters

initially responded to a plane crash. It became much more: a pedestrian bridge blown apart, burned-out emergency vehicles, today's fire crews and a futile attempt to put out the rest of the burning shell of the tower, knowing that those first rescuers on the scene, hundreds of them, lay trapped somewhere inside. A block south, we come upon the other tower, and an army of firefighters, police officers, National Guardsmen and volunteers. It is a monumental effort on a mountain of steel and glass and pulverized concrete. They pass pieces of the building's skeleton hand over hand in a human chain, collecting evidence in a crime scene three blocks wide. We see trauma surgeons, EMTs and paramedics, but they're standing, waiting on the edge of the disaster. There are few rescues and so nothing to do. Instead, just grim discoveries, body parts instead of bodies. (O'Brien, NBC [8:00 a.m.], September 13)

Similarly, Ann Curry's report on that same morning tried to take us "inside" Ground Zero:

The media's been kept far away from the actual Ground Zero area where— where all of this happened. However, earlier, just a few moments ago, I returned from an area where we were able to penetrate all the way to Cortland and Church. And there you can see the rescuers up-close, as we've not seen them until now . . . you can see the intensity of the wreckage here and the smoke still rising, mostly because the wind has been blowing, has been very consistent in moving this debris up into the air. . . . The flag, however, the American flag is still flying high, and the rescuers and the firefighters and the police officers point to that flag and say it is a symbol that their spirit is undiminished and their efforts to find anyone who might still be alive under all this rubble will not stop. We want to also give you an idea that here on the scene, you get a very strong sense from an earlier tour I took, of what these rescuers are facing. . . . Moving toward ground zero is a descent into a kind of hell. The air is thick and toxic, collapsed buildings unstable and dangerous, still, hundreds of rescuers move in. (Curry, NBC [9:00 a.m.], September 13)

Curry's comments illustrate the dramatic news value attached to breaching the perimeter (The "media's been kept far away from the actual Ground Zero area . . . we were able to penetrate . . . and there you can see the rescuers up-close, as we've not seen them until now") and the kind of descriptive language that helps draw the audience into the story and give them a sense of how it feels, looks, and sounds to those involved ("the intensity of the wreckage," "the rescuers . . . spirit is undiminished," "a descent into a kind of hell" where "the air is thick and toxic").

Of course, these efforts at dramatic amplification were not unique to NBC's reporters. In the first week of coverage, hundreds of television news reports on all the broadcast and cable news networks as well as print articles about the events in New York City repeatedly showed or discussed the most horrific scenes from the first few days and focused extensively on the ongoing efforts of rescue workers at the WTC site in order to take their audiences "inside" the attacks and their aftermath.

In addition to delivering live, on-location reports featuring dramatic images and evocative language, both television and print news producers incorporated interviews with eyewitnesses into their scene-setting efforts. Eyewitness accounts are valued as a scene-setting technique because they bring a measure of experiential authenticity to the presentation. Throughout the first week of coverage, those who had a direct connection to the attacks or the response-and-recovery activity (e.g., WTC workers who were present during the planes' impact, emergency responders, civilian responders, public officials, journalists who found themselves near the WTC during the impact or the towers' collapse) were asked to recall their experiences at great length. In fact, one of the first reports on the September 12 *Today* broadcast was entitled "Eyewitnesses Describe the Scene as Planes Hit the World Trade Center Towers." This continued throughout the week's coverage, with eyewitnesses (and also those with a close personal connection to someone believed missing) as the subjects of reports and articles or whose accounts were incorporated into dramatic retellings of these events.

KATIE COURIC: When that plane plunged into the building, leaving that gaping, enormous gaping hole, what did it feel like to you?

DEREK SCHWARTZ (WTC employee who was in his office on the twenty-second floor in the north tower when the attacks began): I thought it was perhaps an earthquake, because the plane, from what I understand, hit the highest part of the building. So I didn't hear the explosion, just the shake, and just such a tremendous shake, you know, the building of that scope and feel it move like it was a flower. I mean, it's just unbelievable. And, you know, one of the colleagues in my office said, "It is a bomb! It is a bomb!" And we tried to run out in the hall, and the whole hallway had collapsed that led to the stairwell. . . . The ceiling collapsed and the wall was blown out and there were wires and water running through it. And he actually tried to run through the hall, of course, and then he saw the hole in the wall and could look straight down the building and got scared and turned back. (NBC [7:00 a.m.], September 12)

News workers also actively sought comment from public officials (e.g., Mayor Rudy Giuliani, Governor George Pataki, U.S. Senators Hillary Clinton and Charles Schumer of New York, Federal Emergency Management Agency Director Joseph Albaugh) and those officially connected to the response in some way (e.g., firefighters, police officers, construction workers, even volunteers) to help set the scene during the attacks or at Ground Zero. Several responders were asked to recount their experiences during the initial moments of the emergency response:

> MATT LAUER: Phil, where were you when the second impact occurred? Or, where were you when the buildings came down?
> PHIL EGUIGUIURENS (emergency medical services worker who participated in the response): Initially, I was in Brooklyn when I saw the first plane hit with my partner, Ellen. That's when we responded. We responded. We headed over to the west side, right in front of the building when the second plane hit, and that's when we had to move and get out of—get out of the scene immediately. Everything just started falling down on top of us. And when we pulled over to . . . Liberty Street, that's when people started coming towards us. And that's when we saw a female that was just completely burned from head to toe. It was a horrible sight. (NBC [9:00 a.m.], September 13)

Meanwhile, NBC's anchors and reporters used interviews with those involved in the response to explain in vivid terms what it was like at Ground Zero:

> KATIE COURIC: Sandy, can you describe what the scene is like? As I said, you all have been in a location that TV crews have not been permitted to be at.
> DR. GELBARD (assigned to a triage unit near the WTC): Well, before you actually get to the site of the wreckage, you pass through about a five-mile radius, and it just looks like a ghost town. The National Guard is all over and this thriving—what was a thriving area is now just all desolate and it is so eerie just to see it. And nothing that you

see on TV, none of the pictures, none of the stories can actually prepare you for when you're actually there. That's all I was thinking. . . . There were some body parts that were removed. But for the most part, it is just a junkyard of scrap metal, like five stories high. And it is a scene of about a thousand rescue workers working together. It is actually unbelievable how well everybody is working together. Piece by piece, little debris by debris, placing it in a pile far away from the wreckage. (NBC [7:00 a.m.], September 13)

MATT LAUER: The *Today* show's Ian Smith went to ground zero at the World Trade Center during the night and he brought a video camera with him to get an inside look at the rescue efforts. This area, by the way, is totally blocked off to the media, so his video captures only what those on the front lines are seeing. Ian, good to see you, good morning. You didn't go down as a reporter. . . . You went down as a doctor.

DR. IAN SMITH (NBC reporter / medical correspondent who used his medical credentials to gain entry to secured areas where the traditional media were not allowed): This here is the beginning. As you can see, this is the north tower, what is remaining up close. And it's just what you see, it's just so unbelievable. The search dogs you see, this is a point outside of the actual, what they call ground zero. This site captured me almost, you know, immediately. To actually see a bus being towed and then to see on it "Call Police," was mind boggling. And this is where I worked in the triage center helping patients. . . . This is the actual ground zero, inside, where only the firemen and the doctors and the police officers are going. And I got to tell you, Matt, the pictures that you see do not at all equal what is the reality, a firemen who's exhausted inside of an ambulance. It's just so tough to see. . . . These guys are out here, and they are taking buckets and they're transferring buckets of debris, by person, by person, trying to find something, trying not to disturb it so much. Because a lot of this is very unstable. When you see it, it's mounds of debris. And they're on top of it, they're trying to get these large structures down. And so the hand work that's going into it is unbelievable. These guys are heroes. And the show of support from everyone, it is so great to see everyone working together like this . . . we're looking for people who have survived. But if you look at the damage that has been done to some of the vehicles—I saw a fire engine that was absolutely leveled, leveled to the ground. And to believe that hopefully someone is alive in this, maybe deep in the voids, but I got to tell you, it looks so bad out there. Just so bad. (NBC [7:00 a.m.], September 14)

Emphasizing Encapsulated Drama

While setting the scene for the aftermath of the attacks, particularly at Ground Zero, was important to the news producers, depicting the drama and horror of the first twenty-four hours after the attacks was a top priority as well. The media went to great lengths to identify and incorporate into their coverage several dramatic and emotionally charged moments from the day of the attacks. Among the more ghastly aspects of the first day's events were reports of office workers who, upon finding themselves trapped in the towers above the point of impact, decided to jump to a certain death rather than face the suffocating smoke and intense heat of the flames. NBC's staff seized on these tales with arguably morbid fervor. NBC's first on-air reports of people jumping or falling from the upper reaches of the towers came during the 10:00 a.m. hour of coverage on September 11:

> I just want to say that some of the descriptions coming from eyewitnesses in Lower Manhattan of these explosions occurring are chilling. One man talked about getting off a PATH train—that's a subway train here in Lower Manhattan—and looking up at the building after the first explosion and seeing people jump out of the windows. We have no idea how high up but hearing people on the ground screaming each time another person jumped out of a window attempting to get to safety and then when the second explosion occurred, he felt the heat of the explosion on the back of his neck. (Lauer, NBC [10:00 a.m.], September 11)

Throughout the 10:00 a.m. hour, NBC's on-air personnel sought more information about these occurrences during live, on-air interviews of eyewitnesses, as evident in the following exchange between NBC's Tom Brokaw and Benjamin Levy, a civilian who worked near the WTC and offered a firsthand account of the chaos after the first crash:

TOM BROKAW: Did you see any people, any casualties, Mr. Levy?
BENJAMIN LEVY: We bumped into a guy from Tower 1 who said that he had a chance to get out of the building after the plane hit the first one. He had a chance to get out of the second one. But he said that

people were jumping out of the windows to get away from the fire. (NBC [10:00 a.m.], September 11)

Brokaw also sought to incorporate information about this issue into an interview during the 1:00 p.m. hour, this time with Robert Harper, who had been on his way to work in lower Manhattan when the attacks began:

> BROKAW: And what about the people who were trying to get out of the building? We had one report of bodies falling through the air and people jumping from windows. Did you see any of that?
>
> HARPER (eyewitness): Absolutely. Absolutely. It was a very traumatic day, I think, having seen that, because where the initial explosion was, there was a lot of black smoke coming out of around the—I believe it was around the seventy-eighth floor, and you saw people jumping for their lives out of the seventy-eighth floor of the World Trade Center. Smoke everywhere, fire everywhere, and people were continuing to jump out of the seventy-eighth floor. (NBC [1:00 p.m.], September 11)

NBC's news personnel attempted to get more information about people jumping from the towers throughout the day's coverage, as exemplified in the following exchange between Matt Lauer, who was anchoring the coverage, and Harry Crosby, another eyewitness to the calamity at the WTC:

> LAUER: Tell me, I know you got fairly close to the World Trade Center towers at the point before they were collapsing, and you explained something, or described something to me on the phone before that stopped my heart and that was the images you saw of people scrambling to escape the flames on one of those towers, and then some of those people actually jumping off those towers.
>
> HARRY CROSBY (eyewitness): Yes, I think the thing that was most harrowing, we tend to ignore common sense. I was about three blocks away. The first building had already been hit. The second building had just been hit. And the impact of the second building, of the plane coming from the second building, came from the south, so to me, where I stood, it looked like a massive explosion. I continued to see people actually go in both directions, oddly enough. I think people were evacuating all buildings. I was actually at that time trying to get to work and—and basically stood and watched, like a deer

in the headlights, people evacuating. . . . The fire was tremendous in the first building, the north most tower, and people could not escape, I think, the heat. They continued to go up, it appears. And there were an enormous number of people that jumped from the building.

LAUER: So you're talking about people jumping from above, probably the eightieth or ninetieth floor, and we've had reports that some people were actually leaving windows in the building holding hands.

CROSBY: They were jumping in pairs. They were jumping—it was raining people. It was amazing to see, and while you think you should turn away and escape, I think everybody was frozen and watching. (NBC [5:00 p.m.], September 11)

Clearly, these tragic accounts became a major focal point in the first twenty-four hours of coverage after the attacks. Active on-air efforts to solicit information about people jumping from the towers continued on September 12, as Couric interjected the issue into a joint interview with a pair of eye-witnesses, Michael George (at his desk on the thirty-third floor of the south tower when the first plane hit the north tower) and David Reck (handing out campaign literature a few blocks north of the WTC when the first plane hit):

COURIC: We heard the most harrowing stories of people witnessing indi-viduals from the building who were on the upper floors, particu-larly the first tower . . . jumping to their deaths, holding hands with other people.

MICHAEL GEORGE: Yeah. I saw—I mean, when we came down the steps, you could just look on to the—the courtyard in between the two towers and that's where a lot of the debris was. And my coworker says, we saw—you know, you could see exactly what you said. It was awful.

DAVID RECK: It was more than just a few people. There were a lot of people that were jumping.

COURIC: Some people estimated 100 to 150 people jumping to their deaths.

RECK: I would say that's about right. (NBC [7:00 a.m.], September 12)

NBC officials were so taken with the account provided by one eyewitness, Harry Crosby, who was interviewed on the first day of coverage, that he was invited to appear to discuss what he saw two more times during the September 12 *Today* broadcast, first with Couric (during the 9:00 a.m. hour):

COURIC: And you actually saw scores, I mean, scores of people doing this [jumping from the towers]?

HARRY CROSBY: Now, I think a lot of people—it was difficult to turn away from. There was an enormous wall of flame beneath the area of impact on the first tower, the northmost tower. The flame was creeping up. And I assume people were caught, unable to proceed down through that area and kept climbing up and up to get away from the heat. And I can only assume the intense heat and smoke inhalation forced these people to do things they would never do. And people were jumping in pairs. People were jumping in streams.

COURIC: They were holding hands in twos and threes . . .

CROSBY: They were in large groups. It was difficult to describe, but intense. And all fell to their death.

COURIC: I know that a firefighter, I heard—again, you know, you hear all sorts of stories, but there was a report that a firefighter was actually killed when someone fell on top of him after plunging, you know, many, many floors. (NBC, [9:00 a.m.], September 12)

And later with Lauer (during the 11:00 a.m. hour):

LAUER: There's a horrible image of what you saw above the area of impact when the fire began to force people to the uppermost floors of the tower.

CROSBY: Yes, we were, most of us, on the West Side Highway, and the first view was really the northernmost tower, which went down last. And people were forced up and were jumping. They were forced, really, to either face heat or smoke inhalation, or jump.

LAUER: And you get the impression these people were not falling. They weren't—this wasn't some injury that was causing them to fall off the building, that there was some conscious decision here, because you've described and other people have described it in some cases, these people were jumping in pairs, in threes?

CROSBY: Yes. Yes, they were—they had made a decision to take—to take that approach, and I think they—they knew that they—they—they were gone, that there really was no other choice.

Couric and Lauer also incorporated still photographs of people falling or jumping from the towers found in that morning's New York–area newspapers into the on-air presentation:

This is quite a photograph in the *New York Times* today. This is a man falling headfirst, presumably to his death after jumping from a window of the World Trade Center. And you actually saw scores, I mean, scores of people doing this. (Couric, NBC, [9:00 a.m.], September 12)

There are some terrible photographs in some of the—and I want to warn people before we put these up, that you know, you may want to turn away for a second—but there are some photographs in the New York newspapers this morning, first is from . . . The *New York Times,* you can see what Harry [Crosby] was talking about. The smoke probably is just above where the area of impact is, and you can see just dozens of people getting to the windows, and probably realizing at this point that the chance for rescue on those floors was very slim. . . . Again, a picture from one of the New York newspapers this morning. You have to wonder if the people in that tower, which again was the second tower to collapse, had seen or heard the first tower go down, and that perhaps forced them to make the decision they made, that they didn't want to go down with the building. (Lauer, NBC, [9:00 a.m.], September 12)

Accounts of people jumping were as horrific and emotionally resonant as any aspect of the attacks, and judging from the extensive efforts to work this issue into the coverage, they were clearly a valued dramatic element to NBC's on-air and production staffs, particularly in the first two days of coverage (a fact attested to by the multiple interviews with Harry Crosby). Again, NBC was by no means the only news entity to feature these horrific moments. On the front page of its September 12 edition, the *New York Times* also included photographs of people jumping from the towers.

It was not long, however, before visual depictions of people jumping were collectively criticized as being in poor taste. As a result, these images were generally dropped from the productions of the mainstream news media by the end of the day on September 12, although they could still be found on the Internet. Verbal accounts of these events were still considered suitable for inclusion in the ongoing coverage for a bit longer, but by the end of the week, they, too, had disappeared from NBC's coverage.[1] Fortunately for news workers, this was not the only available dramatic element.

Tales of narrow escapes and survival became a staple of the week's coverage. NBC's reporters who had been on the scene when the towers collapsed were invited to join the live broadcast to discuss their experiences throughout the first day of coverage. Such stories became even more plentiful in the following days as the news staff were able to find people with a personal connection to these events and learn from them about the many dramatic moments and rumors that were part of 9/11:

> COURIC: You know, Matt, oftentimes in these terrible disasters—and there hasn't been anything like this, certainly, in our lifetime—you hear these miracle stories, and you and I both heard rumors or actually reports, but we can't place them, about one firefighter, and I just have some information about him. It says a firefighter fell 83 floors from the World Trade Center and survived. He was helping to evacuate the building when it collapsed. He plummeted more than 1,000 feet. Rescuers were stunned when they later found him on the ground alive. He told them he, quote, "curled himself into a ball and rolled down floor by floor as the building fell down." A rescue worker said he was conscious, he knew his name and where he lived and how many kids he had. He was just a little uncomfortable.
>
> LAUER: You think about it. He's eighty floors up, but there are floors on top of him collapsing . . . that he survived is beyond a miracle.
>
> COURIC: Anyway, I just thought that was interesting. And since we were trying to find out more about this, I thought I would share it with you and the rest of our viewers. (NBC [9:00 a.m.], September 13)[2]

Monitoring the Ongoing Drama

While the events of September 12 and thereafter may not have offered the same array of dramatic moments as those on the day of the attacks, there still were an abundance of ongoing and new plot lines to be followed. The notion that people might still be alive under the mountainous ruins of the World Trade Center buildings remained particularly appealing to news workers. This was by far the most frequently discussed aspect of the response-and-recovery effort in the week after the attacks. In many ways, the issue of survivors under the rubble and the rush to find them was the perfect story line for this public drama, as it included such elements as the tragedy of innocent victims, enormous obstacles to be overcome, and the heroic spirit of the would-be rescuers. Matt Lauer placed the issue front and center in the very first moments of the September 12 broadcast: "If there is a glimmer of hope, it's this: word is that some victims have survived in lower Manhattan. Police are getting cell phone calls coming from the rubble, and people still are being pulled out alive."

The search for survivors was mentioned near the top of every broadcast during the first week. For example, the September 14 broadcast opened with this report from reporter David Bloom: "The most discouraging, the most disheartening news this morning is that there have been no additional rescues of anyone trapped inside, meaning that the last time any survivor who was actually inside the buildings came out alive was Wednesday, one day afterward, and only five of those, five survivors" (Bloom, NBC [7:00 a.m.], September 14). The September 15 broadcast also began with a report from the field, this time from reporter Pat Dawson:

LAUER: Let's get the latest on the search for the missing and dead at ground zero from NBC's Pat Dawson, who's in lower Manhattan this morning.

DAWSON: Good morning, Matt. Another night of backbreaking work and another night of frustration in the hunt for survivors here. . . . We've spoken to some of the emergency workers here who talked to the searchers, and their mood is growing more somber. Still, the enormous task of digging does go on, even though for seventy-two hours, no one has been pulled from that wreckage alive.

And again on the September 17 and 18 broadcasts, each featuring an on-site report from David Bloom:

Good morning, Matt. We now know that those rescuers have reached down at least six stories below ground level, a battalion chief telling us that he and his men on Sunday were deep, deep beneath the World Trade Center in a stairwell where they found what appeared to be a makeshift torch, which the battalion chief told us that someone had tried to light to guide their way out of the twin towers after the collapse. But there are, as elsewhere, no signs of life. . . . Of course, the rescue and recovery operation here in lower Manhattan began last Tuesday. Today, as it enters its seventh day, no one is resting.

The fact of the matter is these rescuers tell us, and we've heard from other experts, that within seven to ten days, it's still, theoretically at least, possible that someone could still be trapped inside this wreckage. The numbers, though, keep getting more and more grim. Now 211 confirmed dead, 5,422 missing, presumed dead. So it's clearly a dire situation. As Katie mentioned, it's been six days now since anyone was pulled out of the wreckage alive. (Bloom, NBC [7:30 a.m.], September 18)

Hours of coverage were spent speculating about the possibility of people being alive beneath the rubble and how long they could survive in those conditions, recounting previous rescues (of which there were only five, with none after Wednesday, September 12), and detailing the arduousness of the search-and-rescue effort, how the rescuers were going about it, and how they were faring physically and emotionally.

On numerous occasions, NBC's reporters and on-air staff seemed to be trying to will a dramatic rescue story into existence. Whenever there was even a rumor of a possible rescue, the news personnel dropped everything in search of further details or official confirmation, frequently undertaking the messy business of seeking information while on the air. Dozens of reports about rescues (many of which ultimately proved to be grossly inaccurate or false) were based on unconfirmed information. NBC reporter David Bloom scrambled to follow up on a report of a rescue during the September 12 broadcast, during which he interviewed a volunteer at the site who was not even part of the rumored rescue in order to get the story on the air as quickly as possible:

BLOOM: Well, what we're told, Katie, is that they've rescued some firefighters. We don't know how many. We're live right now on the *Today* show. Please, sir, if you could just come over here for just a minute. Thank you very much. Just tell me what happened.

VOLUNTEER RESCUER: I just went up by the World Trade Center to see exactly what happened, and in the process, I saw a lot of people digging out, trying to, you know, get somebody—like they're digging out people out of the rubble, and eventually, when we looked around, there was a guy on a gurney, and they wanted us to form a line to get him out, so that they could get the ambulance. And I just got in the line and helped get him out. And according to one of the firefighters, he was buried for around nine hours. (NBC [8:00 a.m.], September 12)

A glaring example of the media's willingness to follow just about any possible rescue story came in the afternoon of the second day of coverage (September 12) when tales of a dramatic rescue were circulated and dominated the airwaves, with reporters and anchors relaying the information with much joy and optimism. But after a short time, it was revealed that the people who had been pulled from the rubble were in fact firefighters who had fallen into the debris while searching for survivors and had been trapped under the rubble for only a brief period. An important consequence of all the coverage of the search for survivors was that it continued to place the firefighters at center stage of this drama. The FDNY, with its distinctive uniforms and hundreds of members participating in the search-and-rescue effort during each shift, was the most visible organization, and firefighters were often responsible for removing survivors from the rubble or, as was the case with the Wednesday episode, they were sometimes the ones being pulled out from the rubble.

A topic closely related to the search for survivors was the possibility of an enormous loss of life in lower Manhattan as a result of the attacks. Although this was not as often the primary subject in news reports and articles as was the search for survivors beneath the rubble, the death toll at the WTC was nonetheless mentioned in nearly every report and article recounting the attacks or depicting the response-and-recovery effort in lower Manhattan. In any case, it was clear from the outset of the September 12 *Today* broadcast that this would be a point of emphasis in NBC's coverage:

> The early numbers are staggering. Two hundred and sixty-six people on the four hijacked planes are dead, two hit the twin towers of the World Trade Center, one hit the Pentagon and one crashed eighty miles southeast of Pittsburgh. At the Pentagon, up to eight hundred people now feared dead. In New York City, Mayor Rudy Giuliani says the toll could be more than any of us can bear. The New York fire commissioner says that he is missing three hundred firefighters and EMS personnel. Thirty-three New York police officers are missing. Estimates are that there were up to fifty thousand people working in the World Trade Center on Tuesday morning when that attack took place. (Couric, NBC [7:00 a.m.], September 12)

This statement is significant because it shows Couric reverting back to the most alarming figure that had yet been attached to the potential loss of life (50,000), even though this estimate had been quickly rejected as too large and replaced by more modest estimates. Twenty thousand had become the working estimate for much of the September 11 coverage after it was suggested by several officials with the WTC, but it later was replaced for a time to a general estimate of "less than 10,000."[3]

The amount of on-air time and effort spent on calculating the number of people who had died was mainly a result of the fact that the number of dead and missing was the only statistic that NBC had. In discussing the death toll, the anchors and reporters cited the largest reasonable estimate and delivered the numbers in as dramatic a fashion as possible, as evidenced by the following statement by an NBC reporter in lower Manhattan:

Of course, the biggest question here in New York City, how many people may have died in this attack? The latest death toll, of course, is the eighty-two figure in terms of the number of bodies recovered, which you alluded to earlier. But in some potential measure as to the ultimate scope of this tragedy, New York City has now ordered eleven thousand body bags to be delivered. (Bloom, NBC [7:00 a.m.], September 13)

The frequent discussion of the death toll helped promote the firefighters as the stars of this public drama. They were prominently involved in the search for remains, and at that time, they accounted for most of those confirmed missing. Furthermore, when found, they were often the only identifiable remains because of the distinctiveness and heat resistance of their uniforms.

The death toll estimate changed frequently throughout that week, eventually settling between four thousand and five thousand. Once enough official sources had confirmed that the numbers were indeed in that range, the speculation ended, and estimates of the death toll lost much of their dramatic value and were no longer featured as prominently as they were in the first few days of coverage.

Mining for Future Drama

Another way that news workers dramatized their coverage of the response-and-recovery effort was to train their cameras and investigative efforts on those areas and issues deemed most likely to yield a dramatic moment. A look at the entire week of coverage reveals a disproportionate focus on several purportedly imminent dangers at and around Ground Zero, such as the feared instability of "the pile" (the term for the massive mound of debris and rubble on which rescuers were climbing, crawling, and digging by hand), concern about the collapse of other buildings in and around the WTC complex, the heightened hazards resulting from the large rainstorm on Friday, September 14, and the risks of the still-raging fires below the towers' remains.

The dangers posed by the buildings at and around Ground Zero that had been made unstable by the collapse of the WTC towers were mentioned in dozens of reports from Ground Zero in the first few days of coverage:

You can see what is left of the Number Two tower of the World Trade Center, the first to collapse. You can see the cranes that they're now working on to try to remove debris. And the greatest concern that the firefighters, the police and the other rescue workers have told us this morning is their concern that other buildings surrounding this area will collapse. That is why the rescue effort is proceeding so gingerly. (Bloom, NBC [12 noon], September 12)

The greatest concern remains the structural integrity of the buildings that you see around me simply because it makes it next to impossible for the rescue workers to go in safely.... Most especially there were two buildings last night that they were worried about collapsing imminently, and those were the Millennium Plaza and One Liberty Plaza just north of the World Trade Center complex. (Bloom, NBC [7:00 a.m.], September 13)

[T]here are lots of reports of concerns about buildings. And I tell you, looking at the pictures I showed you just a short time ago, you can understand why. There's tremendous instability in the buildings all around. The Millennium building is a hotel—is still standing, but the windows are knocked out and it's clearly an unstable place and a dangerous place for people to be around. Many buildings all around have been damaged severely. (Curry, NBC [9:00 a.m.], September 13)

Reporters and anchors also made sure to discuss the dangers of further collapse in interviews with those participating in the response-and-recovery effort:

COURIC: And, Darren, to add to the almost surreal and horrific nature of this scene, while you all were down there, you were told repeatedly to run because there was a danger of a collapse. And, in fact, you almost became trapped. Is that right?

DR. DARREN FELDMAN (working in a triage unit near WTC): [T]hey felt a building may actually collapse, as it was, like, swinging back and forth. And we had to run. The only way out was basically through our triage center, and so hundreds of firemen and volunteers and paramedics and police officers were running through where we were actually standing, and it's a very narrow area. So it had to be almost single file. But, you know, there was—there was some panic in the air. We actually had to climb out of a window to get out of the area and to, you know, several people were actually injured climbing out, tripping over the scrap metal and so forth. So it was frightening. (NBC [7:00 a.m.], September 13)

Another possible source of future drama was the feared instability of the pile of debris and rubble resulting from the collapse of the WTC towers:

MIKE MORIANA (construction worker participating in the rescue and recovery at the WTC): You're in there, and you're working, and there's about 3,000 people packed on top of a huge debris pile . . . and you're just kind of, literally, crawling through there on your fingers, just trying to pull out whatever you can pull out, and hand it to the guy behind you. Climbing, sometimes you're seventy feet up in the air trying to work on bringing a pile down to size. At one point we were under the steel girders, I think, for like forty minutes last night until they started screaming that something was ready to give away, and we just kind of had to climb out of there as fast as we could. (NBC [8:00 a.m.], September 14)

DR. DARREN FELDMAN (working in a triage unit near the WTC): You know, one minute we're flushing firemen's eyes out because he had gotten some smoke in them, and the next minute there are screams and yells, you know, "Go, go, go!" And you see, you know, all the people who are on top of the debris in that assembly line just running. And, you know, almost like a chaotic situation toward where we were standing as sort of like a refuge place because the debris piles were collapsing. And they were fearful. And, you know, several minutes would go by and then things would sort of go back to normal. (NBC [7:00 a.m.], September 13)

Anchors and reporters seemed to be able to coordinate their dialogue and banter to ensure that the extreme hazards for those working amid the debris and rubble were part of the on-air reports from lower Manhattan, as in the following exchange between Matt Lauer (in-studio anchor) and David Bloom (NBC's lead reporter in lower Manhattan):

LAUER: What are the conditions like for the rescuers actually in the pile of rubble?

BLOOM: The delicate—the incredibly delicate thing is that they believe, and they're finding what they're calling voids, pockets where the buildings have crumbled and yet they're finding space where, as we say, theoretically someone could still be alive inside. So the reason why it's proceeding so carefully, so cautiously with these bucket brigades that we see is because they don't want to collapse any of those voids that might still be there.

Concerns were also raised in many reports about the potential hazards posed by the still-burning fires underneath the massive mounds of debris:

Good morning to you, Matt. Listen, I just took a walk down close to the World Trade Center complex and I can tell you that Building Number Seven, which is the building right behind me, when you get close up to it, you can see that there are several plumes of water still being poured on the hot spots that are still burning now on Saturday after this Tuesday's disaster. So they are still obviously concerned about flareups. You know, whenever they open up one of these pockets and . . . the flames, the heat down below . . . is exposed to oxygen, there is always that risk that there will be flames that come up and the fire continues. But, clearly, they're still smoldering. (Curry, NBC [7:00 a.m.], September 15)

The torrential rainfall that drenched the region on Friday, September 14, created another potential hazard that was seized on as a dramatic element in NBC's coverage. Even though this was a short-lived issue, it was nonetheless repeatedly emphasized throughout Friday's coverage.

The rain is really coming down in sheets. It's really a torrent. There's a lot of wind. But yet, we are seeing, despite the very hazardous conditions inside the site, we're seeing rescuers moving in all morning along West Street here along the Westside Highway. Leading now in behind me is the north building with lots of the north tower that collapsed. There are, we can tell you, hundreds of people on the south tower struggling in their search to find anyone still alive, forming a human bucket brigade, bringing down debris, really—just really working in—in a heroic way with a lot of courage because the situation is so dangerous. There's so much mud, and also the threat of now things being unstablized because the rain is great. (Curry, NBC [9:00 a.m.], September 14)

Mayor Rudolph Giuliani [is] holding a press conference here in New York City at this hour confirming what is evident to those of us out here, and that is that the rescue operation has gotten much more dangerous this morning, and of course overnight, as result of the heavy rains here in New York City over the past many hours. I want to show you a live picture right now of the ongoing rescue effort. What you'll notice, if you've been seeing this picture over the last couple of days, is that there are far fewer rescue workers actually atop the piles of rubble. Still the steel workers, still the cranes, but far fewer, from this vantage point anyway. Some of the rescue workers we've been talking to describing almost the oatmeal-like mush and mud. It's so slippery, they're tripping, falling, they're getting injured, which is why a lot of them have been pulled out. (Bloom, NBC [10:00 a.m.], September 14)

In the end, these dangers never really materialized, although viewers might not have realized this from the manner and extent to which they were discussed in NBC's coverage.[4] Focusing on these possible dangers provided hours of dramatic reportage and an assortment of great visuals and stirring eyewitness accounts, all of which were crucial to helping fill the expanded, all-9/11-all-the-time news hole in the first half of the week.[5]

Perhaps the best illustration of the efforts of *Today*'s personnel to describe the response and recovery at Ground Zero as dramatically as possible (and to indicate some of the elements that they believed had the greatest news value) is an interview of Mayor Giuliani early in the September 12 broadcast (7:00 a.m. hour). The interview is notable not for the mayor's answers but for the questions asked. In this interview, Matt Lauer asked the mayor several questions, the first four of which were like a checklist of the key dramatic elements of NBC's developing 9/11 narrative:

[QUESTION 1:] I know you spent a lot of time down at the scene of the destruction. Can you give me an idea of what you've seen so far?

[QUESTION 2:] There are reports that rescuers are receiving cell phone calls from people who may be trapped in the rubble. What can you tell me about that?

[QUESTION 3:] I want to talk to you about what, in my opinion, is one of the most horrendous parts of this story. Firefighters, police officers, emergency medical technicians, rushing to the scene of this disaster, getting close to the building, in some cases being inside the building, when one of the towers or both of the towers collapsed. Talk to me about the toll this has taken on New York's firefighters and police.

[QUESTION 4:] Yesterday, you said the death toll here may be beyond what we can bear. Is there any way you can even begin to estimate how many people may be in that wreckage?

The first question underscores the scene-setting efforts found throughout NBC's coverage, and the third question shows whom the news producers regarded as the main characters in this public drama. Finally, the second and fourth questions point to the focus on the search for survivors and the death toll.

A Nation's Tragedy

Cultivating Emotionality at Ground Zero

As the week wore on, the heightened drama that characterized the initial postattack period began to wane. This meant that there was more space available as well as great need for 9/11-related reports that were not explicitly focused on the terror of the attacks or the drama of the response-and-recovery operation. This subtle shift in focus already can be seen at various points in NBC's September 12 coverage, but it became more visible during the September 13 *Today* broadcast, as evident in this exchange between Couric and Lauer:

LAUER: Katie, it's important to remember that we're talking about personal stories here. Each person who's lost has families and friends and loved ones.

COURIC: The enormity of this tragedy, Matt, clearly, is very hard to comprehend. The numbers unclear at this point. Thousands, as you know, are feared dead, but I think you and I agree, it's very important to look beyond the numbers to remember the individuals lost, each with his or her own story to tell. . . . [O]f course, we're trying to remember this is not about numbers. This is about people, and the personal stories of those people are very important.

Although most of the analysis in this chapter is of how NBC's news workers identified and described highly emotional themes, I should point out that NBC was by no means the only news organization to place a premium on personalized tales of loss and sorrow; other television networks and print news media emphasized similar news elements. In fact, the *New York Times* made these kinds of stories a cornerstone of its September 11 coverage with its "Portraits of Grief" series.

"Portraits of Grief"

The *New York Times*'s "Portraits" series provides an interesting window into how the print media created emotionally driven news reports. "Portraits," which was a daily feature in the *Times* from September 15, 2001, to December 31, 2001 (and sporadically through February 15, 2002), was between ten and twenty brief biographical sketches and anecdotal tales about those who died in the September 11 attacks. The aim of the series, according to the *Times*'s executive editor Howell Raines, was to provide "snapshots of lives interrupted as they were being actively lived" (Raines 2002, vii). Many of the accounts formed a backstory for the emergency responders, who already had become prominent characters in the mediated public drama of 9/11:

> John W. Perry was not your typical police officer. He spoke French, Spanish, Swedish and Russian, and was learning Albanian. He was a graduate of New York University School of Law. He ran in three marathons and took part in a swim around Manhattan. He was an extra in Woody Allen films. He volunteered one day a week for the Kings County Society for the Prevention of Cruelty to Children. He was in the New York State Guard and was a board member in the New York Civil Liberties Union. He collected bulletproof vests from retired police officers and gave them to officers in Moscow. On the morning of Sept. 11, Mr. Perry was filing his retirement papers at 1 Police Plaza, intent on becoming a medical malpractice lawyer. When he learned of the attacks, he ran the few blocks to the World Trade Center. Colleagues said he disappeared in the rubble when the south tower collapsed, just moments after he tried to help a woman who had fainted. (*New York Times* 2001h)
>
> Raymond R. York spent nearly two decades fighting blazes and loving the New York Fire Department when a shoulder injury 18 months ago forced him into light duty. But he found a second calling, teaching children about fire safety at the Fire Zone at Rockefeller Center. There, he was "Fireman Ray" to the youngsters whom he captivated. But on Tuesday, he learned of the World Trade Center attack from a television crew that was doing a story on the Fire Zone, jumped onto a nearby fire truck and headed downtown. After traffic held him up, he hitched a ride on an ambulance and reached the Fire Department's command post at the trade center. "We're so proud and we just want everybody to know what a great guy Ray was," his wife, Joan, said. "Everybody's saying, 'He's a hero, he's a hero.' He always was my hero. Now the world knows he's a hero." She

described her husband as a man in love with life, a man who insisted on flying the flag. "He was a Little League coach, he was a scout leader—when it came to his kids, he was there for everything," she said. That included building an ice skating rink in the backyard of their Valley Stream, N.Y., home when his son, one of four children, wanted to learn how to skate. (*New York Times* 2001g)

In all, more than 1,800 sketches, or "Portraits of Grief," were featured in the *Times*'s series and eventually were compiled into a book. While firefighters, police officers, and other rescue workers were prominently featured in this series, most of the sketches were of those who worked in the WTC complex or were aboard the hijacked planes:

She was born on Oct. 11, a month too late to get a blurry glimpse of her father. Grace, she was called. When Patrick W. Danahy and his wife, Mary, had discussed girls' names, she suggested Grace. He was hesitant. But Grace is the patron saint of motorcyclists, she told him. (No, really. Look it up.) "It'll have to be," he said. "'She'll look out for me when I go out riding." Mr. Danahy loved motorcycles, and cars. (He bought himself an old Porsche for his last birthday, his 35th.) And mountain bikes. (He did a couple of 100-mile bikeathons.) "He seized any sunny day," his wife said. "He wouldn't waste it inside." But "his girls were his life," she said, "before Grace, a 2-year-old and a 3-year-old. He did a weekly countdown with the oldest, saying on Sunday nights, "Five days to go," and on Mondays, "Four," till he would be home with them. He would often get up at 4:30 to go to a gym. And later, from the 90th floor of 2 World Trade Center—he was vice president for investor services at Fiduciary Trust—he would call and say, "How are my girls doing?" He called and talked to them at 8:30 a.m. on Sept. 11, hanging up just before the first plane hit—and with no bikers' saint to protect him. (*New York Times* 2001f)

Even in grade school in South Bend, Ind., Katie Marie McCloskey and Cherese Djakiewicz were best friends, and somewhere along the way—maybe it was at Indiana University together—they both began sharing a dream: to move to New York City. And so, when Cherese moved to Manhattan a couple of years ago, it was inevitable that Katie would follow. It took a while, but Katie finally arrived to share Cherese's apartment three months ago. Six weeks ago Katie found a job on the 97th floor of 1 World Trade Center, staffing the computer help desk of Directfit Inc., rushing to the aid of employees. Now her sisters, Leslie and Julie, her brother, Noah, and her father, Richard, are in Manhattan searching for her. The other night, they discovered Katie's journal in Cherese's apartment. "She wrote 'I made it!' and that she loved it in New York," said her mother, Anne. Actually, Katie's exact words were that she had found "an awesome job in an awesome place in an awesome city." (*New York Times* 2001g)

There was something about Steven H. Russin that made his wife, Andrea, think of Tom Hanks's character in the movie *Big*. "He always saw things a little bit off, like a child would," she said. She recalled a visit to a gallery in Sarasota, Fla. The couple had no intention of buying any of the expensive artwork, but that did not stop Mr. Russin from questioning the sales staff so intently that they took the couple for serious buyers and invited them to a special back room. There, they drank Champagne. "The rest of us would've walked on and gotten ice cream," she said. "Steve was the type of person who would start asking all sorts of questions, like a child." He had plenty of practice with questions from one particular child, his 2-year-old son, Alec Joseph, and he was very excited that Mrs. Russin was pregnant with twins, who were born on Sept. 15. Early in the morning of Sept. 11, before Mr. Russin went to work at Cantor Fitzgerald, Mrs. Russin sent him to get her a glass of water. Of course, one glass was not enough, she said, laughing. "He said, 'I probably should've brought the pitcher,'" Mrs. Russin said. "I told him, 'That's okay, you'll get it next time.' That was the last thing that I said to him." (*New York Times* 2001e)

These accounts represent more than just a means of memorializing the victims; they also helped build strong and lasting connections between the mediated representations of these events and the members of the media audience. "Portraits of Grief" proved particularly resonant with many in the news audience, as editors received hundreds of e-mails and letters from *Times* readers detailing the strong personal connection they now felt with the attacks and those killed that day:

> Every day, I mourn for the lives lost in the twin towers that you describe in your "Portraits of Grief." I live in San Francisco, and though I did not personally know anyone whose life was taken, your portraits bring to every reader a sympathy for the surviving families and friends. Thank you for making this country remember and for making us feel connected. (*New York Times* 2001b)
>
> I commend you for publishing a "Portraits of Grief" page every day. Reading each profile helps us to better understand the real extent of this

loss. We learn that the victims were more than numbers and names. They were individuals loved by spouses, children, mothers, fathers, coworkers and friends. They laughed, played football, shopped, enjoyed dancing and worked hard. (*New York Times* 2001d)

"Portraits of Grief," the daily glimpses of the victims of Sept. 11, have become compelling reading. They have put those of us who have suffered little or indirectly in touch with those who suffer directly. The profiles give meaning to those who died and make us all aware of their humanity. An Oct. 24 profile ended with a 5-year-old boy quoted as saying he had put Halloween stickers on his bedroom window "so my daddy can see where I am." That statement from little Robert Shay will stay with me forever and help guide me as I stay close to my own little boys. We cannot forget those children who lost a parent in the attack. (*New York Times* 2001i)

In the days following Spetmeber 11, I was strongly drawn to the "Portraits of Grief" featured in the *New York Times*. As I sat there stunned over the tragedy, I felt so very connected to it by being able to share even a small portion of the lives of the people who perished that day. I felt honored and humbled and felt such love for individuals and families I had never met.

I read many of these portraits when they appeared originally in the *New York Times*. Reading them became a daily habit almost a meditation for me. I would read the stories and then keep these people in my heart all day long. Sometimes I will hear a name of someone and remember having read about them.[1]

Cultivating Emotionality on Today

The typical public drama narrative is designed to connect, psychologically or emotionally, its audience to its story and its characters. Although connecting a mediated representation to its audience is important to all media coverage, it is essential to crafting a compelling and sustainable public drama. The goal is to show the audience the significance of the plot or the characters and their actions and to persuade them to believe that what is being presented is important to them or, at the very least, entertaining and worthy of their attention. I refer to these efforts as *cultivating emotionality*.

A public drama is unlikely to take shape, and even more unlikely to be sustained, without an audience willing to immerse themselves in what is being presented. News elements are selected for inclusion partly for their capacity to create an emotional or psychological connection between the audience and the story or its characters. Some of this emotional connection is likely to come from the "scene-setting" reportage, gripping firsthand accounts, and other dramatic elements built into the coverage. News workers also use a variety of other techniques to broaden the story's appeal and increase the likelihood that it will resonate with their audience. This kind of media logic was evident in NBC's coverage of the response and recovery operation at the WTC in the week after the attacks. In this chapter, I describe some of the techniques that NBC's news personnel used to cultivate emotionality in their coverage of the attacks on the WTC.

Highlighting Particularly Sorrowful Accounts

There was no shortage of horrific tales of personal loss in this tragedy, and news workers made sure to incorporate the saddest into the overall 9/11 narrative whenever possible, as the following examples illustrate. Each of these particular reports was presented several times and/or repeatedly referenced throughout the week.

> BOB BAZELL: There was a very sad story at St. Vincent's Hospital where a
> nurse was e-mailing her husband, who was trapped on the upper
> floor of the second building, and the e-mail stopped and she looked
> out the window and saw the building collapse.
>
> BROKAW: Oh my God! You mean a nurse at St. Vincent's Hospital was on
> e-mail to her husband and the . . .
>
> BAZELL: [H]er husband was working in the second tower, the remaining
> tower. He was e-mailing her that he was OK. They were back and
> forth. She was running off to do her duties. The e-mailing stopped;
> she looked out and saw the building collapse. It's one of thousands
> and thousands of stories like that that happened in New York today
> and we're going to hear many more. (NBC [4:00 p.m.], September
> 11)

During the coverage on September 13, another reporter, David Bloom, offered a similarly harrowing tale of loss and tragedy at Ground Zero:

> I spoke this morning to a very badly shaken paramedic who told me a hor-
> rifying story about two brothers here in New York City: one a firefighter,
> one a New York cop. The firefighter raced into one of the World Trade
> Centers just moments before its collapse. The paramedic told me that his
> brother, the New York cop, has been standing a silent, somber vigil at the

spot where his brother died for the last two days, refusing food, refusing water, just trying to stand where his brother apparently died. (Bloom, NBC [10:00 a.m.] September 13)

Later in the week, during the Sunday edition of *Today,* coanchor Soledad O'Brien offered another portrait of one of the many lives affected by the loss of a loved one:

> And welcome back, everybody. We want to share with you, with all this tragedy, the story of baby Hope. One of the victims on one of the hijacked planes was on his way back to California. His wife was expecting. They were about to have a baby. Here is Evelyn Rodriguez, who had baby Hope on Friday afternoon, in her own words. (O'Brien, NBC [9:00 a.m.], September 16)

These stories are universal. One need not be a parent, a nurse, or a rescue worker to empathize or sympathize with those involved, and few people cannot be moved when confronted with examples of tragic and heartbreaking loss like these.

Personalizing the Story

The preceding accounts have a general appeal; other reports provided more personal details. NBC's on-air staff repeatedly reminded the audience that these people were more than a gruesome set of statistics or an anonymous collection of victims. They were the people who died. The people involved in the search and rescue. Those who lost loved ones. All were characters in this public drama, each with his or her own "backstory" and set of experiences to be shared. By framing its coverage in this way, NBC could ensure that these people would be seen by the audience as more than just "those involved."

Personalizing this event required more than just giving a face and a name to those affected, and news workers had to go to great lengths to develop these characters for the audience. Reports about those lost contained names, pictures and physical descriptions, information about where they worked and in what capacity, marital or parental status, some information about those they left behind, brief personality profiles, and other "universal identifiers."[2] These details augmented the public drama by giving it a large cast of characters who were more than just one-dimensional representations (e.g., "victim," "rescue worker"), thereby making them more identifiable to the audience.

The firefighters and police who died or who lost loved ones were presented in ways that made them more than just "firefighters" or "police":

Personal losses from Tuesday's tragedy are making hearts heavy around the country and around the world. Many families are grieving right now, but the horrific events at the World Trade Center are particularly devastating for the Haskell family. Three brothers in the family are New York City firefighters. And all three rushed to the scene when disaster struck. Timothy Haskell is now confirmed dead. Thomas Haskell is still missing. And Kenny Haskell has been assisting in the rescue effort. Kenny, good morning. Our deepest sympathies to you and your family. (Lauer, NBC [7:00 a.m.], September 17)

Similarly, the flight crews aboard the hijacked planes were not just "flight crews," evident in a report from NBC's Bob Faw on September 13:

Flight crews, the first perhaps to comprehend the horror, were among the first to be identified. American Airlines Captain John Ogonowski, whose 767 was the first to crash into the World Trade Center; Victor Saracini, whose United jetliner was the second. That crash in the Pennsylvania woods also claimed CeeCee Lyles, a flight attendant less than a year and a mother. (Faw, NBC [9:00 a.m.], September 13)

Later in the same broadcast, Matt Lauer interviewed the family members of a flight attendant who had been aboard a hijacked plane:

LAUER: We want to turn back now to the human toll of all this. Al Marchand was one of the flight attendants on United Flight 175 from Boston to Los Angeles, the plane that crashed into the second tower here in New York City. His wife, Becky, and son, Joshua, are in Alamogordo, New Mexico, this morning. Becky and Joshua, good morning to you. Our condolences.

JOSHUA MARCHAND [asked to describe his father]: I don't think there's a word in the dictionary that could describe my dad. He's probably the most brilliant person I've ever met in my life. He has had an impact on so many people in this world, in this town, in this entire state. And he's just a great person, and he had a very strong faith in the Lord, and . . .

BECKY MARCHAND: He loved the Lord, and I know that God used him on that flight to help someone receive their eternity. And he said, I don't know how many times after he took this job, that God may have given him this job, because what if he was on a flight somewhere, and the flight was going down, and there was one person on that flight that didn't know the Lord? Then, if he could share with that person before the flight crashed, then his job on earth would be done. And he said that numerous times. (NBC [10:00 a.m.], September 13)

In the same way, the passengers on the doomed flights were more than an anonymous collection of "passengers":

Now the heartbreaking story of two best friends. Last Tuesday, Paige Hackel and Ruth McCourt planned to fly from Boston to Los Angeles, but they couldn't get on the same flight, so Paige boarded American Airlines Flight 11, while Ruth and her four-year-old daughter Julianna got on United Airlines Flight 175. Both doomed flights crashed into the World Trade Center. [A] lot of people talk about putting a face on this tragedy and seeing the faces of Ruth and Paige, such best friends, they called themselves soul sisters, along with [Ruth's] beautiful daughter, Julianna, certainly has struck the hearts of so many people in this country. (Couric, NBC [8:00 a.m.], September 17)

Those lost in the attacks were "personalized" in different ways, the most common of which was to invite the friends and family of a victim to talk about their loved one on the air. Certainly, NBC's reporters and anchors could have gathered basic identifying information (name, picture, age, occupation, marital/parental status, and so on) about them and the details surrounding their deaths (e.g., working in the towers, helping rescue others) off the air and then present it to the audience, but this would not have nearly the same emotional punch as hearing it from those involved, with their words tinged by sadness and tears:

ANNELISE PETERSON (searching for both her brother and her boyfriend): I just cracked. I mean, I just screamed. I just knew that there were these two people, the most important people in my life who were in that building, in those buildings. And I thought to myself, "Oh my God, oh my God." And you think and you think of their face, and you just want them out. You want them out. (NBC [7:00 A.M.], September 13)

When the audience hears a family member say how he or she feels about the sudden and tragic loss of a loved one, it becomes more like a conversation than a newscast, thus allowing the more empathetic among us to consider this scenario in relation to our own friends and loved ones and giving greater emotional resonance to the presentation.

Numerous reports on *Today*, such as the one from Friday's broadcast ("People talk about their loved ones that are feared lost in the wreckage of the World Trade Center"), which offered a composite of profiles of those lost and expressions of grief by their loved ones, existed solely to personalize the events of September 11.[3]

The attacks and their aftermath were also made more personal in less specific ways (i.e., not focusing in detail on one or two individuals), by discussing the victims in relation to general social categories (e.g., occupation, marital status, parental status). For example, on Saturday, an NBC reporter gave an extended report on a New Jersey town located about fifteen miles from New York City from which hundreds of residents commuted daily to work in lower Manhattan's financial district, that had lost more than a dozen of its residents to the attacks on the WTC: "At least eight of the missing have children in local schools, two of them have five children apiece. Two young parents just moved here to take jobs in the financial district" (Dotson, NBC [7:00 a.m.], September 15). The implication for NBC's viewers, as for those who read the *Times*'s "Portraits of Grief," was that these were not just "victims" but people with real lives that were perhaps not so different from their own. An interview on the September 16 *Today* broadcast, with the CEO of Cantor Fitzgerald, a company whose headquarters were in the WTC and which had lost ninety employees, conveyed a similar message:

I have been reaching out all week to each of those families individually . . . talking to the husbands, to the wives, to the children, to the brothers and sisters, who may never see these people again. . . . The loss is so immense, you really can't say it adequately. There are people in our company who have lost not only their husband, but they've lost their mother because their mother worked there, too. There are people that I have talked to who are pregnant and have very young children, four and two. There are people that have teenagers. There are people that have sons and daughters, brothers and sisters. It is immense. The personal loss is so immense. (NBC [9:00 a.m.], September 16)

While these accounts do not discuss particular people in great detail, they do tell the audience something with which they might be able to identify, since most people work or have siblings, spouses, or children or share other features with those lost. Sometimes, however, these attempts by NBC's reporters and anchors came across as forced, resulting in a less-than-genuine emotional moment. This was apparent in Matt Lauer's interview of a woman whose husband was in the towers during the attacks and feared dead. As the interview was nearing its conclusion, Lauer abruptly interjected, "I have to mention, and it pains me to mention [it], you're also pregnant." This was not followed up in any way, and in fact, the interview concluded only seconds later. There were numerous other examples of anchors or reporters mentioning a recent or upcoming birthday, anniversary, birth of a child, or other life milestones regarding a victim when it in fact was not something that would advance the story in any immediately discernable way.

In a few instances, news workers were able to access the personal aspects of 9/11 through the words of those who died in the attacks. Several reports, such as the following from the September 14 broadcast, were based on phone messages left by people who were trapped in the towers and called their spouse or a family member to let them know what was happening or to say good-bye:

LAUER: Shortly after the World Trade Center was first hit Tuesday Mike Laforte, who was working on the 105th floor of that building, left this voice mail for his wife:

MIKE LAFORTE (via voice mail): Franny, I love you. I love you, and Trey and Randy. I love you very much. A plane hit the building. I don't know what's going on. I will talk to you. Love you, bye.

A young woman, Melissa Hughes, who was in the tower when the attacks occurred and called her husband in California to tell him about the perilous situation left a similar message:

LAUER: One woman named Melissa Hughes was attending a meeting on the 101st floor of one of the towers when the planes struck. She left this message for her husband on an answering machine:

MELISSA HUGHES (via voice mail): Sean, it's me. I just wanted to let you
know I love you, and I'm stuck in this building in New York. A
plane hit the building or a bomb went off, we don't know, but there's
lots of smoke, and I just wanted you to know that I love you always.
Bye.

The voice mail left by Melissa Hughes actually became a prominent part of
NBC's coverage for a period of time, with the audio from the message used
in the opening of the September 13 *Today* broadcast and several times on the
following day's broadcast.

For many New York residents or visitors like me, one of the most memorable features of the postattack scene in New York City was the spontaneous
collection of "missing person" fliers that blanketed building exteriors, vehicles, clothing, and public spaces throughout lower Manhattan. While making my way through the streets of Manhattan in the days after the attacks,
I was repeatedly drawn to these fliers and felt compelled to read each one
and commit it to memory (an impossible task given the thousands of postings I encountered along the way). The postings pertaining to missing Cantor Fitzgerald employees moved me the most. I remember being surprised
by just how many postings there were about employees of this firm. I later
learned that this was one of the hardest hit of all the firms, losing more than
seven hundred employees, largely because its offices were located in the upper
reaches of the WTC's north tower, just a few floors above the point of impact.
I was also struck by the demographic features of many of the Cantor Fitzgerald employees depicted in these fliers: Most were male; many were just a few
years out of college (as I was at the time); some were recently engaged or
newly married (as I was at the time); and many of their characteristics were
similar to mine or to those of someone in my circle of friends (as I recall, one
looked eerily like a close friend of mine). This explains how issues or events
can resonate more strongly with exposure to a personalizing agent (for me, it
was the fliers), which is precisely what the media are aiming for.

Injecting Identifiability ("It Could Have Been Me . . .")

NBC's coverage of 9/11 in the first weeks after the attacks emphasized the
sense of arbitrariness that often accompanies death on such a large and tragic
scale. Several reports documented the sad tales of those unfortunate people
who did not work in the WTC complex but happened to be in the towers
that morning (attending a conference or meeting, dining in the Windows

on the World restaurant, visiting a friend who worked in the towers, spending time on the tower's observation deck). Other reports focused on those people who would have been in one of the towers on that fateful morning had serendipity not intervened. In a report on Friday, September 14, entitled "Ordinary Reasons Kept Many People from Being in the World Trade Center Tuesday Morning,"[4] NBC reporter Bob Faw told viewers about dozens of people who would have been in the WTC during the attacks had it not been for chance encounters or random life moments. They included a CEO from a firm located on floors 101 to 105 (above the point of the plane's impact) who was not at work because it was his daughter's first day of school, and he wanted to be with her; a woman who was originally scheduled to be a passenger on one of the doomed flights but had changed her ticket to a cheaper flight; a woman who had been fired from her job in the WTC on Monday, September 10, and therefore did not have to report for work on Tuesday; people who overslept that morning or whose subway was minutes late or who uncharacteristically stopped for a cup of coffee or to chat with a friend. By working these anecdotal tales into the coverage, news workers were able to impress upon the audience how seemingly random all this was.

Nationalizing the Narrative

Another technique that NBC used to give the coverage a broad appeal and cultivate emotionality was to present 9/11 as affecting everyone throughout the United States. The way the news networks titled their coverage (e.g., "Attack on America") helped accomplish this, but the message was also conveyed in reports that included explicit or implicit claims that no matter where their audience lived, these events were consequential for their region, state, community, or neighborhood. Members of the media audience were told that though they may not have been directly affected by these events (i.e., physically present at one of the attack sites or losing a friend or loved one in the attacks), they should be concerned simply as American citizens or as members of a particular social category or group. We can see these attempts to nationalize the narrative in Katie Couric's comments on Thursday's broadcast:

> Matt, there's been so many acts of small kindnesses and big kindnesses. I'm just reading about a jar in the front of a supermarket in Illinois. They collected $118,000. Two postal workers left $760 from their colleagues. An army recruiter emptied his wallet and went back to the bank to give

more. . . . And I know, both you and I thought this was so poignant: an ad taken out by the people of Oklahoma City. "New York City & Washington, DC, Oklahoma Cares. You stood with us in our darkest hour. Now, we stand with you." And that's from the people of Oklahoma and the Oklahoma City National Memorial. (Couric, NBC [9:00 a.m.], September 13)

Reports throughout the week (with titles like "Impact of Attacks on New York and Washington Being Felt Nationwide" and "Repercussions of Tuesday's Attack on America") detailed the national aspects of this story. A report during Saturday's broadcast reinforced the idea that this was a national (and even international) story, not just a New York City story:

At West Point, 3,500 cadets act out of a tradition of respect, never seen publicly before. The academy allowing pictures of this ritual for the very first time. Uniforms of another type, another bond, American Airlines flight attendants honor colleagues lost among so many victims. An outpouring overseas as well. A moment of silence in London. Another observed at the Eiffel Tower in Paris. Flowers and sympathies on display in Germany. Expressions near and far that acknowledge the unthinkable loss and encourage comfort in coming together. . . . After tragedies like these, there are often symbols. Of course, with hostages, we've seen yellow ribbons, there were the teddy bears at the fence in Oklahoma City. At least in the last several hours, it seems candles are a symbol of this tragedy. Across New York and neighborhoods far from here, we've seen candles lit in the night hours. Also, across the country, because the whole nation was attacked and feels personally affected by this, there isn't one place for that spontaneous memorial, so candles across the country seem to be, at least in these hours, a way for people to show a sign of togetherness and respect for the dead. (O'Donnell, NBC [7:00 a.m.], September 15)[5]

Interestingly, the efforts of NBC's news workers to cultivate emotionality became more pronounced as the week went on. What accounts for this? One factor, which was briefly discussed at the beginning of this chapter, is that the terror and rapidly changing series of dramatic moments and warnings that characterized the initial coverage had begun to subside as the week wore on. When coupled with still-expanded news holes and continued uncertainty about how or how much to attend to non-9/11 matters, the need for other kinds of stories to sustain the news cycles became clear. By identifying and developing a series of sorrowful accounts and tragic tales of lives lost, the media were able not only to honor those lost but also to present a wealth of new material for reports and feature stories. It also often takes time to craft an emotional story, as the facts must be ascertained and interviews must be conducted first. In fact, it was not uncommon for accounts and reports that had strong emotional appeal to be repeated in part or in full in the same broadcast or presented multiple times throughout the week.

A number of researchers have found that the amount and form of the media coverage after the attacks produced an immediate, tense, and lasting emotional connection between the audience to this public drama and those involved in it (Brown, Bocarnea, and Basil 2002; Carey 2003; Cohen et al. 2003; Debatin 2002; Seeger et al. 2002; Smelser 2004). The fact that the media, particularly the televised media, were immediately able to provide live coverage of the attacks and their aftermath contributed greatly to the strong emotional connection from the audience to this public drama and the short time in which that connection was formed.

In those first hours after the attacks, the television audience was repeatedly exposed to some of the most harrowing images ever broadcast. These included the crash of the second of the two planes (which was shown live on television and hundreds—if not thousands—of times thereafter on tape, frequently in slow motion and in still frames) and the live feed of the post-attack scene, with people jumping from the burning towers, the buildings slowly teetering back and forth before crumbling into massive piles of debris and dust, the frantic postcollapse search for survivors, and numerous other harrowing moments. The volume and ferocity of these images, coupled with the live and unyielding coverage, may have formed a strong and lasting emotional connection to these events by enabling audience members to become, as one media scholar noted, "sympathetically absorbed in the creation of a community feeling that is based on identification with the victims" (Debatin 2002, 167–68).

Emotionality can be shown in a variety of forms. The audience can demonstrate connection to public drama by watching or reading about it. The structural capacities and technological capabilities of the modern mass media permit tens of millions of Americans to participate symbolically, cognitively, or emotionally in an unfolding public drama. Nowhere was this more evident than after the September 11, 2001, terrorist attacks, which gave rise to an unparalleled level of audience interest in media presentations of the events and their aftermath. In a survey of post-9/11 media usage, the respondents reported being mesmerized by the events of 9/11 and compulsively following news coverage for days on end (Carey 2003). Indeed, the events of 9/11 aroused strong emotions, typically in the form of ambiguity and uncertainty, which the public tried to remedy by turning to mass media for information.

Emotionality can also be manifested in ways not involving the consumption of media content. This, too, was made clear in the aftermath of September 11 when activities such as praying (individually or collectively), attending memorial services, making donations (money, blood, clothes, garden tools for digging at the site, safety equipment, or other supplies), visiting the WTC site in New York City, participating in a candlelight vigil, or displaying an American flag are indications of how people participated as a broad community after September 11.[6] Many people demonstrated their newly found patriotism by buying and/or displaying an American flag on their home, vehicle, or person, as Couric observed on the September 18 broadcast:

> It is the eighteenth day of September, the year 2001. You're looking at a live picture of the Eder Flag Manufacturing Company, which is outside Milwaukee. They have been making flags there for more than a hundred years, and in the wake of last week's terror attack, they have been sewing 200 to 250 flags an hour—lines outside the factory four blocks long. Amazing the demand for flags here in this country.

Part III

America's Heroes

New York's Firefighters in the Spotlight

No individual or group (other than, perhaps, Osama bin Laden and al-Qaeda) received more frequent and prominent attention in the extensive postattack coverage than the firefighters of New York City. Within hours of the attacks, as information began to surface about what had happened and more about the magnitude of the destruction and loss of life in New York City became known, it became increasingly clear that the FDNY would be central to the developing story of September 11. Right after the attacks, many of the most visible "front-stage" aspects of the emergency response—evacuating the occupants of the buildings, extinguishing the fires engulfing the towers, conducting postcollapse search and rescue—were part of the firefighters' instrumental capabilities and organizational routines. Then, as media began to frame these events in the days after the attacks, the firefighters fit the media logic and news routines that news workers were using to give shape to the coverage. The FDNY offered the first semblance of "hard" news and "dramatic facts" that the press so desperately needed to fill the suddenly available broadcast and print space.[1] The firefighters' willingness to enter the smoke-filled, unstable towers and their refusal to give up the search for their fallen comrades in the mountains of rubble and debris were amenable to dramatic amplification. The details of their tragedy also were suited to cultivating an emotional connection with the media audience.

Discovering the FDNY

The story of the firefighters offered captivating visual images, sensational headlines, dramatic story leads, and other raw materials that the media could use to make sense of what was happening on the day of the attacks and, later, to craft a public drama around the response and recovery at Ground Zero. The media's tendency to emphasize sensational occurrences and details (i.e., when something is "first" or "biggest" or "most") found a ready-made story in the calamitous damage suffered by the FDNY, particularly the tremendous loss of life. One out of every eight people killed in the attacks was a firefighter, with a total of 343 deaths. Moreover, nearly one out of every thirty-three members of the FDNY were killed on September 11, 2001, more than thirty times greater than the number of firefighters ever lost by the department in a single event and greater than the combined total of all FDNY line-of-duty casualties in the previous one hundred years (Von Essen and Murray 2002, xiv). The total even exceeded the number of firefighters killed in the line of duty throughout the entire nation in most years (usually around one hundred). In addition, the FDNY lost much of its specialized equipment (twenty-seven fire engines, thirty ladder trucks, and dozens of other department vehicles were damaged or destroyed), and their organizational structure and institutional knowledge were all but obliterated (ninety fire officers of varying rank, including the chief of the department and the first deputy fire commissioner, died, and several firehouses lost all but a few members).[2]

When gathering information, news workers typically seek those who are officially linked to the issue or event of interest (i.e., a FEMA official following a U.S. disaster or legal experts during the coverage of high-profile criminal proceedings). In the chaos of the attacks and the immediate aftermath, city officials were on the move, in meetings or unaccounted for and therefore not available to the media. The perimeter that had been established around the WTC complex made Ground Zero off-limits to the media, so news workers could not acquire firsthand accounts of the initial response-and-recovery activity. In addition, there really were no outside "experts" available to talk about the activity at Ground Zero (because there had never been an event quite like this, not many people could speak with the authority that comes from experience).

In order to solicit official comments on what was happening, news workers turned to the rescue workers involved in the emergency response. Immediately after the towers' collapse on September 11, a staging ground was established south of the WTC site where rescue workers could prepare to enter the site or be debriefed and decontaminated after leaving it. By noon that day, reporters from dozens of broadcast and print news organizations had identified this as a potential source of information about the emergency response and had stationed themselves near the staging ground.

Initially, the reporters tried to talk to all the main players at Ground Zero: Mayor Rudy Giuliani, police officials and officers, firefighters and FDNY leaders, and even volunteers. But it quickly became apparent that the firefighters could provide the most detailed accounts of activity at Ground

Zero. For instance, the mayor's primary role was to coordinate the entire city's response to the attacks (of which the work at the WTC site was only one aspect), so he was away from Ground Zero quite often and thus was unable to provide dramatic first-person accounts like those of the firefighters. The police also were also unable to give reporters the kinds of details about Ground Zero that the firefighters could, because most were assigned to guard the perimeter around the site and were generally not directly involved in what was happening within the site. It thus became a common practice to question the firefighters as they entered or left the WTC site, making them the unofficial spokespersons on the magnitude and scope of the tragedy and the activities taking place at Ground Zero.

As the media continued to latch on to the firefighters and promote their exploits, their role in the response-and-recovery effort (and, by extension, in the public drama) was further cemented when Mayor Giuliani publicly declared that the firefighters were in control of the Ground Zero site.[3] This decision had more lasting consequences than emergency management officials had originally foreseen when, within the first few days after the attacks, the rapidly growing support for the firefighters made it almost impossible for the mayor or any other public official to reverse the earlier decision to put them in charge of the site.

From there, the lionization of New York's firefighters gained momentum as news workers discovered that they could supply the kinds of news elements needed to sustain the continued demand for 9/11 coverage. The firefighters proved to be almost ideal public drama characters, as their "everyman" quality was easy for the audience to identify with; their stories were both tragic and inspiring; and their efforts in the face of unspeakable danger were easily linked to idealized morality and cultural values (e.g., heroism, courage, self-sacrifice). Anchors, correspondents, and field reporters from network and cable news outlets, as well as from the print and radio news media, repeatedly referred to firefighters as "heroes" and "pillars of American virtue."[4]

The Narrative Appeal of the FDNY

The firefighters' narrative capacity made them ideal for filling the vast post-9/11 news holes. Each firefighter killed in the attacks and the colleagues and loved ones they left behind could provide source material. The dramatic elements and numerous avenues for the cultivation of emotionality that the firefighters offered gave the media a way to help personalize the attacks and their aftermath.

By September 12, 2001, less than twenty-four hours after the attacks, entire newspaper articles and televised news segments were focused exclusively on the firefighters. There were stories about the selfless actions of more than a hundred off-duty firefighters who immediately put on their gear to join in the response, with some even abandoning their vehicles on bridges or in tunnels (owing to the gridlock there) and traveling more than a mile on foot to the WTC site. Some firefighters climbed the towers' stairwells to help evacuate wounded office workers and try to put out the fires (there were some particularly "Hollywood" moments depicted in these stories, such as the spontaneous cheering and applause that reportedly erupted among office workers in the stairwells when a group of firefighters moved past them on their way up the stairs).

The September 13 broadcast of *Today* (12:00 noon) featured a report, entitled "Salute to NYC Rescuers," that was primarily a glowing tribute to the New York City firefighters (who by that point were fast becoming the representative image of all "rescuers"). In addition to the reporter's fawning narrative, the report featured the most dramatic images from those first few days and evocative on-screen accounts from eyewitnesses who were in the stairwells of one of the towers when firefighters passed by them or from firefighters involved in the response and recovery at Ground Zero:

> KATIE COURIC (coanchor): New York City's firefighters and police officers are fondly known here as the city's finest and bravest with very good reason. When others race away from danger, they rush in, but in the World Trade Center disaster, that, of course, had tragic consequences. 'Dateline NBC's Dawn Fratangelo has their story.
>
> DAWN FRATANGELO (reporter): [A]fter the first plane slammed into the World Trade Center, and when those 911 calls started pouring in, New York's firefighters and police couldn't stand around in shock like millions of other New Yorkers. . . . They had a job to do, a job that would cost many of New York's finest and bravest their lives. . . . As the towers were burning, hundreds of firefighters and police were sent into the buildings. The firefighters were from some of the city's most elite rescue units, teams of six who were specially trained in building collapses. While thousands of office workers were running down the stairs, hundreds of firefighters were running up.
>
> [UNIDENTIFIED WOMAN 1]: I guess it was about the twenty-seventh floor, the firemen started coming up into the building. And I just felt that they were very brave and, you know, we were kind of clapping for them and wishing them luck on—on their way in.]

DAWN FRATANGELO: In one fell swoop, entire on-duty companies from fire stations throughout New York were engulfed in the rubble of the collapsed buildings, all just doing their jobs, now all just gone. The numbers keep adding up, seven from a rescue squad, eight from a ladder company. And from here, a captain and a beloved chaplain. . . . For ten years, Mychal Judge, Franciscan father and fire buff, ministered to the men and women of the fire department. Yesterday, he answered the call quickly and died in his line of duty, giving divine comfort. . . . Their colleagues left behind feeling they need to do something, anything. So first thing this morning, they board a bus heading for Ground Zero to find the fallen. . . . It's their second nature. In an emergency, police respond. Firefighters rescue, and even after an unimaginable toll, they're still at it. (NBC [12 noon], September 13)

Many of the most gripping tales of escape and rescue involved the firefighters, such as those who survived because the slow pace at which they carried a woman down the stairwell left them at a location in the stairwell that miraculously had enough structural integrity to protect them from more than one hundred floors of rubble that rained down during the collapse:

The six firefighters would have moved faster if they hadn't stopped to help a weary woman trying to flee. They would have moved slower if they hadn't been able to coax her along, to tell her that if she wanted to see her children and grandchildren again, she had to keep moving down the stairs. . . . It was that precise intersection of rescuers and rescued, that destined bit of timing, not a few seconds less or more, that enabled them all to survive inside a twisted stairwell of the World Trade Center when the north tower crashed down on them. The woman and the firefighters, in the actions each took, saved each other. . . . They realized that if they had been going a little faster, they would have been below the second floor, possibly in the lobby. If they had been slower, they would have been above the fifth floor, where the stairwell was severed. At the time of the collapse, as far as anyone knows, people higher and lower did not live. . . . "It was a freak of timing," Captain Jonas said. "We know the people below us didn't fare well. Above, to my knowledge, none got out. God gave us courage and strength to save her, and unknowingly, we were saving ourselves." (Kleinfield 2001, B1)

Dozens of articles and reports and books describing the general culture of firefighting and the "brotherhood" of the FDNY and the familylike atmosphere in its firehouses were written, as well as reports about how individual firefighters were coping with the loss of so many colleagues, close friends, and/or family members.[5] Examinations of how the FDNY (as an organization) dealt with the enormity of what had happened, and numerous articles and reports explored how the wives, sons, daughters, parents, siblings, and other loved ones remembered the deceased and/or how they were coping in their absence.

The press's collective valorization of the firefighters continued for weeks and even months. The firefighters were discussed in television reports and newspaper articles in only the most glowing terms. One *New York Times* reporter referred to them as "knights in shining fire helmets," and an article in the September 23, 2001, edition of the *Times* had the headline "Just Regular Guys in the Urban Wild, until the Bell Rings" (Brown 2001; O'Donnell 2001).

The Visual Appeal of the FDNY

In addition to their narrative appeal, the firefighters were involved in some of the most stirring visual moments of 9/11. Firefighters were frequently visible in on-location news reports as they worked in the massive mounds of debris. When news personnel were able to get inside the perimeter and bring back images of what was happening there, firefighters were usually a dominant presence in the footage. The bright yellow lettering on their black coats sometimes seemed like the only bit of color against a backdrop of gray ash. In fact, FDNY personnel were at the center of two of the most captivating images from 9/11: the still photograph of the flag being raised at Ground Zero and the photos and live footage capturing the ceremonial removal of firefighters' remains from Ground Zero.

On the afternoon of September 11, 2001, a mere seven hours after the attacks, a photographer from a local New Jersey newspaper took a picture of three firefighters—exhausted, grief stricken, and covered in ash—lifting an American flag from the periphery of the towers' wreckage and planting it upright in the ground. The resemblance of this image to the photograph and memorial from World War II of six U.S. Marines raising an American flag on Iwo Jima allowed the media to enhance their framing of the firefighters, transforming them into an enduring symbol of American strength, pride, and resolve in a moment of crisis.[6] This image quickly found its way to televised news broadcasts, newspapers, magazines, clothing, hats, billboards, advertisements, and commemorative memorabilia, many of which are still available today. The rapid diffusion of this image further bolstered the firefighters' prominent position in the media presentations of Ground Zero and helped strengthen their connection to several culturally valued forms.

The ceremonial removal of firefighters' remains from Ground Zero provided a similarly captivating set of images that evoked such culturally valued themes as honor and sacrifice for the collective good and also strengthened the media's positive presentations of the firefighters and their audience's reception of them. Any time that a firefighter or other rescue worker spotted what appeared to be a helmet, coat, boot, or some other possible sign of firefighter remains, all operations at the site came to a halt. Cleanup efforts stopped as firefighters, using garden tools and handheld picks, carefully shifted the dirt and searched the area around the potential remains (Lipton and Glanz 2002b). If the remains did belong to a firefighter, they were collected and placed on a stretcher, which was then covered with an American flag in preparation for a ceremonial removal from the site, with the flag-draped stretcher carried out between two lines of firefighters standing at attention and saluting the remains of their fallen "brother." A removal ceremony took place each time the remains of a firefighter were discovered, sometimes several times in a single day, as happened on October 1, 2001, when the remains of approximately fifty people who had died in the attacks, including twenty-five firefighters, were discovered in an area where a stairwell of one of the WTC towers had once stood.[7]

The press increasingly promoted the firefighters as the lead characters in the public drama at Ground Zero. This in turn brought the firefighters to the broader audience, which is important because moral currency is inherently social, as its value as a symbolic commodity is linked to its collective recognition. The extent to which the media's audiences were exposed to and accepted the media's uniformly positive framings of the firefighters was closely related to their willingness to recognize the firefighters as possessing a symbolic, legitimate, and valuable commodity. But the media were not the firefighters' only champions, as they also received extensive support from key political and cultural elites.

Support from Political Elites

America's mainstream press was clearly a significant force in directing an astounding amount of attention toward the FDNY, but they were certainly not alone in promoting their heroic exploits. Firefighters also benefited from the support of key figures in both the local and national political scenes. Some of this support was inadvertent, such as when Mayor Giuliani delayed changing the official designation of the WTC site from a "rescue operation" to a "recovery operation." The mayor's lack of decision helped maintain the firefighters' dominance long after the response-and-recovery operation had begun to shift away from their instrumental capacities. Even though the last rescue of a living survivor took place on Wednesday, September 12, more than a week later the official designation of the WTC site remained that of a "rescue" operation. Not until October 31, 2001 (seven weeks after the attacks), did Mayor Giuliani publicly acknowledge that Ground Zero was no longer principally a rescue operation (Smith 2002; Steinhauer 2001).

Much of the political support directed toward the firefighters was more explicit. In the tumult of postattack politics, government officials tried to frame 9/11 in ways consistent with the dominant political and economic considerations. That is, they tried to create an environment of consensus and unconditional support, often discussed as "patriotism," in which they could implement their agenda (particularly a sustained military response) with as little public opposition as possible. The significance of their efforts is in both the support and the location of these actors in society's power structure. Indeed, as sociologist Gary Alan Fine and others have noted, the location of supporters in the institutionalized power structure is often more important than the support itself: "Stories must be accepted and spread by those with economic, political, social and/or cultural capital, capable of making their accounts part of cultural discourse" (Fine 1999, 244).[8]

Emile Durkheim stated that the presence of moral exemplars or heroic figures (particularly in a time of crisis or societal shift) can help affirm boundaries, strengthen collective identity, and promote solidarity and consensus. After the attacks, political elites quickly realized that the emerging media narratives about firefighters could help create the kind of context that would best suit their goals, so they used firefighters—just as the media narratives had done—as symbols of idealized notions of virtue, courage, and morality to which all people should aspire. President Bush repeatedly promoted the firefighters as moral exemplars, as evident in a speech given in November 2001: "We have gained new heroes. Those who ran into burning buildings to save others: our police and our firefighters" (*New York Times* 2001c). Months later, when he delivered the commencement address at Ohio State University and wanted to promote a new, idealized cultural ethos of selflessness, civil service, and sacrifice for the greater good, Bush again cited the New York City firefighters as the ultimate example of such a culture:

In the last nine months, we've seen the true character of our country. We learned of firefighters who wrote their Social Security numbers on their arms with felt tip pens—to mark and identify their bodies—and then rushed into burning buildings. We learned of the desperate courage of passengers on Flight 93—average citizens who led the first counterattack in the war on terror. [Applause.] We watched the searchers, month after month, fulfill their grim duty—and New Yorkers line the streets to cheer them on their way to work each morning. And in these events, we relearned something large and important: the achievements that last and count in life come through sacrifice and compassion and service. (White House press release 2002)

All kinds of politically powerful public figures described the firefighters' actions at Ground Zero as being more than "just" emergency response, disasters, terrorism, or any other such categorizations. Indeed, their rhetorical efforts helped ascribe a symbolic meaning to the firefighters, connecting them with stable, culturally valued forms already embedded in the American mind (i.e., patriotism, bravery, resolve in times of crises). Consider a sermon delivered in New York on Sunday, September 16:

I will never look at a firefighter the same way again. What is in someone, hundreds of them, to compel them to run into a burning building while everyone else is running out, just to save people they don't even know? Their bravery has become part of our collective national legacy. Their bravery dignifies us all. (Niebuhr 2001, A8)

Mayor Giuliani repeatedly placed the firefighters on a pedestal, most notably in his address at a FDNY promotion ceremony on September 16, 2001:

I want you to know that the prayers of every single New Yorker, I believe every single American, are with you. Your willingness to go forward undaunted in the most difficult of circumstances is an inspiration to all of us. It sends a signal that our hearts are broken, no question about that, but our hearts continue to beat, and they beat very, very strongly. . . . Winston Churchill, the leader of war-torn England who saw his country through the Battle of Britain with bombings every day, once said, "Courage is rightly esteemed the first of human qualities because it's the quality which guarantees all others." Without courage, nothing else can really happen. And there is no better example, none—no better example of courage than the

Fire Department of the City of New York. . . . So you're all my heroes. You have been from the time I was a little boy, and from the day that I became the mayor of New York City. (*New York Times* 2001a)

This is not to say that government leaders were writing the scripts for 9/11 and the media were simply reading them. Rather, government officials were taking steps to ensure that the dominant media narrative contained certain key words and themes that could both implicitly and explicitly support their agendas.[9]

Political elites also took steps to ensure that the mainstream coverage included the notion of collective victimization, and they helped craft the narrative through press conferences, official statements, and media appearances to facilitate the transformation of the grief and pain associated with that victimization into a desire for revenge and support for military action.[10] A study of mainstream television's coverage of 9/11 reveals the presence of hegemonic narratives in that coverage, which proved ideally suited to certain political goals (i.e., unifying the nation and creating a supportive context for sustained military action). The study's authors concluded that "American television networks participated in a patriotic reconstitution of American self-identity using a reservoir of images, ideas, and narratives against which the attacks could be contrasted and understood" (Martin and Phelan 2003, 168). Politicians and media figures even labeled moderate acts of self-sacrifice and giving—and even shopping—as commensurate with patriotism and community.[11]

It is clear that the FDNY's rise in status did not just happen but was deeply embedded in the media organizations' and political elites' political, economic, and entertainment considerations. Tales of 9/11-related heroism, in which firefighters were often the protagonists, were repeated by political elites in an effort to create broad support for sustained military action. By connecting the media coverage to their broader political and economic considerations, political elites gave their audiences guidelines for framing and talking about these events in ways that were consistent with the agendas and ideologies of government officials and political elites.

Support from the Popular Culture Industry

Popular culture had a unique place in the aftermath of the attacks. Rather than being derided as trivial and inconsequential, it was seen by many people as an important component of America's return to normal, which in turn helped give it greater symbolic weight. Some popular culture moments in the fall of 2001 (e.g., benefit concerts, professional sporting events, and television programs) were even heralded as important reflections of the "American spirit" that would help a wounded nation begin to heal. The popular culture marketplace was flooded with products related to the attacks—books, television programs, magazines, songs, movies, toys, clothing, hats, greeting cards, bumper stickers, comic books, pins, key rings, flags, stamps, and just about every kind of collectible, souvenir, or other object one could dream up. These became more than just simple objects to be watched, adorned, worn, displayed, or otherwise used; instead, each became a sort of vehicle through which people could come to grips with what happened and begin to make sense of it. Many of these cultural productions were explicitly linked to the firefighters and helped promote them as central figures in the public drama at Ground Zero.

Within months of the attacks, several dozen 9/11-related books were released, and many of these were entirely about the firefighters. Dramatizations and documentary portrayals of the attacks or their aftermath were broadcast on television or made available for sale in the home video market. They emerged in waves throughout the first year, peaking in September 2002 in the lead-up to the one-year anniversary of the attacks. Some of these productions (e.g., CBS's "9/11" or HBO's "In Memoriam") focused exclusively on the firefighters.[12] The popular media's support of the firefighters was evident in other ways as well: firefighters appeared on the covers of news and entertainment magazines, had songs written about them that were played on the radio, and stood beside Mayor Giuliani and members of the NYPD while the mayor delivered the opening monologue during the season premier of *Saturday Night Live* on September 29. They were the principal figures in televised concerts held to raise money for victims of the attacks (e.g., the "America: A Tribute to Heroes" telethon on September 21, 2001, and "Concert for New York" and "Come Together," each held in New York in October 2001) and were a focal point for dozens of auctions, art exhibits, and charity events throughout New York City.

Some of the most symbolically powerful support for the firefighters came from professional athletes and comic book writers. Athletes repeatedly said things like "What we do is just a game, those guys [firefighters and other rescuers] are the real heroes." A sign at a National Football League game in October 2001 read "Football has players, America has heroes." Players and coaches in all sports frequently wore FDNY and NYPD hats and shirts on the sidelines and in the locker rooms, and firefighters and other rescuers were repeatedly featured in emotional and patriotic ceremonies during sporting events, often standing on the field at ballparks and stadiums throughout the nation during the fall of 2001 while crowds cheered their presence and reveled in patriotic songs and speeches. A particularly powerful symbolic moment took place during a nationally televised football game in Minnesota between the New York Giants and the Minnesota Vikings, when a group of New York firefighters brought a tattered flag that had somehow withstood the devastation at the WTC to midfield for a ceremony.

Comic book writers, illustrators, and publishers made it their mission to promote the firefighters (and, to a lesser extent, others involved in the rescue efforts) in the months after the attacks. A November 2001 issue in the Amazing Spider-Man series featured superheroes alongside firefighters combing through the rubble and debris at the WTC site (Barnes 2001). Entirely new titles were created and released, several of which focused exclusively on firefighters. *Heroes* (released just over a month after the attacks) featured a firefighter cradling a victim of the WTC attack on its cover with the caption: "The world's greatest superhero creators honor the world's greatest heroes" (Lew 2001, A28). The support of athletes and superheroes was significant because these figures have traditionally been used as exemplars of America's shared cultural notions of a heroic figure, which gave greater weight to their claims about the firefighters' heroism and noble spirit.

The popular culture industry also supported the firefighters in the form of clothing, toys, and collectibles. Within weeks of the attacks, T-shirts, hats, key rings, decals, pins, and other merchandise recognizing the attacks and/ or bearing the FDNY or NYPD logos were available on street corners and at retail stores. The public snatched these items up as quickly as they were made, spending millions on them through the end of 2001 alone (Wyatt 2001). Manufacturers offered as much firefighter-related merchandise as the market could bear. The shoe designer Steve Madden created sneakers called "the Bravest" (a regional nickname for the FDNY), selling more than 35,000 pairs in less than four months after the attacks (Barstow and Henriques 2002). The top-selling costumes throughout much of the nation for Halloween 2001 were those of firefighters and other rescuers, while toy fire trucks, police cars, and other products that could be related to the attacks were brisk sellers in the 2001 holiday season. Fisher-Price, a leading toy manufacturer, added new characters with direct ties to 9/11 to its "Rescue Heroes" line of toys: a police officer ("Jake Justice"), an emergency medical technician ("Matt Medic"), and a New York City firefighter ("Billy Blazes") (Hayt 2002; Kovler 2001).

After the attacks, the usual array of collectibles advertised in the Sunday newspapers included a miniature teddy bear dressed like a firefighter and carrying an American flag, dubbed "My Brother, My Nation," and a figurine featuring a firefighter standing behind a winged angel, entitled "Angel of Protection" (S. Elliott 2001, 2002). The FDNY also benefited directly from the intense demand for firefighter-themed products by bolstering their existing merchandising infrastructure and extending their commercial licensing reach. Before the attacks, the FDNY operated a single store located in Manhattan's Rockefeller Center named the "Fire Zone," which sold officially licensed FDNY merchandise (with profits directed to their Fire Safety Education Fund). After the attacks and the collective valorization of the firefighters, sales at the Fire Zone skyrocketed to more than $19,000 a day (the pre-9/11 daily sales average was about $700) in late October and nearly $25,000 per day during the 2001 holiday season (Bellafante 2001; Wyatt 2001).

The support that firefighters received from officials and organizations representing the media, politics, and popular culture was not entirely altruistic. Each supporter had its own reasons for promoting the firefighters: the media because the firefighters fulfilled their needs for the amount and types of stories they sought; political figures because promoting the firefighters advanced their political agendas and helped create the best possible climate in which to act politically and militarily; and the popular culture industry because the firefighters represented a marketable commodity that could turn a profit. Cumulatively, they created a broad base of support celebrating them as the embodiment of all that was pure and good about America. Firefighters were depicted as heroes and their activities at Ground Zero were described with overtones of bravery, valor, and altruism. Once applied, heroism became the dominant frame through which firefighters were viewed. Indeed, virtually all that they did at Ground Zero in the ensuing weeks and months was labeled by the media as further evidence of their heroism.

The abundance of positive portrayals offered by the media, politicians, celebrities, corporations, and the rest created a cultural context in which dissenting views of firefighters were not allowed. Frames inconsistent with the hero frame were glossed over or ignored altogether by the media, political and cultural elites, and the public at large.[13] The facts as we now know them, however, show that the firefighters did not always act responsibly in their initial foray into the towers or during the recovery effort at Ground Zero. Many firefighters ignored emergency response protocols on the day of the attacks.[14] Some of those in charge of the initial response allowed long-standing rivalries with police and city administrators to adversely affect many important decisions and actions (Dwyer, Flynn, and Fessenden 2002; Smith 2004). Moreover, the evidence suggests that many firefighters did not take the necessary safety precautions while searching for remains on "the pile" in the months after the attacks (Flynn and Dwyer 2002; Langewiesche 2002). There even were claims that the FDNY treated non-firefighter remains differently.[15] Nonetheless, the mainstream media generally ignored these improprieties and continued to promote the hero frame.[16]

Firefighter Agency

The firefighters' status was not just thrust on them by external forces; they did not simply sit back and reap the rewards of the broader political and social climate that supported the spread and entrenchment of their hero label. Rather, the firefighters themselves engaged in a range of symbolic actions and communicative strategies that contributed to their ascent up the status hierarchy.

Mediated events or episodes can have "reciprocal effects," meaning that the media coverage reacts to what is being covered and ends up changing its nature and affecting the actions of its principals, or characters (Lang and Lang 1986). In some instances, the principals in a high-profile media moment have something to gain or lose through their involvement and, if they realize this, may try to sway the media audience in their favor. Thus, some people who suddenly become media darlings may try to transform this attention into some sort of political leverage. For example, Todd Gitlin found this in his analysis of the Students for a Democratic Society (SDS) movement. The SDS leaders had not started out seeking the spotlight, but once they were caught in its glare, many of those who could (i.e., leaders and charismatic figures) attempted to make the most of it.[17]

A similar phenomenon can be applied to the FDNY in the wake of 9/11, when the firefighters became a focal point of the dominant "reality" created around what was happening at Ground Zero and took steps to maintain that reality for as long as possible. At some point during the response-and-recovery operation at Ground Zero, firefighters became aware that they had something to win or lose, and so they began to implement rhetorical strategies and engage in symbolic actions designed to maintain the initial organizational structure at Ground Zero (which was distinctly favorable to them) and to curry the favor of the public drama's audience.[18]

Initially, the FDNY's skills and resources closely matched many of the most pressing needs at the WTC site, so it was generally assumed that their centrality to what was happening at Ground Zero was a necessary feature of the emergency response. If their status at the site was questioned, and it rarely was, they could simply appeal to their instrumental compatibility with the response-and-recovery effort. But eventually the site changed in ways that diminished the instrumental rationale for the FDNY's prominent placement. As September turned to October, the main tasks at the site increasingly revolved around heavy construction and large-scale debris removal, tasks that were, obviously, not as closely aligned with the skills and abilities of the FDNY. But rather than accept their declining instrumental significance and retreat to the sidelines, firefighters began to wage a symbolic battle around activity at the WTC site.

Both the rank-and-file and administrative officials from the FDNY became more vocal in their defense of what they perceived as the moral significance of their activity at the site. The need to honor fallen comrades by continuing to search the site until all remains were found was a cornerstone of the FDNY's moral claims, and the universal firefighter credo of "never leave a man behind" was frequently invoked through statements like "our 'brothers' are in there" or by suggesting that to stop the search before every last remain was recovered was akin to leaving dead soldiers behind on the battlefield (Smith 2002). During a November 2001 rally held at Ground Zero to protest the city's decision to reduce the number of firefighters per shift at the site, the father of a missing firefighter (himself a retired fire captain) offered a prime example of the nature of the FDNY's morally based domain claims: "My son Tommy, from Squad 1, is still in that building, and we haven't gotten to him yet" (Barry and Flynn 2001, A1). These initial moral claims were a marginal success. The firefighters maintained a strong presence at the site, but they never fully regained control of it to the extent that they had in the first weeks. Although they remained a central part of postattack activity at Ground Zero, the firefighters and FDNY officials were not content with their reduced role and feared further marginalization if they did not act.

As the emergency response at Ground Zero continued, the firefighters became more aggressive in their efforts to defend their moral right to remain involved in the emergency response. This often took the form of attempts to denigrate their opponents (in the dispute about their numbers at the site, it was Mayor Giuliani and other top city officials) by publicly impugning their motives and questioning their agendas. These efforts were intended to lend greater symbolic value to the firefighters' moral claims and bolster their position at Ground Zero.[19] FDNY officials publicly called into question the values, motives, and interests behind many of the decisions made by city officials with regard to Ground Zero, often intimating that the city's approach to the site was devoid of feeling and needlessly callous and overly rational. Whenever possible, the FDNY took advantage of opportunities to publicly deride administrative actions and portray them as nothing more than attempts to transform what they felt should rightfully be considered "sacred ground" into a construction site, a tourist spot, a touchstone for the revitalization of lower Manhattan, or other "soulless," bureaucratic ends.

Another way that firefighters worked to neutralize threats to their standing (both instrumental and symbolic) at Ground Zero was to try to gain the favor of the broader public, often by playing to their "hero" image and "celebrity" standing.[20] Over time, firefighters became aware of the crowds of supportive onlookers at the Ground Zero perimeter and began to interact with them more frequently, often leaving their posts or using their breaks to meet with them, shake hands, and pose for photographs. Firefighters appeared as guests on various morning news and entertainment programs and on cable news broadcasts throughout the day, sat for interviews with reporters for leading newspapers and magazines to have entire feature stories written about them (often posing for pictures to accompany the process), attended prominent events (e.g., sports and benefit concerts), and even embarked on a "Thank you, America" bike tour across the United States.[21]

Firefighters frequently invoked their widespread public support in various disputes with city administrators. FDNY officials also staged numerous protests throughout the first year after the attacks, often enlisting citizens as participants and calling on those who were sympathetic to their plight to show their support.[22]

The firefighters' efforts to maintain a prominent placement at the WTC site were about more than just staying involved and maintaining a role in the emergency response, having a particular number of firefighters on each shift, or having a say in how the site was being handled. These were attempts to remain symbolically bound to the sources of their newfound status. In this way, we can see an interesting duality in the firefighters' agency in the production of their moral currency. Many of their efforts were symbolic strategies designed to help them maintain a central role in the response-and-recovery operation at the WTC site. At the same time, they also undertook various actions and rhetorical strategies that were intended to appeal to the broader media audiences. To have a prominent place in either the response and recovery or the public drama meant having a place in both. If the firefighters lost their central role in the response-and-recovery operation, they might be confined to the margins of the public drama. At the same time, their starring role in the public drama represented their strongest leverage for remaining integrated in a response-and-recovery operation with rapidly shifting needs.

Tangible Reflections of Collective Valorization

Clearly, the support for firefighters had both broad and far-reaching consequences. The public's charitable response immediately following the attacks was unprecedented. It is estimated that nearly $2.5 billion was raised for 9/11-related charities in the first year after the attacks (GAO 2002; Strom 2002).[23] The American Red Cross raised the most, nearly $1 billion, followed by the September 11 Fund's more than $500 million. But while the overall response was impressive, there were several well-documented inequities in how this money was distributed. For instance, more charitable funds were directed toward groups and organizations related to response-and-recovery efforts in New York City than toward other 9/11-related charities.

There also was a disparity in the New York/WTC–related charitable response. Nearly three hundred charities were created to address the disaster in some way, many of which were intended solely for rescue workers in New York City and their families (Strom 2002). Those classified as "first responders" or "rescuers" (e.g., FDNY, NYPD, EMS, Port Authority) became a special class of victims whose efforts were generally framed as more noble, selfless, and valorous than those of civilian victims (i.e., WTC office workers and passengers on the planes) and, therefore, more worthy of financial compensation. It is estimated that the survivors of the more than four hundred uniformed rescuers killed in the WTC attacks received nearly $1 million in donations per victim, an amount nearly seven times higher than the per-victim average awarded to survivors of civilian victims (Fessenden 2002).

Even in the "first responders" category, the distribution of charitable resources was uneven, with firefighters receiving a disproportionate share of the money directed to this group. More outlets for donations were established for firefighters than for other rescue workers. Accordingly, the families of the 343 firefighters received three times more money in charitable assistance per victim than did the families of the thirty-seven Port Authority officers who died in the attacks (Barstow and Henriques 2001). An even more startling disparity can be found between the firefighters' families (each of whom received about $1 million) and the families of the eleven WTC security guards who were killed in the attacks, with the latter receiving less than $20,000 in compensation per victim (Greenhouse 2001).

FDNY officials reported receiving many more supplies and gifts than they could use in the emergency response or maintain in storage (Bovino 2002). Firehouses throughout New York City were inundated with all sorts of gifts and trinkets, including hundreds of paintings, children's drawings, handwritten notes, teddy bears, sculptures, ceramic figurines, and statues. Several New York City streets were even renamed in honor of some of the firefighters killed in the attacks.[24] As celebrities-in-the-making, firefighters received the full media treatment reserved for popular figures of the moment. Pictures of FDNY personnel and stories of their exploits quickly found their way to the front pages of newspapers throughout the nation. They appeared on morning news programs, graced magazine covers, and were invited as distinguished guests to a wide range of public and private events. Firefighters and their families received free tickets to dozens of concerts and sports events, and they were showered with lavish trips to cities and small towns throughout the nation and the world.[25] All the gifts, trips, and dollars given to the firefighters demonstrate just how powerfully the mediated representations of firefighters resonated with the 9/11 audience.

This powerful resonance also is evident in the many instances of spontaneous, firefighter-directed collective behavior in New York City: People placed flowers, candles, and notes of condolence outside firehouses throughout the city; spur-of-the-moment vigils in remembrance of the firefighters killed in the attacks often were held near the Ground Zero perimeter; and roadside memorials gradually were placed around the damaged fire department vehicles that remained in the streets around the WTC site. A few *New York Times* reporters noted that it was not unusual to see New York City residents lining the streets near Ground Zero to cheer the firefighters (and others involved in the emergency response) as they went into or out of the WTC site. Some news reports said that patrons in restaurants would stop eating and conversing when firefighters passed by so that they could wave, clap, and whistle to show their support (Kuczynski 2001). A *New York Times* article in January 2002 depicted a similar scene at a local grocery store:

> On a recent night at the Fairway market on Broadway, hungry West Siders were pushing and shoving, but all were abiding by the unwritten rule: get a number, eyeball the selections, shout out an order, take the food, run for safety. Three New York City firefighters, in full garb, wandered into this scene, obviously not knowing the protocol. They looked uncharacteristically bewildered and perhaps a little cowed as they waded through the sea of people and looked for the number dispenser. The deli man yelled "next"

and a customer spied the firefighters just as she was ready to shout her order. In an instant, she motioned to the firefighters and asked whether they would like to take her place. A hush fell over the scene, the firefighters sheepishly shuffled forward to order and there was a round of applause from the crowd. (Nemy 2002, B2)

This kind of treatment continued for months, with firefighters receiving kind words, hugs, and other gestures of thanks at nearly every turn.

To the Stars Go the Spoils

Moral Currency and the FDNY

Within hours of the attacks, it became increasingly clear that New York City's firefighters occupied a unique place in these tragic events. As the media and their audiences learned about the enormous loss of life among their ranks and witnessed their resolve as they combed every inch of Ground Zero for the remains of their fallen "brothers," the firefighters became part of both the developing media narrative and public consciousness. By the close of the first week, the frequent and uniformly positive portrayals of the firefighters had become staples in the mainstream coverage of September 11. This continued in the next months as firefighters were transformed into "America's heroes" and positioned as moral exemplars for modern times.

As I discussed in the previous chapter, the firefighters' positioning as the stars of the mediated public drama and the iconic representation of September 11 was not an accident. The media, political officials, cultural elites and other social actors sought to capitalize on the firefighters' narrative and visual resonance in order to serve their own interests. These efforts helped create a context that supported the notion of firefighters as heroes, and this support gave the firefighters substantially greater prestige. In this chapter, I explore how the firefighters leveraged their exalted status, which I term *moral currency*, in the response-and-recovery operation at the World Trade Center site and in other political and social realms. *Moral currency* is a symbolic resource that gives its holder broad authority that can be used to influence a range of social processes. Much of this chapter concerns how the firefighters "spent" the moral currency they accrued in the wake of the attacks.[1]

Using Moral Currency in the Public Drama

The firefighters were able to use their accrued moral currency to influence activity at Ground Zero and maintain a prominent position in the public drama even after the instrumental justifications for their presence had greatly diminished. Within days of the attacks, Mayor Giuliani had granted the FDNY operational command of response-and-recovery activity at the WTC site. In addition to a great deal of administrative control, the FDNY had a substantial physical presence at the site. It was not uncommon to see more than two hundred firefighters searching through the debris and rubble during a single twelve-hour shift during the first week of the operation.

On October 31, 2001, more than seven weeks after the collapse of the towers, the city announced its plans to reduce the number of firefighters, New York City police officers, and Port Authority police officers at the site during each shift. The plan was to decrease the number of firefighters allowed at the site at any given time from its current level of sixty-four to twenty-five. They would be accompanied by twenty-five New York City police officers and twenty-five Port Authority police officers. Before this announcement, the FDNY was generally perceived to be the lead agency at the WTC site, although this perception was false, as the city's Department of Design and Construction (DDC), in conjunction with the Mayor's Office, had managed much of the recovery operation since late September. However, in the interim, the FDNY remained in putative control of the site, largely because the mayor and other city officials were either unwilling or unable to revoke control of the site that they had ceded to the firefighters in those first days, presumably for fear of public backlash and reproach.

As the instrumental justification for their presence at the site diminished, the firefighters began to invoke their newfound status as a reason for maintaining their prominent position in the organizational hierarchy of the response-and-recovery effort. This was about more than just maintaining a role in the emergency response or having a particular number of firefighters at the WTC site. The symbolic value of the firefighters was inextricably bound to Ground Zero, which, as the main stage on which this public drama was playing out, had become a kind of highly symbolic "charismatic property" (Shils 1965). If removed from their prominent positioning at Ground Zero, the firefighters would be in danger of being relegated to the margins of this public drama.

The firefighters vehemently opposed these changes to their presence at the site. The official reason given for the reduction was safety: Mayor Giuliani insisted that it was exceedingly dangerous to have an unregulated number of firefighters and other rescue workers walking over the loose debris and working close to the heavy excavation equipment. The mayor also suggested that the firefighters had demonstrated themselves to be too emotionally vested in the response to be objective. The firefighters countered by suggesting that the city was guilty of treating the hallowed grounds of the site as "just another construction site" and derisively referred to the city's approach as a "full-time construction scoop and dump operation" (Barry and Flynn 2001, A1). They claimed that the mayor and other proponents of this shift were motivated more by political and economic concerns, such as cutting costs, reopening the area to make it accessible to businesses as quickly as possible, and even completing the cleanup by the close of Giuliani's term as mayor on December 31, 2001, than by trying to find the remains of fallen heroes.

To give symbolic voice to their displeasure, the firefighters organized a protest at Ground Zero to be held on November 2, 2001, two days after the city announced its intention to reduce the number of rescue workers at the site. But upon arriving at Ground Zero, the protestors' progress was halted by police officers and steel barricades at the perimeter of the site. When the police refused to allow the firefighters to continue their protest inside the perimeter, a brief scuffle—an exchange involving a few punches and many profanities—ensued between the police officers and the firefighters. Afterward, the protestors filed out of the restricted area through an impromptu honor guard created by dozens of applauding construction workers and other bystanders. Buoyed by the support of this audience, the firefighters marched toward city hall threatening to rouse thousands more protestors and to rally firefighters from other cities, while also screaming through bullhorns for the ouster of Mayor Giuliani and Fire Commissioner Thomas Von Essen (Barry and Flynn 2001).

Within a few days of the protest and conflict with police, the city had arrested fifteen firefighters and union officials involved in the protest and filed charges against many of them. Included among the arrestees were the president of the Uniformed Firefighters Association (UFA) and the president of the Uniformed Fire Officers Association (UFOA). The firefighters were undeterred. Noting a readiness to "mobilize to defend and support their view of the sacred ground," leaders from the UFA and UFOA threatened to call on the International Association of Firefighters to recruit firefighters throughout the nation to participate in a much larger protest with thousands of demonstrators (Flynn 2001, D3). They also decided to cancel a public memorial for firefighters scheduled for November 18, 2001, at Madison Square Garden and vowed that any such ceremony would not take place until a new mayor was in office.[2]

Although they were furious, city officials ultimately dropped all the charges and acquiesced to the firefighters' demands to maintain their presence at Ground Zero. In fact, less than one week after the protest, the mayor had agreed to double the number of firefighters allowed at Ground Zero per shift and announced that city officials were considering a plan to reduce the amount of earth-moving equipment at the site, a move that would slow down the cleanup operation considerably but would lessen the likelihood of accidentally removing body parts before they could be identified.[3] Firefighter union officials responded by saying that the increase (from twenty-five to fifty) was much too small, and they demanded that more firefighters be allowed to dig for remains at the site during each shift. By November 15, 2001, the number of firefighters per twelve-hour shift had been increased to sixty-five (one more than the number of firefighters permitted per shift before the reduction on October 31). Union officials and representatives of the fire department declared this new number to be acceptable but hinted that they might seek further increases in the near future. The number of New York City and Port Authority police officers remained at twenty-five each.

Despite having much less justification for active involvement in the cleanup effort, the firefighters were nonetheless able to leverage their moral currency to maintain a prominent position in the public drama at Ground Zero.[4] This ensured that Ground Zero, the main stage of this public drama, would remain their primary base of operations, although the firefighters also began to move beyond the site.

Leveraging Moral Currency beyond the Public Drama

The FDNY and its members also used their higher status to gain a voice in various political disputes, policy development discussions, and other situations in which they otherwise might have had little or no influence before that September day. For instance, firefighters tried to use their moral currency to enhance their bargaining position in contract negotiations with the city. Union leaders for the firefighters had agreed in principle on a contract with Mayor Giuliani in July 2001 and had planned to present a draft of that contract to union members on September 14, 2001. But those negotiations were shelved after 9/11, and talks did not resume in earnest until several months after the attacks. When the contract talks were reopened, several high-ranking officials from the firefighters' unions argued that the contract tentatively agreed on with the mayor the previous July should not even be put before the firefighters for a vote. Instead, they suggested that the firefighters should try to negotiate a more generous contract, since they were at that time being hailed as national heroes.[5]

Firefighters also invoked their status to try to prevent structural changes to the FDNY (e.g., closing firehouses, relocating entire squads, decreasing the number of firefighters per engine) proposed by city officials, who faced a tremendous postattack budget deficit that necessitated considering a wide range of ways to cut expenditures. One option was to close certain firehouses and transfer their members to other firehouses throughout the city. Squad 1 in Brooklyn had lost nearly half of its firefighters (twelve of twenty-seven) in the collapse, and the city, in conjunction with top-level officials in the fire department, proposed that the fifteen remaining members be reassigned to five other squads throughout the city that had also lost some of their members (LeDuff 2001). Firefighters were fervently opposed to this idea, and they quickly gathered support from the ranks of the fire department and the larger community and held a rally to protest the possible reassignment. Within twenty-four hours, the fire commissioner had informed the fifteen firefighters that Squad 1 would remain operational and that they would not be reassigned.

A similar scene unfolded in April 2002 when Mayor Michael Bloomberg (whose term began on January 1, 2002) gave to city agencies a list of potential emergency budget cuts that would be considered if the city did not receive the expected financial assistance from the federal and state governments. One of the items on this list was to close as many as ten fire companies. Officials from the firefighters' union quickly informed the mayor that closing even one firehouse, let alone an entire fire company, would be completely unacceptable to the union and its membership, and they invoked the status of the firefighters by threatening that "we will go to the streets on this matter, we will go to the public" if the city continued to pursue the closings (Steinhauer 2002, B1). Other potential budget cuts under consideration that involved the FDNY—reducing the number of fire marshals by half, removing one firefighter from some engine company crews, and closing some less active firehouses at night—elicited similar moral outrage from the firefighters, with one fire chief claiming that firefighters were "all up in arms," wondering "how can this happen after 9/11?" and the president of the UFOA referring to the proposed cuts as "the equivalent of cutting the military after Pearl Harbor" (Cooper and Flynn 2002, B1).

The FDNY as well as individual firefighters attempted to use their heightened status in other ways outside Ground Zero. When efforts to honor FDNY firefighters with a bronze statue based on the iconic flag-raising photograph were revealed to include plans to make the statue ethnically and racially diverse (instead of the three white firefighters who raised the flag, the statue was to feature one white, one black, and one Hispanic firefighter), firefighters mobilized to prevent the statue from being erected. More than one thousand firefighters signed a petition noting their objections to any statue that did not represent the flag-raising moment exactly as it happened (Flynn 2002a). Other examples of how firefighters and those close to them (i.e., widows and other family members) used their new status to gain influence in various political and social realms include trips to Washington, D.C., to put pressure on the government's investigation into the attacks, efforts to persuade political leaders to provide more funding for New York City's recovery, efforts to raise money for the wives and children of firefighters killed in the attacks, and steps to substantially extend the FDNY's licensing and marketing arm (Flynn 2002c; Lauro 2002; Lipton 2002b; Zinser 2002).

A good example of the firefighters' far-ranging attempts to use their moral currency can be seen in the case of Joseph Finley, a New York City firefighter who, after being placed on disability because his lungs were injured so severely by the fumes and dust he inhaled while working at Ground Zero, attempted to trade on his FDNY membership to jump-start a run for Congress. What makes this a particularly brazen attempt to capitalize on the public adoration of firefighters is that although Finley was seeking to represent his home district in Long Island (about thirty-five miles from Manhattan), he made the announcement at the Manhattan firehouse at which he had worked (and which had lost nine firefighters on September 11) until the attacks. It further became evident that this was little more than an attempt to capitalize on the public's high regard for the FDNY when he spent more time during his campaign appealing to his twelve years as a New York City firefighter and his links to the events of 9/11 than to communicating the initiatives he would undertake were he to be elected (Lambert 2002).[6] Over time, the firefighters continued to use their moral currency for their own benefit, both inside and outside the public drama at Ground Zero. The firefighters also shared their moral currency with certain individuals, groups, and organizations.

"Symbiotic Lending" of Moral Currency

Those with moral currency can be valuable to other social actors. Borrowing from the status of another can give greater visibility or credibility to those who become associated with it. Likewise, the bearer of moral currency can benefit by extending this prestige to others as an interest-gathering deposit—like a line of credit—to be drawn on later as needed. As the FDNY's collective valorization intensified in the weeks and months after the attacks, many individuals, groups, and organizations tried to align themselves with the firefighters or, more appropriately, with the firefighters' image. During this time, symbiotic relationships were forged between the firefighters and key public figures, political officials, and social institutions.

Within days of the attacks, a mutually beneficial relationship began to form between President George W. Bush and the FDNY. The cornerstone of their symbiotic relationship was an impromptu meeting at Ground Zero on September 14, 2001. Although other individuals and groups also shared in this moment—Mayor Rudy Giuliani, New York Governor George Pataki, other elected officials, and several construction workers assigned to the WTC site were also in attendance—the prevailing image from this meeting at the pile was the president with one arm draped over the shoulders of a firefighter and a megaphone in his other hand, pronouncing the nation's gratitude to the firefighters and other rescue workers and declaring his intent to use military force to bring to justice the perpetrators of the attacks, all while military fighter jets were screaming overhead and the assembled audience of firefighters, construction workers, and other rescue personnel chanted "USA! USA! USA!" in response to the president's remarks (McFadden 2001). The press presented video and still photos from this meeting often in the following weeks and months. The frequent presentation of the images from this moment in television and in newspapers and magazines enabled the president and the firefighters to draw on the public affection and adulation for the other and add it to the outpouring of public support that each was already receiving.

The FDNY also figured prominently in many of the president's speeches and public proclamations. One of the president's political tasks, in addition to overseeing the domestic recovery and directing the military response abroad, was to demonstrate his close connection to the symbolically rich events in New York City. Bush's initial unavailability on September 11 (although he did provide statements in press releases during the day, he did not make his first public appearance until early in the evening) had created an opening for visible leadership that, in the estimation of various journalists and pundits, had been admirably filled by Rudy Giuliani. Many citizens had a lingering sense that New York City's mayor was leading the post-9/11 recovery, especially as it pertained to the events in New York City. The challenge for the president, then, was to position himself as a sympathetic supporter of those affected and humanize his connection to the events (i.e., to send a message of "I don't just care because I am president, I care because I, like you, have been deeply affected on a human level by these events").

One way that Bush was able to draw a more explicit connection between himself and the WTC attacks was to align himself with the firefighters. During a visit to New York City in early October, the president organized and paid for a pizza lunch with firefighters in a Manhattan firehouse (Bumiller 2001). Then, when Bush delivered his State of the Union address in late January 2002, he made sure to place members of the FDNY in the audience. And when Bush wanted to affirm his pledge of $20 billion in aid for New York City, he flew to New York so that he could make the announcement while standing on a stage alongside a collection of New York City firefighters and police officers (Nagourney 2002a). During each visit to Ground Zero, the president also made sure to include photo opportunities with firefighters and other rescue workers. The president reminded the public of this relationship with the heroes of the moment whenever possible in an effort to bolster the favorable alignment of his administration, New York City, and its firefighters.

The president was not the only political figure who saw the value of aligning with the firefighters. Mayor Giuliani also created a symbiotic relationship with the FDNY. Like the firefighters, Giuliani had enjoyed a dramatic rise in public support. He appeared on the cover of dozens of national magazines, was regularly scheduled on talk shows, was named "Man of the Year" for 2001 by *Time* magazine, and even was given an honorary knighthood by the British government. Giuliani drew on the adulation for firefighters by appearing with them at press conferences, at their colleagues' funerals and memorials held in their honor, at sports events and benefit concerts, and other public appearances, such as when the mayor invited firefighters to join him on stage (along with members of the NYPD) as he delivered the opening monologue for the season premiere of *Saturday Night Live* on September 29, 2001.

The main way that the FDNY (and other rescuer groups) benefited from their alignment with Giuliani was in charitable ventures. He spearheaded the Twin Towers Fund, which raised hundreds of millions of dollars for uniformed victims. For the FDNY, the fund-raising function of the symbiotic relationship was evident in a letter sent to the mayor by the firefighters' union in February 2002 requesting his presence at a charity golf tournament to raise money for the union's Widows and Children's Fund. The letter concluded with "Rudy, your presence will assure the FDNY of a successful turnout" (Barron, Cardwell, and Nagourney 2002).

In addition to developing mutually beneficial relationships with a range of individuals, groups, and organizations, the FDNY and its personnel came to be associated with several key moments in the nation's recovery and with various efforts to reintroduce the routine features of pre-9/11 life. The firefighters lent their prestige to numerous symbolic moments and events in ways that granted them a prominent placement in the media's presentations of a broad range of 9/11 story lines. On September 17, 2001, a firefighter was one of those chosen to ring the opening bell when the New York Stock Exchange (NYSE) resumed operations. The NYSE borrowed the firefighters' image to show that they were still strong and viable and would not be bowed by the terrorist attacks, much as the firefighters had not yielded on the morning of September 11. In return, the firefighters were able to stand on the world stage during an important occasion for the national and international economy.

The firefighters also aligned themselves with America's professional sports leagues, which were being celebrated as an enduring and vital American institution in the late summer and fall of 2001. Shortly after the attacks, it was decided that all professional sports contests in the United States would be postponed indefinitely. However, by the next weekend, politicians, pundits, public officials, celebrities, and professional athletes all were declaring that the resumption of professional sports could help heal the collective psyche and aid America's recovery from the attacks. Sports, it was said, would be an important diversion from the somber scenes unfolding in New York City. By Monday, September 17, Major League Baseball was ready to resume its scheduled games, and the National Football League would return to its scheduled contests on Sunday, September 23. But sports proved to be much more than a mere diversion. As Robert Brown pointed out, "Once the games returned, rather than offering escapist retreats from the tragedy, they communicated a wealth of messages directly addressing the tragedy and its impact" (2004, 120).

Firefighters were part of baseball's pregame ceremonies throughout the nation during that first week. Before a single pitch had been thrown in any of the Major League ballparks that evening, it was readily apparent to all involved that the stadiums had been transformed into forums for the display of patriotic fervor and nationalistic pride. Stadium concourses were lined with red, white, and blue bunting; patriotic T-shirts were available for sale at many ballparks; and miniature flags were given out in others. In many stadiums, firefighters and other emergency response personnel stood on the field as patriotic songs were sung, images from the WTC and other patriotic moments were featured on the large scoreboards, and chants of "USA! USA! USA!" rang throughout the stadium (participating firefighters were typically from the host city's fire department, but FDNY personnel did travel to some of these cities to participate in the ceremonies).

On September 17, during the ceremonies before their game in Atlanta, players from the New York Mets wore hats with the letters FDNY, NYPD, and New York City Emergency Medical Services (EMS). A few days later, on September 21, the Mets became the first team to host a game in New York City, and the scene was more patriotic revival than baseball game. The pregame ceremony featured members of the NYPD and FDNY, a stirring rendition of "God Bless America" sung by Diana Ross, and a salute to the September 11 victims and their families. During the seventh-inning stretch, Liza Minnelli sang "New York, New York." To this day, many baseball teams continue to reserve the seventh-inning stretch for a performance of "God Bless America" or other patriotic anthems in place of the typical pre-9/11, entertainment-oriented songs and activities. Ceremonies and remembrances for the victims of the terrorist attacks were held during the first game at each home stadium for all of the teams in Major League Baseball, and FDNY personnel participated in many of those ceremonies.

Similar scenes unfolded throughout the nation as the National Football League resumed its games several days later. During a pregame ceremony before the New York Giants' first football game after the attacks, on Sunday, September 23, in Kansas City, Missouri, the team lined up behind more than 150 members of the FDNY and NYPD.

The Challenges of Symbiotic Lending

Although it offers the prospect of great mutual benefit for both parties, symbiotic lending is often a very tenuous proposition. Not all the firefighters' symbiotic transactions were as mutually beneficial as those they enjoyed with President Bush and Mayor Giuliani. The reason was that in many instances, the firefighters' value as a symbolic commodity was significantly more valuable to the other party in the symbiotic relationship than to the firefighters. But even those alignments offered some benefit to the firefighters.

Parties who enter such relations must maintain a tricky balance between aligning closely enough with the other so as to obtain the benefits of their status and not aligning so closely that they cannot immediately distance themselves should the other do something that could hurt them or upset the audience. For instance, Mayor Giuliani and the firefighters had a difficult relationship, often going from standing side by side and praising each other at one moment to being heatedly at odds with each other at the next. They fought over the numbers of firefighters at the site, the distribution of funds, firefighter contracts, and so on, but all the while they also worked together closely to raise money, to represent the city, to mourn the loss of firefighters (and other rescue workers), and to show a brave and united front to the nation and world. When the mayor left office on December 31, their relationship happened to be on the upswing. So the mayor was again singing the praises of the firefighters, and he was in turn saluted by the FDNY with a recording of Carly Simon's "Nobody Does It Better." Giuliani took notice of the fleeting moment of goodwill by remarking, "I just better get out of here . . . quick" (Cooper 2002, B1). This comment underscores just how tenuous symbiotic relationships can be.

President Bush enjoyed a similarly tenuous connection with the firefighters. Although he had shared his status with the firefighters and benefited from their prestige in the months after 9/11, he was heavily criticized for what firefighters claimed were blatant attempts to capitalize on the tragedy of 9/11 and the firefighters' losses for his own political gain. One particularly vivid illustration of this came in March 2004, during the president's campaign for reelection, when firefighters criticized him for using their image without consent. Bush had released a series of television advertisements, some of which featured images of 9/11. Included among them was footage of firefighters removing shrouded remains from Ground Zero. The International Association of Firefighters, rival politicians, and relatives of those killed in the WTC attacks immediately and resoundingly criticized the advertisements as an attempt to capitalize on a national tragedy for political gain. Bush's representatives responded with the argument that the advertisements were meant only to highlight the president's role in the nation's recovery from and response to 9/11. The advertisements represent both an attempt to invoke the public's adulation and approval of the president (his own moral currency), which was arguably at its peak in the months after September 11, 2001, and a somewhat unsuccessful attempt to invoke the symbiotic relationship that the president enjoyed with the firefighters in the months after 9/11.

Attempted Appropriation of Moral Currency

The firefighters could not possibly align themselves with all the potential suitors who came calling; there were simply many more parties seeking to benefit from their prestigious standing than they could willingly accommodate. The goal of those seeking to cultivate symbiotic relationships with the firefighters was to create a symbolic link to the firefighters' iconic image that indicated some sort of natural allegiance or connection between them. The consent of the firefighters would help, but it was not necessary. A wide range of individuals, groups, and organizations tried to use the firefighters' status for their own benefit without the permission of the firefighters.

There is an adage that "any publicity is good publicity." From this perspective, the attempts by others to associate themselves with the imagery of the FDNY would be beneficial to the firefighters, as it would provide publicity and help keep the firefighters in the media's spotlight and in the collective consciousness. But unlike the symbiotic relationships that they had willingly formed, the firefighters did not have any authority over how their image would be used by these other parties. If another individual or group were to use the firefighters' image in a way that the public deemed unfavorable, it could lower the firefighters' status. Thus, the firefighters and their union leaders were quick to denounce many of the attempts by those who sought to "borrow" some of the firefighters' status.

As the "heroes" of 9/11, the firefighters and their image became a valued asset for various political campaigns. By early November 2001, candidates in many of the nation's top media markets had produced commercials that referred directly or indirectly to the events of 9/11, often, emphasizing the firefighters (Berke 2001). Rather than the usual focus on local matters, such as public works, infrastructural needs, and budgetary concerns, many candidates centered their campaign ads on images of the American flag and firefighters and other rescue workers to highlight their qualifications for protecting the public.

In some cases, the FDNY and the firefighter unions willingly aligned themselves with certain political figures and provided their endorsements, but in other instances, political figures merely appropriated the image of the firefighters to bolster their campaigns. Consider the 2001 race for governor of New Jersey between Jim McGreevey and Bret Schundler. McGreevey had been endorsed by the unions representing state firefighters, police officers, and Port Authority officers, a fact that he promoted in his campaign advertisements (Halbfinger 2001). One television commercial featured McGreevey wearing a red, white, and blue tie standing in front of an American flag while images of firefighters and other rescue workers—FDNY personnel standing by their fire engines, police officers walking with construction workers, and so on—appeared on the screen. Schundler released a somewhat similar television commercial featuring several images of firefighters, including a clip of FDNY personnel working amid the smoke and debris at the WTC site and President Bush at Ground Zero with his arm around the fire chief while shouting into a megaphone. Officials from the firefighters' unions (along with union leaders representing the NYPD and Port Authority, whose members were also featured in the commercial) criticized Schundler's commercial as a crass ploy to align himself with the heroes of the moment, calling it a "clear attempt to capitalize politically on the tragedy that has touched the entire nation" (Halbfinger 2001, D5).

The incumbent New York governor, George Pataki, repeatedly traded on his connection to 9/11 and attempted to parlay the status of firefighters and others involved in the emergency response into political gain during his reelection campaign leading up to the November 2002 election. When addressing his constituency and other potential supporters in public forums, he often spent more time praising firefighters and other rescue workers than discussing his next term's agenda, policy goals, or other typical campaign topics.[7] Not only did Pataki join the chorus of voices touting the firefighters and police as heroes in hopes of crafting a real or, at least, perceived allegiance with them, but he also appealed to other potential political supporters by trying to transfer some of the FDNY status to them. He did this by stating that he viewed the 9/11-related efforts of these other groups to be on par with those of the more celebrated groups (i.e., firefighters and police) and suggesting that if elected, he would spread that word to the masses. For instance, in April 2002 Pataki visited the union hall of the New York City sanitation workers and told those in attendance:

> Let me tell you, there are quiet unsung heroes of September 11 and afterward as well. I was down there, in the evening of September 11, when dust and debris covered lower Manhattan from one river to the other. And it wasn't just the police officers and the firefighters and the emergency service workers. You were out there, too. You were the ones who cleared the streets so emergency workers could get to Ground Zero. (Nagourney 2002b, B1)

The governor used a similar tack when addressing workers at the New York Mercantile Exchange in September 2002, telling them they should be praised simply for their willingness to return to work so close to the WTC site: "We know that those who worked here also are heroes. You had to have the guts and willingness to come back."[8]

Attempts to appropriate some of the firefighters' status and create a link to their iconic imagery were not limited to New York City and surrounding regions. Shirley Clarke Franklin, then a candidate for mayor of Atlanta, Georgia, ran a commercial promoting her candidacy in which she emphasized that she had received the endorsements of the local police and firefighter unions.

The commercial featured the American flag, the faces of Atlanta firefighters and police officers, and the words *courage, valor,* and *trust* interspersed throughout. Franklin appeared on screen only at the end of the commercial, stating, "I am honored and humbled to be endorsed by our police and firefighters. They make us proud" (Berke 2001, B6). Early in November 2001, in the state of Washington, ballot initiative 747, a proposition to place limits on property taxes (the initiative, if passed, would have limited property tax increases to 1 percent a year unless otherwise authorized by public vote), was being hotly contested. Those who opposed a limit on annual property tax increases claimed that invoking the human face of the firefighter would increase the likelihood of winning, so they released a televised advertisement featuring images of firefighters from beginning to end and with narration stating, "They're always there for us, putting their lives on the line. Now they need our help" (Verhovek 2001, A8). Four different firefighters appeared during the commercial, one of whom, speaking directly to the camera, stated that limiting the revenue stream from property taxes would "jeopardize our training, equipment, and safety, so vote no on 747" (Verhovek 2001, A8). This issue, which had only an indirect link to public safety or firefighters and no link whatsoever to New York City or the FDNY, illustrates both the value of the firefighters' status after September 11 and the lengths to which people would go in trying to create a link between themselves and firefighters.

Further Exploration of Moral Currency

Judging from this evidence, many of the firefighters' efforts clearly were successful. But the firefighters did not win every contest. They did not enjoy carte blanche to shape the activity at Ground Zero exactly as they wished, nor were they able to make public officials give in to their every whim. This suggests that there are limits on the symbolic value of moral currency.

The value of moral currency has certain structural limits. Put simply, one cannot ask for what is not available or realistically possible. Consider the firefighters' efforts to use their moral currency for greater leverage in their negotiations with the city on a new contract. Despite their best efforts, the city's budgetary crisis, which predated the attacks and was greatly exacerbated by them, represented a structural limitation on just how valuable the FDNY's moral currency was. In the end, the contract offered to and signed by the firefighters was only a nominal improvement over what they had been offered in July 2001 and was roughly the equivalent of the contract the NYPD had received after 9/11 (Fahim 2005; Greenhouse 2002). There were similar structural limits (i.e., budgetary constraints) on just how successfully the FDNY could leverage their moral currency regarding the city's attempts to close or relocate firehouses and fire companies. Despite the opposition of firefighters and their attempts to leverage their moral currency in these contests, some firehouses were closed and changes were made in the structural allocation of FDNY resources throughout the city.[9]

Certain cultural factors also may cap the overall value of moral currency and restrict how it can be used. Moral currency is inherently social, and its value as a symbolic commodity is linked to the collective recognition of that value. Status gained through involvement in public drama is the product of an unpredictable, emergent, and dialectic process built on the interplay between the performances of social actors and the valuations of social audiences. This means that the actions and rhetorical efforts of status seekers can be only as effective as the audience permits them to be; it is up to the audience to collectively ascribe legitimacy to that status and determine its exact value. Thus, the processes by which moral currency is created cannot be set in advance, and there is no guarantee that it will remain viable for any length of time. Furthermore, the outcome of any attempts to leverage such status derived from public drama (moral currency in our discussion) are similarly emergent and not fully controllable. Thus one must be careful with leveraging attempts so as to avoid overstretching their status and seeking more from them than they can deliver.

These potential limits on the use of moral currency are evident in the case of Joseph Finley, the firefighter who was put on disability owing to respiratory damage from his work at Ground Zero and who tried to use his FDNY experience and 9/11 connections in a run for Congress. He was soundly defeated by his opponent (Ryan 2002). Although Finley's loss can be attributed to his lack of political experience or the fact that he was competing against a well-regarded incumbent, the main reason for his defeat was that many people were critical of his motives and concerned that he was using the post-9/11 public adulation of firefighters for personal and political gain. In other words, Finley may have stretched his moral currency further than the collective audience was willing to permit.

The FDNY and firefighters also lost favor with others connected to the events at the WTC site—the rescue workers who toiled alongside them for months and months, the families of some of the firefighters killed in the attacks, the families of non-firefighter rescuers killed in the attacks, and the families of civilian victims who died in the towers—who felt that the firefighters were using their new status to unfairly influence the response-and-recovery effort at Ground Zero, the distribution of charitable funds, the design of a memorial at the site, and several other issues. This raises the possibility that overusing moral currency or using it in ways deemed inappropriate by the collective audience can diminish its symbolic value.

The case of the firefighters may also show the potential connections between how moral currency is produced and its long-term viability for its holders. Typically, those who achieve significantly high moral standing do so because they are intimately connected to culturally valued social institutions (e.g., the presidency of the United States carries with it a certain measure of moral prestige that is extended to those who hold that office). Moral prestige is "usually (even if not invariably) mediated by organizations and institutions" in the words of John Kane, who added that "for most individuals . . . such moral capital as they enjoy in political life is largely a function of their membership in larger collective entities—parties, movements, governments, even nations" (2001, 35).[10] The connection to the institution provides stability to the form and force of the moral prestige. Even as individuals come and go from institutional roles, the institutions and organizations (often) remain committed to the core values that give the stature its moral base. But can significant moral currency exist outside this institutional base?

The firefighters' moral currency originated in a particular series of events. It is what we might call "event-based" moral standing, located in a particular historical epoch (after September 11) and contingent on social processes (i.e., symbolic communication) to remain viable. The firefighters accrued moral currency through their prominent placement in the response-and-recovery effort at Ground Zero and their successful "starring" performance in the mediated public drama surrounding that effort.[11] The question is whether event-based prestige is different in form or force from that whose foundation is found in long-standing cultural institutions. Is event-based moral currency more ephemeral (without opportunities for institutional replenishing)? Does its symbolic potency or the arenas in which it can be wielded have limits? Is it a more tenuous form, perhaps requiring more careful management? Can it be overused or underused? Does it dissipate with time, as the source event fades into the recesses of collective memory?

Instances in recent years seem to indicate that the FDNY's symbolic leverage may be on the wane, that it no longer affords them the level of access to and influence in administrative matters and decision making in local, state, or national affairs that they enjoyed in the first year or so after the attacks. For instance, in April 2005, New York City Mayor Michael Bloomberg announced a new command structure for disaster response in the city that would give the

NYPD authority to direct the work of all city emergency agencies (including the FDNY) at virtually every disaster scene involving hazardous materials (Confessore 2005; O'Donnell 2005b). The revised structure angered FDNY officials, so they used a variety of techniques, including calling on their 9/11 status, both before and after the announcement, to try to force the mayor to change the policy (Farmer 2005; O'Donnell 2005a). Efforts to convince the mayor to reverse course on this policy were unsuccessful. This was a victory for the NYPD over their chief rivals and a resounding loss for the FDNY, as well as a clear indication that public officials no longer were as reluctant to enter into a symbolic struggle with the "heroes of 9/11." It seems that while the firefighters still enjoy a higher status and political import relative to their pre-9/11 position, their status is not nearly so secure as it was right after the attacks.

September 11 and Beyond

Public Drama in the Twenty-first Century

"There's only three things [Rudy Giuliani] mentions in a sentence: a noun, a verb, and 9/11. There's nothing else." These were the words of Senator Joe Biden, invoked to communicate his perception of Giuliani's qualifications (or lack thereof) to serve as president of the United States.[1] Biden's comment gained a laugh from many as it made the media rounds. Lost amid the obvious humor and political partisanship, however, was a more subtle message: September 11 remains a vital political resource for those who are willing and able to use it.

The symbolic value of September 11 has been a central theme in this book. I have tried to show how people—the firefighters, President George W. Bush, Mayor Giuliani, and a number of other political officials and citizen activists—have drawn on "9/11" to shape public opinion, evoke sentiments, reinforce or communicate ideologies, attract attention, frame issues, and advance domestic and international policies in the years since the attacks.[2] More than that, I have tried to explain how and why September 11 became such a potent political and moral commodity.

My argument is built on the simple idea that the story of September 11 did not have to be told as it was. The meanings that would be applied to the attacks and their aftermath were not intrinsic to what happened. Instead, the series of observable events that took place—planes crashed, buildings fell, thousands of lives were lost, a massive response-and-recovery operation was initiated, and so on—acquired meaning through the interplay of cultural values, rhetoric, and social action. In other words, the dominant narrative of September 11 was socially constructed.

The story was crafted and told in a way that made these events a shocking and traumatic threat to the moral order and cultural fabric of our society. At the same time, the "American spirit," along with the "warriors" (soldiers) and "heroes" (firefighters and other rescue workers) who were said to embody that idealized ethos, were offered as the antidote to the impending cultural doom. To a great extent, this transformation was driven by the media, although it was also facilitated by the actions and discursive practices of political and cultural elites and, not to be overlooked, the willing complicity of much of the media audience. To borrow from sociologist Neil Smelser's exploration of September 11 as a "cultural trauma," September 11 was not born as "9/11"; it was made into it through a "complex process of selective remembering and unremembering, social interaction and influence, symbolic contestation, and successful assertions of power" (2004, 279).

As a result, we now have an ideology of September 11, a rigidly bounded system of meaning and rhetoric that in the words of Jean Bethke Elshtain, "discounts or dismisses whatever does not 'fit' within it" and "has very little use for accurate descriptions of what is going on" (2003, 16). The dominance of the framings offered by the media and political elites (and, just as important, facilitated by several other institutions and social actors) means that "9/11" has become a morality tale about patriotism, loss, victimhood, and heroes. Moreover, other interpretations that ought to be more strongly considered (e.g., international relations, U.S. military policy, government inefficiencies, "turf battles" among law enforcement and other service agencies) have been glossed over or ignored by political leaders, the mainstream media, and much of the public.

> The general reaction to 9/11 throughout the American mass media and political establishment lacked critical self-reflection. It was a wholesale attempt after 9/11 to better "sell" what America was really about, rather than question whether U.S. foreign policy had fueled distrust of the country before the attacks. Instead, the government joined forces with the public relations industry to promote a positive image of the United States throughout the American press and abroad (Dimaggio 2008, 265).

Efforts to draw on the meanings of September 11 to achieve various symbolic and tangible outcomes continue today in a variety of political and social arenas. The attacks, which occurred less than a year into President Bush's first term in office, were a central component of his and other political officials' support of the ongoing military campaigns in Afghanistan and Iraq and the more nebulous "war on terror." Indeed, fear-inducing references to September 11 were a valuable rhetorical device in the 2004 campaign that resulted in Bush's reelection to a second term. John Kerry, Bush's Democratic rival, who many believed could win the presidency, repeatedly suggested that the release of a new videotape by Osama bin Laden just days before that election revived the fear-based sentiments of September 11 and resulted in Bush's reelection: "It [the tape] changed the entire dynamic of the last five days. We saw it in the polling. There was no other intervening event. We saw the polls freeze and then we saw them drop a point, because . . . it agitated people over 9/11" (Johnson 2008, AA2).

The rhetorical use of "9/11" also is illustrated by Bush's remarks in support of the Protect America Act (a surveillance bill) on February 13, 2008, which opened with the following: "Good morning. At this moment, somewhere in the world, terrorists are planning new attacks on our country. Their goal is to bring destruction to our shores that will make September the eleventh pale by comparison" (White House press release 2008a). Vice President Dick Cheney used similar rhetoric to support the Bush administration's surveillance policies in a speech he gave just a few weeks earlier:

As with any legislative matter, there will be points of agreement and points of disagreement. I prefer to begin with some points of fact. The United States of America has not experienced a catastrophic attack since the morning of September 11th, 2001. In the days following 9/11, we had to assume that another attack was imminent. We proceeded on that basis, mobilizing against the danger, and using every legitimate tool at our command to protect the American people against another attack. It is a fact, as well, that the danger to our country remains very real, and that the terrorists are still determined to hit us. They are fanatical in their hatred. They likely have operatives inside the United States. And they have tried many times to cause more violence and death in this country. Nobody can guarantee that we won't be hit again. Our intelligence agencies have made clear that we're in a heightened threat environment, with a "persistent and evolving" terrorist adversary. And so the relative safety of the six years and four months since 9/11 is not an accident. It's an achievement. (White House press release 2008b)

September 11 also was used in the 2008 presidential election by the candidates of both parties to bolster their positions in discussions of national security, foreign policy, civil liberties, and a host of other issues. The events of that day were a linchpin in the campaign of Rudy Giuliani, who frequently referred to the September 11 attacks—or, more precisely, to his much-lauded performance as mayor of New York City during the crisis—in his political speeches and campaign appearances. The former mayor's repeated and unsubtle efforts to use 9/11 to advance his candidacy did not go unnoticed (as evident in Senator Biden's comment). Throughout 2007 and 2008, countless segments of the *Daily Show*, a satirical but increasingly influential forum for political commentary, examined Giuliani's propensity for mentioning September 11 in nearly any forum and with regard to nearly any issue. An article in *USA Today* summed up the sentiments of many reporters, commentators, and pundits: "Giuliani has made his experience during and after the 9/11 attacks the centerpiece of his campaign for the Republican presidential nomination" (Moore 2007, 2A; see also Barrett 2007; Bone 2007).

Even after Giuliani ended his campaign in 2008, September 11 continued to be an issue. John McCain and Barack Obama, the Republican and Democratic presidential nominees, respectively, made sure to schedule an extended visit to Ground Zero on the seventh anniversary of the attacks. And after Sarah Palin was tapped as the Republican vice presidential nominee, campaign officials also scheduled a visit to Ground Zero for her, within weeks of her arrival on the national political scene. There, she stopped at the WTC site, visited the memorials, and met with local firefighters at a nearby firehouse. More than just a visit, Palin used her time at Ground Zero to reaffirm the retributive framings in the 9/11 narrative and the connection between September 11 and the ongoing military conflicts:

> I agree with the Bush Administration that we take the fight to them. We never again let them come onto our soil and try to destroy not only our democracy, but communities like the community of New York. Never again. . . . I wish every American would come through here. I wish every world leader would come through here, and understand what it is that took place here and more importantly how America came together and united to commit to never allowing this to happen again. (Berger 2008)

The use of September 11 is, of course, not confined to those seeking political office, as I demonstrated in regard to New York City's firefighters using their newly acquired prestige in the wake of the attacks. Even today, whenever someone mentions September 11, he is implicitly referring to the range of shared sentiments and meanings of these events that we understand as "9/11." We can see this in the death and "contested heroism" of James Zadroga, a New York City police officer who responded in the September 2001 emergency at the WTC site. His death in 2006 was believed to have been caused by respiratory problems he developed while working at the site. If this were the case, he would be the first confirmed case tying the death of an emergency responder on September 11 to an illness related to those events. This designation would, of course, make him an important symbol in the battle waged by those seeking more compensation for health-related expenses incurred by those who participated in the emergency response.

Most people thought that Zadroga's death was indeed a direct result of his role in the 9/11 response. Others, however, including New York City's chief medical examiner, believed that his death was due to the intravenous ingestion of ground-up prescription pills. In affirming the chief medical examiner's findings, New York Mayor Michael Bloomberg explained that those findings suggested that Zadroga was "not a hero," which set off a storm of complaints from Zadroga's family, police officials, and local citizens who wanted to protect not just Zadroga's legacy but the sanctity of 9/11 heroes as a whole (Harris 2007). Amid the ensuing battle over Zadroga's "contested heroism," the case became more about public perception and post–September 11 symbolic politics than about forensic science (Kahn 2008). This story also serves as further testament to the still-strong symbolic potency of all things September 11 and its continued viability as a rhetorical device that can be used as part of a broader array of discursive strategies.

The framing of 9/11 as a public drama with iconic heroes and melodramatic notions of good versus evil continues to shape how people think and talk about September 11. We can see this in the media coverage on the anniversary of the attacks, which each year serves to affirm the public drama narrative as much as it does to commemorate the attacks.

The coverage on the seventh anniversary, September 11, 2008, is a good example: In this collection of seemingly straightforward commemorations was an abundance of evidence illustrating just how fully and effectively the public drama narrative had been cemented in collective memory about September 11. MSNBC developed a special interactive "Where Are They Now?" feature for its website that resurrected and reinforced the character-driven personifications that characterized the postattack coverage. The section began, "Seven years ago, their images were everywhere. Find out what has happened to them . . . since." Included in the list of ten people were Rudy Giuliani, Bob Beckwith (the retired New York City fireman who stood next to President Bush on a burned-out fire truck at the WTC site while the president spoke through a bullhorn and whipped the crowd into a patriotic fervor), the three firefighters who raised the American flag at Ground Zero, Osama bin Laden, and Lisa Beamer (the widow of a passenger on flight 93, which crashed in Pennsylvania) (see MSNBC 2008).[3] On that same seventh anniversary, President Bush's commemorative remarks to the nation unintentionally demonstrated the extent to which the media's dramatic amplification of 9/11 had taken hold: "On a day when buildings fell, heroes rose." As I have noted, once the media-fueled dramatization and personification took over, we were left with a Hollywood-like version of September 11.

Public Drama in a Mediated Social World

The pervasiveness of public drama in the mainstream media was caused by the economic, technological, and cultural shifts in the news industry, shifts that have fundamentally altered how news producers and their audiences gauge "newsworthiness." This, in turn, has noteworthy implications for the kinds of news items that are selected for attention and how they are molded into news. Consequently, packaging and presenting news as a dramatic and emotional story (i.e., public drama) has become an increasingly valuable means of creating news that can attract and retain an audience while also satisfying news organizations' profit-oriented goals. The prominence of public drama in the news cycle is that it "sells"; audiences seem to enjoy news that offers entertainment and style. As a result, we now can find public dramas in the lead stories on the morning and prime-time news programs, in the headlines of Internet news websites, on the covers of popular magazines, and in the front pages and section leads of newspapers.

Seeking a Broader Understanding of Public Drama

For this book, I adopted a constructionist approach, in which detailed analysis of a single topic is the norm. By examining the media's coverage of the attacks and the emergency response at Ground Zero, we can better understand how and why this coverage took the shape that it did while also gaining an appreciation for the role of public drama in the broader, mass-mediated culture. My analysis of the media's coverage contextualizes public drama within the overlapping cultures of news work and news consumption. The fact that such an overtly consequential historical moment would be organized and packaged for public consumption as a public drama says much about the primacy of this form of news in the contemporary media.

We still have, however, much to learn about public drama. For instance, I have used sociological literature and the patterns of the mainstream media's post–September 11 coverage to identify some of the strategies and techniques that news workers use to find "suitable" news elements and bring them together into a long-running news story. But there remains much to discover about how public dramas are constructed. Examining a range of public dramas will undoubtedly reveal additional strategies and techniques that news workers employ to uncover dramatic elements, cultivate emotionality, and select the focal points of that coverage, the plot lines to be shaped and followed, and the characters to be fleshed out.

We also need to know how audiences absorb public drama. Future research should look at how audience members understand and use the meanings ascribed to an issue, event, or individual through public drama. The messages of a public drama carry a great deal of symbolic influence, so it is important that we learn how these messages are received and entered into people's daily interactions. What specific meanings do people receive from a particular public drama? Are some meanings readily accepted while others are questioned? Which and why? What do people do with the acquired meanings? Do the meanings directly affect news consumers (i.e., spur them to action), or do they exert more general "ripple effects" over time, perhaps gradually creating meanings that shape the appraisals of similar social phenomena from the past or in the future? As we become better able to specify the ways that public dramas shape meanings and, more important, how they may be manifested in individual perceptions, decisions, or action, we can better assess the role of public drama in social life.

We also should know how the impact of public drama extends beyond the media and their audiences. As my analysis has shown, the dominant meanings of high-profile public dramas can serve as resources for social actors who are not connected to the public drama (or the media that produce it) but nonetheless co-opt these meanings and symbols for their own ends.[4] Once established, the dominant meanings and the main characters promoted in a high-profile mediated representation become valued symbolic resources for those who are able to align with them. The public drama of O. J. Simpson in the mid-1990s became a resource for claims makers whose agendas included domestic violence, institutional racism, media ethics, the judicial system, or any other issue that could be directly or indirectly linked to that public drama. Similarly, the public drama of the beating of Rodney King by four Los Angeles police officers in the early 1990s appealed to those making claims about racism in society, constitutional rights, police brutality, racial profiling, and other related issues.

The larger point is that high-profile media stories can, and often do, become "symbolic of perceived social problems in a given time and place, engaging a broad range of participants" in discourse, policy, or action (Chancer 2005, 7).[5] Several recent high-profile public dramas have become "typifying examples" and "landmark narratives" for certain issues, providing the dominant frames through which news workers and the general public understands and responds to similar issues or events (for more on landmark narratives, see Lee and Ermann 1999 and Nichols 1997, and for examples, see Lowney and Best 1995). Columbine has become the standard reference for how to think and talk about school shootings (perhaps to be joined by Virginia Tech). Hurricane Katrina has quickly emerged as a referential event not only for subsequent hurricanes and emergency response protocols (especially in the Gulf region) but also for government ineptitude or malfeasance.

Another aspect of public drama that deserves future consideration is the nature of the media attention it receives, that is, the *amount of coverage* (total hours of coverage or number of stories, reports, features, etc.), *level of coverage* (local, regional, national, international), and *duration of coverage* (how long it remains in the news cycle), which may be important to how a public drama unfolds and the meanings that emerge from it. The amount and scope of media exposure help determine how big a public drama's audience can be, how easily audience members can access media narratives, and what resources are available to cover a story (i.e., national and international news corporations have fewer monetary restrictions in deciding what and how much to cover than do most local media outlets). Some public dramas attract a great deal of media and audience attention, sometimes dominating the headlines for weeks. Other public dramas are prominently featured for just a few days before disappearing (owing to the resolution of suspense, lack of compelling plot points, absence of interesting characters, or other factors that decrease their dramatic appeal).[6] For instance, several years ago the saga of the "Runaway Bride" overtook the news cycles of national news organizations, particularly television, for several days.

When Jennifer Wilbanks disappeared from her Georgia home on April 26, 2005, it sparked a nationwide search and extensive media coverage. The speed and extent of the media response may be partly attributable to the fact that Wilbanks's home was in a suburb of Atlanta (also home to CNN). The media coverage quickly took on a familiar plot structure, with much speculation about her fiancé's possible culpability in her disappearance. Three days later, Wilbanks called her fiancé and told him that she had been kidnapped and assaulted. But the police were able to trace Wilbanks's call to a pay phone in Albuquerque, New Mexico, where local authorities found her and took her into custody. When questioned by the police, Wilbanks admitted that she had fabricated the entire story, and she had run away voluntarily to escape the pressure and uncertainty associated with her upcoming wedding, which was scheduled for April 30, 2005. These revelations stripped the story of much of its drama and compromised the initial plot around which the coverage had been framed (as a mysterious disappearance with the possibility of foul play). Accordingly, in early May, the case of the "Runaway Bride" began receding to the margins of national news cycles and out of public consciousness.[7]

It is difficult to ascertain what effects these variables—the amount, level, and duration of media coverage—may have on the form and force of a public drama, given that my case study, September 11, did not have the typical amount and duration of media coverage. The media's and audience's attention to the attacks and their aftermath was in many ways unprecedented, replacing nearly all non-9/11 content for more than a week. Even after non-9/11 topics, issues, and events reentered the mainstream news cycles, 9/11 still affected the entire media landscape. Stories and reports about the attacks and their aftermath remained in local and national (and even international) news cycles throughout 2001 and into 2002.

A well-crafted public drama that lasts a long time and is popular with the media audience is likely to contribute to the frameworks of meaning through which similar events or issues, in the past or the future, are understood and acted on. Expanding the range of public drama cases permits us to expand the conceptual framework and, in turn, to develop the tools needed to identify public drama and its causes, characteristics, and consequences so that we may better understand its role in social life. Further refinement and expansion of this public drama framework may also help news consumers become more critical, to be more judicious in their consumption and use of news productions, and to question what is being emphasized and why, and what is being excluded and why. This is important not just to deconstruct the media coverage of future issues and events but also to uncover the misrepresentations of past events (e.g., Columbine, O. J. Simpson, the death of Princess Diana, the Oklahoma City bombing).[8]

Next I provide a brief examination of some of the patterns in the media coverage of Hurricane Katrina, which I hope will underscore the importance of developing additional case studies and comparative analyses of public drama to find out how their meanings filter into other political and social realms. Hurricane Katrina ravaged parts of Louisiana, Mississippi, and other areas in the Gulf Coast region in August 2005. The mainstream media's coverage of the hurricane and its devastation reveals many of the pillars of public drama. Like September 11, it received tremendous media attention, captivated the nation, and contained an abundance of news elements around which news workers could create a dramatic and emotional narrative. Katrina even enjoyed an advantage over September 11 because the media had advance warning of the impending hurricane and arrived on scene before the storm made landfall, which offered plenty of opportunities to speculate about the potential scope and magnitude of its destructive path.

Media swarmed to the region (no doubt spurred on by the success of the long-running coverage of September 11). The hurricane dominated the media for several weeks and remained in the forefront of mainstream news cycles for months. As the coverage took shape, it began to reflect the dominant media logic of the day (i.e., emphasis on drama and emotion and an inclination toward rendering the news in story form) and eventually exhibited the characteristics of a public drama. As one study of post-Katrina media framings found,

> Initial media coverage of Katrina's devastating impacts was quickly replaced by reporting that characterized disaster victims as opportunistic looters and violent criminals and that presented individual and group behavior following the Katrina disaster through the lens of civil unrest. Later, narratives shifted again and began to metaphorically represent the disaster-stricken city of New Orleans as a war zone. (Tierney, Bevc, and Kuligowski 2006, 60–61)

When viewed as a public drama, we could consider the dominance of these framings in the mediated Katrina narrative as evidence of the media's efforts at dramatic amplification and cultivation of emotionality. In the aftermath of Katrina, news workers feverishly mined the disaster and the emergency response for the most dramatic and emotional angles. Their efforts, as demonstrated by an analysis of media coverage of Katrina conducted by Kathleen Tierney, Christine Bevc, and Erica Kuligowski, enabled them to "find" some of the most powerful images and prominent story lines in all of the Katrina coverage (2006). For instance, a series of horrific accounts about what was happening in New Orleans (e.g., widespread looting, sexual assaults in the Superdome, several homicides and sexual assaults in the city's convention center and other locations used to house those who were not able to evacuate before the storm hit) became part of the central story line. The problem was that many of the more sensational of these news items proved to be nothing more than disaster myths and unfounded rumors.

The larger point, however, is that it did not matter that these reports were never officially corroborated, because their prominence in the earliest accounts of the situation in New Orleans drove the initial narrative and gave news workers the dramatic and emotional building blocks they needed to fill post-Katrina news cycles. Of course, the disproportionate emphasis on drama and emotion required a trade-off, in the form of highly skewed reporting and false assumptions about what was actually happening in New Orleans and what should be done in response. All of this led Jim Lehrer, a respected journalist and host of PBS's *NewsHour*, to refer to the initial post-Katrina coverage as "one of the worst weeks of reporting in the history of the American media." Clearly, the mainstream media treatment of Katrina highlights the constructed nature of media coverage and underscores the dangers of a media logic that adheres to a story-first, entertainment-like ethos and favors news elements with the most drama and emotion.

The media's reliance on the dictates of public drama can also be seen in their disproportionate focus on New Orleans. Most of the television reports included live shots from the city (usually from the French Quarter or other tourist attractions); similarly, much of the print news tended to focus on the hurricane's impact on New Orleans. Certainly, some areas of New Orleans were substantially affected by the hurricane and flooding (e.g., the much-publicized Lower Ninth Ward), but many areas in the region were affected just as much or more than New Orleans. By considering the coverage in relation to the public drama framework laid out in this project, we can better understand the reasons for the extensive focus on New Orleans, which came at the expense of other, harder-hit regions.

The rapid and rigidly bounded funneling of media attention toward New Orleans reflects the fact that like New York City after September 11, the city offered some of the most accessible, dramatic, and horrific images and moments. New Orleans also offered a range of news elements that could be used to cultivate emotionality. The city is a major tourist destination and so is a setting with which many members of the media audience could identify, thereby enhancing the emotional potential of coverage of or from this area. Audience members could see reports or stories about New Orleans and remember their own experiences with that city to feel more connected to the event than they might if the coverage had been focused on more remote, rural areas that few in the media audience had ever heard of or visited.[9]

Conclusion

The media are essential to the formation of a public drama. The productions of the mainstream media provide information, set agendas, and constitute shared experiences for many. People rely on what they see, hear, and read from the press as a basis for activity, as a reference point for defining the situations they find themselves in, and as a way to make sense of politics, the economy, and other issues and events of the day. The ever-increasing media saturation of contemporary society means that there always are a multitude of public dramas unfolding at the national, regional, and local levels, with many more issues and events available to be discovered and treated accordingly by the media. Public dramas often occupy prominent positions in the news cycles of television (e.g., morning network news programs and evening talk-news hybrids) and other media (covers of news and entertainment magazines, section leads in newspapers, headline links on Internet news sites). As public drama continues to gain favor among media officials and their audiences as a vehicle for packaging and presenting news, it may increasingly change the media landscape as well as how members of the media audience understand and respond to those events, issues, and individuals brought to them through public drama.

We should acknowledge the prevalence and importance of public drama, through which we experience and ascribe meaning to issues, events, individuals, objects, and other aspects of the world around us. We learn about our culture and social institutions through public drama. It can shape how we understand current events and remember historical moments. Public drama can influence the development and application of certain policies. Individuals can acquire a new status through their involvement in a public drama, moving from being unknown to becoming a celebrity, from being famous to infamous, or from being popular to reviled, depending on what part they play and how the audience receives their performance.

Public drama can take shape around almost anything; there is no limit to what can become public drama, nor is there anything about certain events, issues, objects, or individuals that guarantees their transformation into a public drama. The number of public dramas in play at any moment, coupled with their prominence and prolonged placement in mainstream news cycles, means that it is now exceedingly difficult for news consumers to remain informed about current issues and events without encountering public drama. But even if we cannot avoid public drama altogether, we can at least be aware of it. We can know that when events, issues, individuals, and information are deemed newsworthy, primarily because they fit a format that favors dramatic, emotionally gripping narratives and images, we are likely to get a significantly slanted picture of reality.

Notes

1. This is seen as particularly beneficial to those who wish to find news outside what is produced by the "mainstream" media. Some people also believe that the expansion of the traditional media and the introduction of a host of "new" media democratize news making by creating new and exciting avenues for people outside the news industry to contribute to the information mix (such as the "citizen"-produced journalism found on certain Internet "blogs").

2. As I discuss in chapter 2, these individuals do not assign valuations of newsworthiness or construct the news in a vacuum; instead, their actions are guided by a particular cultural logic for making news within the broader structural (e.g., economic and technological) inducements and constraints in which they operate.

3. While other historical events may have attracted a similar level of coverage in the short term (e.g., the *Challenger* disaster in 1985) or maintained the interest of media officials and media audiences over an extended period of time (e.g., the O. J. Simpson saga), no other event in history has garnered the combined amount and duration of coverage than that generated by the September 11, 2001, terrorist attacks.

4. This combined approach is the same as that used in other media research. Findings reported elsewhere (Gitlin 1980; Jacobs 2000) suggest that network television news and the *New York Times* are similar enough to be analyzed together.

5. Some of this research is discussed in detail in edited volumes about the media and 9/11 (see, e.g., Chermak, Bailey, and Brown 2003; Greenberg 2002; Grusin and Utt 2005; Noll 2003).

6. Audiences tend to look to television first because it offers instant information to its audiences, is readily available throughout the day, provides what seems like a real-time window into an event, and wraps its offerings in a thrilling technological bundle of moving pictures, graphics, and sound that enhances its appeal to its audience. "Because of its ubiquity, accessibility, and technological ability to broadcast in 'real time,' television has in contemporary times served as the principal media choice during national crises for most Americans" (Ruggiero and Glascock 2002, 66). See also Carey 2003; Greenberg, Hofschire, and Lachlan 2002; Rainie and Kalsnes 2002.

7. Kirsten Mogenson and her colleagues (2002) conducted a content analysis of the first eight hours of September 11 coverage on the major news networks (ABC, CBS, NBC, CNN, and Fox News) and found that 34 percent of NBC's total coverage during that period focused on what was happening at the WTC (this was more than any other

broadcast or cable news network). In comparison, the other broadcast news networks (ABC and CBS) focused 23 percent and 28 percent, respectively, of their total coverage in the first eight hours on the World Trade Center. The two cable news networks examined in this study, Fox News (32%) and CNN (31%), focused almost equally on the WTC (although still slightly less than NBC did).

8. The *Today* broadcast schedule for September 12 to 18 was as follows: September 12 (7 a.m.–1 p.m.), September 13 (7 a.m.–1 p.m.), September 14 (7 a.m.–12 noon), September 15 (7 a.m.–9 a.m.), September 16 (9 a.m.–10 a.m.), September 17 (7 a.m.–1 p.m.), September 18 (7 a.m.–10 a.m.). The September 18 broadcast marked the return to the customary *Today* format (i.e., thirty-minute segments, with commercial breaks and weather and local news updates spaced throughout the broadcast).

9. The site attracted more than 1.1 million unique visitors per day, an 83 percent increase, in the weeks after the attacks (MLM 2001).

10. For more information on postattack patterns of media use, see Abel, Miller, and Filak 2005; Carey 2003; Downey 2001a; Poindexter and Conway 2005; Ruggiero and Glascock 2002; Seeger et al. 2002.

CHAPTER 2

1. The media's agenda-setting function has been a central focus of media research for several decades. See Bunis et al. 1996; Cook et al. 1983; Lambeth 1978; MacKuen and Coombs 1981; McCombs and Shaw 1972; Roberts and Bachen 1981.

2. A large body of research explores the extent to which media direct the attentions of their audiences and help set the parameters and content of public discourse. See Brewer and McCombs 1996; Dearing and Rogers 1996; D. Elliott 1989; W. Gamson 1992; Jacobs 2000; Katz and Lazarsfeld 1955; Liebes and Katz 1990; McCombs and Shaw 1993; Molotch and Lester 1975; Tierney 1994; Turner and Killian 1987.

3. Francis Polletta argues that for audience members, frames are "interpretive schema that enable individuals to locate, perceive, identify, and label occurrences within their life space and the world at large" (1998, 139).

4. From this perspective, a media representation is never a direct or particularly accurate reflection of the objective reality of its subject matter. Rather, the media translate and transform the subject matter in accordance with their own needs. For more on this, see Best 1990; Edelman 1988; Lester 1980; Stallings 1990; Tuchman 1978.

5. James Hamilton (2004) argues that since the 1970s, the mechanisms for determining what is to become news have been increasingly shaped by this profit orientation and other market forces.

6. These economic shifts have been accompanied by a series of changes pertaining to how news audiences are conceptualized and targeted to receive the news and other media offerings. The contemporary news audience has become more and more commodified and segmented so that its members can be more effectively delivered, or "sold," to advertisers.

7. Certainly, most of this "new" media space has been allocated to decidedly non-news content, but it has also been the breeding ground for novel, and increasingly influential, vehicles for news delivery (e.g., Internet-only news websites like slate.com, the websites of traditional news sources, often-visited blogs like the *Drudge Report*, podcasts).

8. Bogart (1981, 34) initially outlined the concept of the news hole to refer to newspapers' organization and space allotments, but the concept is now generally understood to include all kinds of print and broadcast news products.

9. Philip Jenkins stresses the need to acknowledge the range of "formats for storytelling available in modern media" (1989, 112), as do Lull and Hinerman, who suggest that "most media scandals are multimedia events: the tabloid press, trash TV video, on-line services, mainstream news, event radio—all construct versions of the story fitting to their technologies and audiences" (1997, 17).

10. The Project for Excellence in Journalism (PEJ) is a research organization that empirically assesses the performance of the press. Since 2006, it has been affiliated with the Pew Research Center in Washington, D.C.

11. For more on the "culture of news work" and its various habits, strategies, informal routines, and journalistic norms, see Altheide 1976; Fine and White 2002; Gans 1979; Jacobs 1996; Oliver and Myers 1999; Peltu 1985; Snyder and Kelly 1977.

12. Schechter's comments were featured in a *New York Times* article (Scott 1998) about the media coverage of the Monica Lewinsky scandal (which centered on accusations that President Bill Clinton had had a sexual relationship with a White House intern).

13. A study of cable news content found that 68 percent of the segments were repetitious accounts of previously reported stories, without any new information (PEJ 2004). Thus, despite having twenty-four hours of programming space to fill each day, cable networks consistently draw on only a few topics to fill that space.

14. Television is uniquely situated in this regard, as television news coverage can be made to seem more robust by interspersing existing information with video images, remote interviews, and other production techniques.

15. A poll conducted by the PEW Research Center for the People and the Press (2004) found that 21 percent of people aged eighteen to twenty-nine obtained most of their information about the 2004 presidential campaign and the candidates from comedy programs like *The Daily Show* and *Saturday Night Live*.

16. A well-crafted public drama can reinforce or alter existing systems of meaning (Van Ginneken 2003), help maintain existing societal power arrangements (Edelman 1988), shape public opinion (Brown, Duane, and Fraser 1997; Dayan and Katz 1992), influence the development or implementation of social policy (Lull and Hinerman 1997), and mold collective memory (Chaney 1993; Dayan and Katz 1992; Olick 1999; Olick and Robbins 1998). By directing "the attitudes of an audience toward a version of cognitive reality and moral order" (Gusfield 1981, 177), public drama can fundamentally influence how we view our past, present, and future and how we think about various events and topics.

17. While not a full-blown public drama, the prolonged period of media coverage and political scrutiny stemming from Janet Jackson's "wardrobe malfunction" during the 2004 Super Bowl illustrates the media practice of linking the media narrative to broad cultural values. The repercussions of this brief moment continued to reverberate for years after it occurred. It had a substantial effect on the media industry because it focused public attention on the network television's standards and practices and gave ammunition to those who wanted to portray certain media content as the enemy of common morality and shared values.

18. Similarly, Fine and White suggest that media coverage can facilitate "the creation and the recognition of social bonds and communal care that might otherwise be attenuated" (2002, 58).

19. A high-profile public drama can also alter the media landscape. The public drama that emerged following the sinking of the *Titanic* in 1912 was a key factor in the transformation of the *New York Times* into a global media powerhouse, and the Watergate scandal helped transform the *Washington Post* into one of the nation's elite newspapers (Heyer 1995; Nichols 1997).

20. Public drama's culture-shifting capacity also was evident in the Watergate scandal, which had all the earmarks of a mediated public drama, albeit in a much more "primitive" media age. Although numerous events contributed to "Watergate" as a public drama, the Senate hearings received extensive media coverage (thus rendering the hearings as, in a sense, the "main stage" on which this public drama unfolded). As a rule, Senate hearings are rather tedious, mundane affairs, so coverage of them is generally not expected to receive high levels of viewership or readership. But the Watergate hearings regularly managed to attract a large proportion of the population because these hearings, and the events leading up to them, were amenable to presentation in dramatic form, and these dramatic elements came to define how the media packaged and presented the hearings and, consequently, the way that Watergate has been defined in collective memory. See Schudson (1992) for a detailed examination of the cultural and structural productions in the Watergate hearings.

21. For example, in a crime-related public drama, the cast would likely include offender(s) and victim(s), lawyers, family members, the spokespersons, witnesses, relevant experts and professionals, and the neighbors and friends of those involved.

22. A number of sociologists and other analysts have explored how media might enhance the status of those depicted in their coverage. Gusfield contends that "a public issue has status implications insofar as its public outcome is interpretable as conferring prestige upon or withdrawing it from a status group" (1986, 173), and Jacobs suggests that "depending on how they are defined, linked together in story or plot, and the things that determine what is or is not in the narrative, events can have important consequences for social identities and social actions" (2000, 8). In his discussion of pseudoevents, Boorstin showed that participation in mass-mediated representations could serve as a means of "fabricating well-knownness" (1978, 46) for the relatively obscure or as a means of increasing the public presence of those who were already well known. Klapp argues that mediated representations can wield "a creative power to make and break statuses, to give and take prestige, to generate enthusiasm . . . and to create new identities" (1964, 257).

23. In some ways, the power of public drama to confer status is a by-product of the overall media logic—the systematic processes by which media gather, organize, and transmit news—that governs most news work. News work is organized to give greater priority to some sources of information over others (i.e., those that are closely connected to the issue or event of interest, preferably if such connections stem from their official, professional capacity). As a result, we often come to understand an event or issue largely through its participants. "Collective memory is known through its dramatic personae. Much historical memory is a pageant of prominent persons who exemplify the issues with which they are associated" (Fine 1999, 229). Similarly, Gitlin found that media depictions of the SDS movement were framed around the movement's characters, rather than the issues that gave rise to the movement or the goals they sought: "The all-permeating spectacular culture insisted that the movement be identified through its celebrities" (1980, 153). The way public drama is constructed dictates that the media select for characters that closely match

prefabricated images of what a participant in that particular type of public drama should appear to be.

24. As Herbert Gans (1979) noted in his seminal book on the organization structures of the media industry, the media seek to construct stories, whenever possible, around characters with whom the audience is likely to be at least somewhat familiar.

25. I position visibility, because of its ready availability, as the most banal and least valuable of the status rewards available through participation in public drama and other mediated representations. If virtually anyone can attain visibility (whether their deeds are trivial or of great social importance), it would not seem to offer much value to its holder if possessed in moderate amounts (other than the opportunities it creates for gaining more visibility). I recognize that such valuations are subjective. For example, many of the social actors discussed by Klapp (1964), J. Gamson (1994), and Scanlon (1989) viewed recognition and even a small measure of fame as a highly desirable end goal.

26. Those with ownership may come to be perceived as the representative faces and voices for certain issues (Nichols 2003), and they may become the "mass-mediated fountainhead of authoritative moral and technical excellence" (Gitlin 1980, 267) on the matter. Ownership is similar to Nichols's notion (2003) of a "single-issue" symbol, that is, any representation that immediately brings to mind a particular issue.

27. Joel Best suggests that holding owner status can become self-reinforcing, that "once the media have used particular activists or experts as sources for one story, they are more likely to seek out the same sources for future, related stories" (2008, 142).

28. Other co-owners of this issue include Marc Klaas and Erin Runnion (each of whom was the parent of a child victim). More recently, Beth Twitty (the mother of Natalee Holloway, an Alabama teenager who disappeared while on a school trip to Aruba in 2005) has been included in several news reports regarding child safety.

29. Kane contends that "moral reputation inevitably represents a resource for political agents and institutions, one that in combination with other familiar political resources enables political processes, supports political contestants and creates political opportunities" (2001, 2). The notion that status represents a viable social and political resource is widely supported by sociologists and other analysts (Dayan and Katz 1992; Goffman 1959, 1969; Molotch and Lester 1974; Thye 2000).

30. In his research on how social problems are constructed and communicated, Joel Best states that "insider claims-makers" (i.e., those with direct or indirect access to key institutional actors, such as political leaders or media officials, who can help make or disseminate a claim about a particular social problem) enjoy certain advantages in the construction of social problems (e.g., easier access to press coverage) (1990, 109). The possession of moral currency can help turn "outsiders" into "insiders," at least for a limited time. Robert Stallings implies in his study of risk that a high-profile media story can raise the status of certain participants and that "a dramatic event gives different claimsmakers and risk definers access" (1990, 91) to the larger public arenas (Hilgartner and Bosk 1988) in which social problems (Miller and Holstein 1989) take place.

31. The differences between ownership and moral currency as they relate to public drama are similar to Nichols's distinction (2003) between "single-issue" symbols (representations that immediately bring to mind a particular issue) and "generalizable" symbols (representations that can have significance for issues beyond those to which they are directly linked).

1. *Nancy Grace* provided the most intensive coverage of the Caylee Anthony story, far outpacing the coverage offered by similar criminal justice–oriented cable news programs (e.g., Fox News channel's *On the Record* with Greta Van Susteren, MSNBC's *The Abrams Report* with Dan Abrams) and the networks' morning news programs. In fact, *Nancy Grace* discussed the Caylee case more times than the morning programs on NBC (70), ABC (30), and CBS (20) combined. But as these numbers reveal, the story still had a significant presence on these programs, especially in December after the discovery of a child's remains and the subsequent confirmation that they were, in fact, Caylee's.

2. *Nancy Grace* bills itself as "television's only justice themed/interview/debate show, designed for those interested in the breaking crime news of the day." It airs nightly on CNN's Headline News network, with original episodes typically aired from Monday to Friday.

3. It is believed that Caylee actually disappeared on June 9, but the local authorities were not notified until July 15, after which it became an official law enforcement investigation and, ultimately, available to the press.

4. Of the morning news programs on network television, *Today* provided the most coverage of this story. CBS's *The Early Show* discussed the story seven times in July, although it did not provide any coverage until July 22, five days after the story first broke. ABC's *Good Morning America* first mentioned this story one day sooner than CBS (July 21), but it had only three discussions for the remainder of July. These figures were obtained through a review of the complete broadcast transcripts retrieved from the Lexis-Nexis searchable database.

5. Much of the discrepancy in the amount and frequency of coverage is that *Nancy Grace* has a much narrower range of topics and stories to cover than do the networks' morning news programs.

6. The Caylee Anthony saga was discussed on only two broadcasts of *Nancy Grace* during the week of October 27 to 31, when it was briefly replaced with another public drama involving the murder of the family members of actress/pop star Jennifer Hudson.

7. On Thursday, December 11, a child's remains were reported found near the Anthony home. That evening, *Nancy Grace* achieved its highest-ever ratings, surpassing the previous high in October 2008, which was also during the ongoing coverage of the Caylee Anthony saga (Media Bistro 2008).

8. In other words, the "carrying capacity" of the news media is limited. *Carrying capacity* (Hilgartner and Bosk 1988) refers to the finite amount of time, space, and other resources that the various public arenas, such as the media, have available for social issues.

9. This simplification of the narrative is similar to what Allport and Postman (1947), in their analysis of rumor transmission, referred to as the "leveling," "sharpening," and "assimilation" that make rumors more interesting and easier to tell and understand as they are passed on over time. Klapp also referred to this process as "funneling," in which "whatever is needed to make a good story is abstracted from all of the information that is available" (1964, 60). Van Ginneken termed such enhancements of narrative appeal as "selective articulation" (2003).

10. In his examination of the burgeoning "convergence culture" that has grown in relation to the new media and technology, Henry Jenkins (2006) argues that the circulation of media content has become increasingly contingent on the active participation of consumers.

11. This view finds support in Nimmo's contention (1984) that televised news programming is often more fable than fact and in comments offered by William Gamson and his colleagues regarding the media coverage of the 1991 Persian Gulf War: "The spectacle of seeing journalists donning gas masks during the Persian Gulf War overshadows the reality that there was no chemical attack" (1992, 386).

12. According to Joel Best, "the press favors stories that promise to capture the audience's attention—stories with elements of novelty and drama" (1990, 110). Similarly, Murray Edelman noted that "the logic that explains official, public, and media attention to political problems does not turn on their severity but rather upon their dramatic appeals" (1988, 28). Todd Gitlin suggested that an emphasis on drama has been inextricably woven into the fabric of modern media logic, pointing out that "from the media point of view, news consists of events which can be recognized and interpreted as drama" and "the traditional narrative structure of a news story selects for dramatic (preferably melodramatic) conflict" (1980, 146, 90).

13. The Internet's video-streaming capacity makes it increasingly effective for this, although there often is still a lag.

14. A report by the Project for Excellence in Journalism (PEJ 2004) indicates that 62 percent of broadcast time in 2003 was "live" in the form of interviews and reporters' "stand-ups" in the field at a dramatic location, a telling indicator of the importance that media officials place on "setting the scene" and creating for the viewers a feeling of "being there."

15. Other prominent media stories in which this technique was evident include the 2001 anthrax attacks and events involving the "Beltway Snipers" in October 2002.

16. Indeed, as sociologist Todd Gitlin argued long ago about media coverage: "A dramatic piece is a dramatic piece," so the way to get an audience to pay attention is to create an "emotional event with emotional people" (1980, 86).

17. Media officials have an added incentive in trying to direct their audience toward a public drama and its characters: if they are successful, they may be able to sustain that audience for their other news and entertainment programming.

18. Schudson argued that the "experiences of audiences with mass media provides people a sense of connection to the collective whole that few other institutions today can rival" (1986, 46). Along these same lines, Hoffner and her colleagues suggest that "mass media coverage of news is uniquely suited to arouse emotions" (2002, 230).

19. Horton and Wohl's (1956) notion of "para-social interaction" is among the earliest and best known explorations of the connectivity between media figures and their audiences. *Para-social interaction* refers to the purported existence of a media user's psychological involvement with a media personality. In a para-social relationship, audience members come to see these media personalities as friends with whom they can feel comfortable, which increases their likelihood of tuning in to watch their "media friend," their willingness to listen to what these personalities have to say, and the overall enjoyment they derive from their encounters with the media form with which the personality is affiliated.

20. The authors found that a key factor in the transformation of Floyd Collins (a caver trapped in a coal mine in rural Kentucky for seventeen days in 1925) from an unknown small-town resident into a national media star was the ability of newspaper readers to relate to him as a person. This "relatability" was, in large part, a product of the press's crafting of the entrapment and subsequent rescue efforts as a human-interest story.

CHAPTER 4

1. E-mail systems and cellular phone networks were severely taxed on September 11, with many unable to function well, if at all. These limitations also may have helped many people move to more traditional information sources, such as television and radio. For more on communication and information seeking after the attacks, see Carey 2003; Rappoport and Alleman 2003; Vengerfeldt 2003.

2. Carey (2003) reports that one-third of citizens in the EDT zone knew about the plane crashing into the WTC by 9:00 a.m. (i.e., within fifteen minutes of the first crash) and that 90 percent knew by 10:30 a.m. A survey of East Coast college students (Hoffner et al. 2002) found that 73 percent of the respondents knew about the attacks within an hour of their occurrence; a survey of Midwest college students (Kanihan and Gale 2005) found that 62 percent of the respondents knew within one hour; and 97 percent knew within three hours. A sample of more than three hundred Michigan residents found that the news had spread nearly completely within two hours of the attacks (Greenberg, Hofschire, and Lachlan 2002) and, in a sample of New Mexico residents, within three hours (Rogers 2003; Rogers and Seidel 2002).

3. A Pew study (Rainie and Kalsnes 2002) found that four out of five Americans turned to television as their main source of information on September 11. Ruggiero and Glascock's study (2002) reported that 92 percent of respondents were following the attacks on television on the evening of September 11. Greenberg, Hofschire, and Lachlan (2002) surveyed 314 Michigan residents on September 12 and 13, 2001, 88 percent of whom cited television as their main source of information in those first three days. Stempel and Hargrove (2002) conducted a national phone survey on October 20 and 31, 2001, in which 69 percent of the respondents stated that television had been the most important source of information for them since the attacks.

4. Jones and Rainie (2002) reported that more than 53 million people, about half the entire Internet-using population, sought information about the attacks online at some point during the three weeks following the attacks.

5. Throughout the day, CNN.com had 11 million unique visitors (six times its normal number of visitors), and MSNBC.com drew more than 9 million visitors (twice what it receives on a typical day) to its site (Carey 2003).

6. Although moral shocks may engender outrage and political action, they do not have to do so. What is important from a public drama perspective is that they capture people otherwise apathetic or unaware as a way of focusing on an event or issue. Whether those same people come to care about the issue and become politically active are significant questions from a social movement perspective, but they are not necessary components of a moral shock as it pertains to public drama.

7. In this way, moral shocks create a condition akin to Sandra Ball-Rokeach's (1973) notion of "pervasive ambiguity," which is characterized by individual and collective

difficulties in defining a situation, which then inhibit people's ability to cognitively or affectively process an unexpected or threatening event or social situation.

8. Sixty percent of the respondents in a study by Greenberg, Hofschire, and Lachlan (2002) reported that the image of the plane hitting the towers resonated most strongly for them.

9. I was not alone in being profoundly affected by these images, as 15 percent of the respondents in the Greenberg, Hofschire, and Lachlan (2002) study indicated that the images of the towers crumbling resonated most strongly for them.

10. Estimates of the death toll from the WTC attacks fluctuated widely in the first months after September 11. By late 2001, it had settled at slightly more than 2,700. In 2004, it finally seemed to rest at 2,749 (Lipton 2004), but two official victims have been added to the list in the years since, and as of July 2008, the official death toll for the WTC attacks was 2,751 (Dunlap 2008).

11. The most apt historical parallels to the level of postattack coverage are found in the media coverage of the assassination of President John F. Kennedy in November 1963. Although that event occurred in a much less complex media environment, the media's response was similar to that after September 11 in the event's dominance of television and print news. In 1963, newspapers canceled advertisements to make room for extra news content, and the television networks pulled all commercials and aired special coverage in place of scheduled programming. As with 9/11, NBC news was exclusively of the assassination, broadcasting continuously for nearly forty-two hours (Zelizer 1992).

12. This also calls to mind the response after the Kennedy assassination. According to Zelizer (1992, 62), the television audience grew dramatically during the weekend after the assassination and peaked on Monday, when an estimated 93 percent of households with televisions watched the funeral procession to Arlington National Cemetery. More recently, the reading of the verdict in the O. J. Simpson trial and the funeral of Princess Diana attracted similarly large audiences, with Nielsen estimating that 91 percent of U.S. households with a television tuned in for the verdict. Princess Diana's funeral is estimated to have drawn 2.5 billion viewers worldwide.

13. These figures come from research conducted by Cohen and colleagues 2003 and Stempel and Hargrove 2002 and 2003, respectively.

14. These surveys were administered by the Pew Research Center for the People and the Press. For more information, see PEW 2001a and 2001b.

15. I use *retaliation* rather than response here because an overwhelming amount of evidence suggests that the response to these events was never really in doubt. Within hours of the attacks, "hawkish" statements abounded about the need to seek justice, hunt and punish those responsible, and formulate a retribution strategy organized around military action.

16. Others have argued that the primacy of this kind of framing greatly influenced the way that many Americans came to understand and interpret these events and, as a result, allowed President Bush and other political officials to use 9/11 to reinforce their ideology, shape policy, or justify a broader military agenda. Kellner (2003), Mayer (2006), Simpson (2006), and Welch (2006) are among those who examined some of the ways that September 11 has been used by U.S. government officials, political elites, and other social actors to gain political advantage or to justify domestic or international policies and actions.

17. Breithaupt (2003) also found that America as a victim was a prominent frame in the mainstream media coverage, although he offers different reasons for such a framing,

suggesting that it was constructed so that the media could then position themselves as a source of healing for the traumatized victim (America) or victims (American citizens).

18. In all, *Today* offered twenty-nine hours of coverage from September 12 to 18, with the daily coverage as follows: September 12 (7 a.m.–1 p.m.), September 13 (7 a.m.–1 p.m.), September 14 (7 a.m.–12 noon), September 15 (7 a.m.–9 a.m.), September 16 (9 a.m.–10 a.m.), September 17 (7 a.m.–1 p.m.), and September 18 (7 a.m.–10 a.m.). The September 18 broadcast marked the return to the customary *Today* format (i.e., thirty-minute segments, with commercial breaks and weather and local news updates spaced throughout the broadcast). The total number of coded items exceeds 100 percent because some *Today* reports were equally focused on more than one coding category. For instance, the September 12 *Today* broadcast featured a report entitled "Rescue Efforts at the World Trade Center Disaster Site; President Bush Back in Washington Vowing America Will Win against Terrorism; Authorities Identity at Least Five of the Hijackers." This report devoted roughly equivalent attention to each topic reflected in the title, so I coded its content as belonging to both the Dealing and Healing category (specifically, New York City / Ground Zero) and the Responsibility and Retaliation category (specifically, How should the U.S. respond? and Who did this?).

19. This is consistent with Lang and Lang's (1986, 277) finding that developments occurring in more remote locales are less likely to receive publicity—unless they have unusually dramatic features—than things that happen near the centers of power (e.g., Washington, D.C., Los Angeles, New York City).

CHAPTER 5

1. Steve Barkin discussed the effect that NBC's *Today* had on the news industry in American Television News:

> The *Today* show, which premiered on January 14, 1952, embodied a mixture of some attention to "serious" issues with subjects that were trivial, profane, or merely diverting. The combination became prototypical for broadcast journalism, especially for the evolution of every morning program and the later generation of television news magazines. (2003, 122)

2. This is difficult to verify, as NBC officials do not disclose the profitability of news programming. However, recent estimates suggest that NBC's news programming, which includes its broadcast news division (*Today, Nightly News,* and *Dateline*), its cable news channel (MSNBC), and its Internet news site (MSNBC.com) contribute up to a half-billion dollars in profits per year to the parent corporation (NBC Universal) (Carter 2009).

3. When Mogenson and her colleagues (2002) interviewed executives at CNN and the Fox News channel, they offered similar assessments of how the chaos of the day affected their networks' coverage. One noted that they "did not have time to ponder the consequences of their coverage . . . or even to coordinate the messages being delivered," and another pointed out, "There was no time to consult a plan or analyze events: You acted on instinct and relied on experience to get the job done" (2002, 107, 111).

4. On the morning of Saturday, September 15, the television networks reintroduced commercials for the first time since the attacks. Later that day, NBC included commercials as part of both its *Today* and *Nightly News* broadcast coverage of the attacks. While this period of commercial-free broadcasting was generally considered unprecedented in

the media age, it was not without historical parallels. The Persian Gulf War featured long periods of uninterrupted news broadcasts, although the commercial-free standard was not adhered to as rigidly during that period as it was after September 11 (Kirkpatrick and Elliott 2001). Similarly, commercials and other non-news content were largely absent for several days following the assassination of President Kennedy in 1963.

5. I organized NBC's September 11 coverage into thematic segments rather than a strictly chronological analysis of each report as it appeared in the broadcast. After numerous analytical passes through the data, I was able to identify four chronological periods: 9 a.m. to 12 noon ("morning hours"), 12 noon to 3 p.m. ("early-afternoon hours"), 3 p.m. to 6:30 p.m. ("late-afternoon hours"); and 6:30 p.m. to 12 midnight ("evening hours"). Although there is some overlap from one period to the next (similar topics, shared on-air personnel and reporters), each contained a distinct thematic orientation and collection of coverage framings.

6. Even though the word *apparent* suggests that the administration was not yet prepared to label this a terrorist event, its use was immediately rendered superfluous when the next sentence of Bush's brief statement included a pledge to "hunt down and to find those folks who committed this act."

7. "TWA Flight 800" is a reference to a commercial aircraft that exploded and crashed into the Atlantic Ocean about ten minutes after takeoff from New York's John F. Kennedy International Airport, killing all 230 people aboard. While the official explanation for the crash came to rest on faulty wiring, there was much initial speculation that it was struck down by a terrorist attack, by either a missile or the detonation of a bomb onboard. Couric probably thought of this because of the shared characteristics of these events (i.e., both involved airliners, New York City, and presumptions of possible terrorist activity). Couric's mention of the Murrah Federal Building was meant to invoke the horrific bombing in Oklahoma City in April 1995 (it is more commonly referred to as the "Oklahoma City Bombing"). The fact that Couric mentioned this as a historical parallel is not surprising, given that the bombing, which killed 168 people, had been the most deadly attack on U.S. soil before the attacks on September 11.

8. Although technically false, reports of car bombs—which were quite frequent in the first hours after the attacks—were not entirely unfounded. There were explosions throughout lower Manhattan on September 11, but city officials determined that they were caused by exploding gas lines under the streets of lower Manhattan and by cars near the WTC site that had overheated and exploded.

9. By this point, it was no longer enough to show the same images of this horrific moment. NBC producers had acquired footage of the attacks from a variety of vantage points and angles from other networks and from civilians who had recorded the events on personal video cameras, and this hour marked the first of many times these "new" images of the attack were featured.

10. Those featured on the air as official sources in the early afternoon hours whose selections can be seen as a manifestation of the terrorism frame include James Baker, former secretary of state; Sandy Berger, former national security adviser in the Clinton administration; Paul Bremer, chairman of the National Commission on Terrorism; Martin Fletcher, NBC's Middle East correspondent; Lee Hamilton, former chairman of the House Intelligence Committee; Ray Kelly, former NYC police commissioner; Anthony Lake, former national security adviser in the Clinton administration and terrorism expert;

Neil Livingston, expert on international terrorism; U.S. Senator John McCain; Warren Rudman, former senator and co-chairman of the U.S. Commission on National Security; General Norman Schwartzkopf, famed commander in the first Gulf War; U.S. Senator Richard Shelby, vice-chairman of the Senate Intelligence Committee; and Alex Standish, editor of *Jane's Intelligence Digest*. Some of these sources appeared on the air several times on September 11 and in the following weeks.

11. Although he is speaking of the firefighters, Brokaw mistakenly referred to them using the familiar nickname of the NYPD ("New York's finest") instead of that of the FDNY ("New York's bravest").

CHAPTER 6

1. Reports of people jumping or falling from the burning towers were discussed in passing on the September 13 edition of *Today*. The first report was by a psychiatrist citing it as one of the many horrific images that could cause emotional and psychological trauma; then it was mentioned by a rescue worker in his account of the scene in the streets before the towers collapsed; and finally, during the September 14 *Today* show. This was a report on life for those who resided in a nearby neighborhood, in which one resident described what it was like to see people jumping. Otherwise such reports were completely absent from the rest of the first week's coverage.

2. More information about this alleged event was never found, which led many people to question the veracity of the account. This was not the only unproven account or rumor to emerge during the initial coverage. In fact, many of the rumors bandied about in the first day or so after the attacks proved to be inaccurate. But that does not undermine the fact that the media eagerly seized on all potential news elements. Once included as part of the story, many of these examples became permanent themes in the developing narrative, rendering their actual veracity of secondary importance.

3. Official estimates of the death toll at the WTC stood at more than 6,700 in late September and did not fall below 3,000 until January 2002. Today, the official WTC death toll stands at just below 2,800.

4. In fact, the emergency response, recovery, and cleanup at Ground Zero resulted in remarkably few injuries, given the size and scope of the operation. Not a single person was killed during the search for survivors or the cleanup of debris at the site, and there was a relatively modest number of injuries (none of which was classified as "serious") during the more than eight months and 1.5 million work hours at the WTC site (LeDuff 2002a).

5. By Saturday, September 15, NBC had begun airing commercials, and some programming unrelated to the attacks, such as childrens' programming and general talk shows, had resumed.

CHAPTER 7

1. These last two testimonials about the personal significance of the "Portraits" series are not from letters submitted to the *Times*; they are from a pair of customer reviews on Amazon.com (online retail website) of the book *Portraits: 9/11/01: The Collected "Portraits of Grief"* (*New York Times* 2002).

2. Personality profiles contain statements like "He's a great man, very adventurous person, the daredevil of the family. He loved his boats, his motorcycles, loved to go fast,

take his chances"; "My brother was my best friend. I love him so much. We did everything together. We grew up together, and we used to share a bed because we have so many in our family"; "He was such a people person, and he was always wanting to know how everybody was . . . he was just the kind person that lit up the room, you know."

3. I should emphasize again that attempts to personalize this tragedy were not unique to the *Today* broadcasts. NBC's *Dateline* programs repeatedly did this, as did the newscasts and news magazines on other networks. The *New York Times* developed a twelve-part series based on its "Portraits of Grief" series to provide more detailed stories about a dozen selected victims and the family and friends forced to carry on in the wake of their death. In their ongoing coverage of September 11, other national newspapers and magazines also regularly featured in-depth profiles of victims and their relatives, as well as the people involved in the ongoing recovery operation.

4. This report was repeated later in the Friday *Today* broadcast, under the heading "Some People by Twist of Fate Weren't in World Trade Center during Attack on America."

5. A number of reports on *Today* throughout the week conveyed the emotional impact of these attacks on countries and regions throughout the world, including the following: "Support for America All over the World, People Laying Flowers at U.S. Embassies, Grieving for Victims" (NBC [8:00 a.m.], September 12); "Israeli Foreign Minister Shimon Peres Expresses His Sympathy for the People of New York" (NBC [9:00 a.m.], September 12); "British People Express Sympathy and Support to Americans Following Terrorist Attack" (NBC [9:00 a.m.], September 14); and "People Pulling Together All over the World in Support of New Yorkers following Attack on America" (NBC [9:00 a.m.], September 14).

6. Cohen and her colleagues (2003) found that 66 percent of respondents donated money to various 9/11-related causes or organizations; 20 percent donated blood; 31 percent attended a memorial service; 18 percent attended a candlelight vigil; and 73 percent reported purchasing or displaying an American flag. Rogers (2003) found that people reacted in highly emotional ways that did not involve turning to the media after 9/11.

CHAPTER 8

1. An essential guideline of news work is the need for stories that can be put together and made available to the audience as quickly as possible (Klinenberg 2002; Tuchman 1972). This can become even more urgent when faced with unanticipated complex events. When "breaking" news or an audience's demand for news reaches a certain level, there is simply not enough time to wait to find out all the facts, so news producers must construct stories around the information that they believe to be most accurate.

2. Some high-ranking FDNY officials estimated that the department lost more than 4,400 years of collective experience in the attacks, with one suggesting that "it is going to take us a couple of generations, at least, to get the Fire Department back to where it was prior to 9/11" (Baker 2002, sec. 1, 41).

3. During an emergency response, one of the most pressing needs in the first hours after a crisis is establishing an organizational structure close to the crisis zone. Such a structure proved to be particularly difficult to establish for the WTC because of the characteristics of the event and the fact that the tremendous loss of personnel and other resources (particularly the Emergency Operations Center, EOC, which was located in

the WTC complex, was rendered uninhabitable by the attacks) far exceeded the city's planning and emergency response capabilities in many areas. Firefighters thus were seen as a suitable choice to coordinate the initial stages of the emergency response because their instrumental capabilities closely matched many of the on-site needs, and unlike the thousands of volunteers who had converged on lower Manhattan wanting to help, they were accustomed to a command-and-control structure and therefore more likely to follow orders (Langewiesche 2002). For further discussion of the justifications for placing the FDNY in charge of operations at Ground Zero in the first hours and days after the collapse, see also Smith 2002 and Von Essen and Murray 2002.

4. A pair of comments offered by NBC reporter Ann Curry—"What they are doing here is no less than heroic" ([9:00 a.m.], September 14)—and NBC anchor Katie Couric—"You're looking at a live picture from lower Manhattan, where . . . incredibly heroic rescue workers are hoping against hope to find survivors of Tuesday's disastrous attack" ([8:00 a.m.], September 15)—are typical of the many compliments about the firefighters offered by NBC's news personnel (and those of other news outlets) throughout that first week (and beyond).

5. *Firehouse*, by the noted historian David Halberstam (2002), is a good example of both the general focus of these books and the surprising speed with which many of them came to market. *Firehouse* chronicles the lives and careers of thirteen members of a firehouse (Engine 40, Ladder 35) located on Manhattan's Upper West Side after twelve of the thirteen perished during the WTC response. It was published in May 2002, a mere eight months after the attacks.

6. The visual resemblance of these two moments (along with the somewhat similar context of conflict and war in which each occurred) enabled the media to establish a link between them. As a result, the meanings being ascribed to the firefighters could be fused with the meanings that were attached to the Iwo Jima moment. The references to the attack on Pearl Harbor and the recent appreciation of the "Greatest Generation" may have also helped link between these events and World War II.

7. By January 2002, many city officials, construction executives, union leaders, and others were hailing the cleanup effort at the WTC site as an industry model for efficiency, speed, and safety (LeDuff and Greenhouse 2002), but the body-removal rituals continued to be carried out even as the work at the site became increasingly efficient and "construction oriented" over time.

8. Minna Bromberg and Gary Fine (2002) explore how and why political actors try to institutionalize reputations for their own gain. Jeffrey Olick contends that "powerful institutions clearly value some histories more than others, provide narrative patterns and exemplars of how individuals can and should remember, and stimulate memory in ways and for reasons that have nothing to do with the individual or aggregate neurological records" (1999, 342).

9. Philip Patterson identified a similar process in the aftermath of the Chernobyl disaster, which was the "convergence of a specific event with cultural and governmental needs as filtered through a mediated reality that was ripe for a particular interpretation" (1989, 144).

10. Fritz Breithaupt argued that the media were only too willing to cosponsor the victimization frame being promoted by political elites because such a frame would allow the media to position themselves as key components of the national healing process:

In general, what might be the most unique and notable aspect of the media's response to the terrorist attacks is the therapeutic mission the media seem to have assigned to their reporting: to further the healing and reconcile the loss. This is not limited to a few exceptional productions, but includes standard reporting. The new role of the news media is to be a friend and therapist. (2003, 72)

11. Even the simple act of spending money in New York City was offered as virtuous behavior by President Bush, Mayor Giuliani, and other political leaders.

12. Television and documentary films that focused on firefighters generally dealt with either the firefighters' actions and role during the attacks or how they were dealing with the loss of so many of their own in the months after the attacks. The 9/11 programming reached its peak in the weeks leading up to the one-year anniversary of the attacks. For a detailed listing of some of the television programs and documentaries on September 11, 2002, see James 2002a, 2002b.

13. This rejection of dissension extended well beyond the firefighters to encompass virtually all matters related to 9/11. "There was no significant divergence in the reactions of government and community leaders, the media, and the public in assigning meaning to the events as a national tragedy and outrage" (Smelser 2004, 280). Similarly, Debatin contended that "the call for patriotism and counterstrike led very quickly to a situation in which critical words were stigmatized by the government as unpatriotic and intolerable, even when they were clearly satirical" (2002, 173–74). Numerous celebrities and politicians were chastised by the Bush administration and leading political figures and were rendered pariahs by many in the mainstream media for comments that contradicted the dominant 9/11 narrative. For instance, Bill Maher, a popular political satirist, comedian, and television host, was blasted for suggesting that the U.S. military's use of missiles to strike targets from a distance was more cowardly than the terrorists' acts on September 11. The show, which he hosted, on which he made these statements was eventually canceled. Senator Tom Daschle and television news anchor Peter Jennings faced similar scorn for their criticisms of the war in Afghanistan in March 2002 (Debatin 2002). The post-9/11 context parallels other historical moments. Examples are the "red scares" of the first half of the twentieth century, Senator Joe McCarthy's hunt for "Communists" between 1947 and 1954, and the "New Left" in the late 1960s discussed by Gary Alan Fine (2005).

14. Firefighters are required to report first to their firehouse. On 9/11, however, many off-duty firefighters reported directly to the WTC and, in some cases, immediately entered the towers' stairwells without first alerting the on-site incident commander of their presence (Dwyer and Flynn 2002; Lipton and Glanz 2002a). This meant that not only was the commander not aware of how many firefighters were at the scene, but many firefighters lacked the proper equipment to communicate with their colleagues, carry out their tasks, or protect themselves. Some FDNY and city officials have speculated that the number of off-duty firefighters who died in the attacks (60) was so high because the attacks occurred during a shift change at firehouses throughout the city.

15. Langewiesche (2002) claimed that other workers at the site began to resent the firefighters because of what he described as their cavalier, "bag-em-and-tag-em" approach to the bodies and remains of those who were not firefighters, an approach in marked contrast to the painstakingly methodical search for firefighter remains and the elaborate rituals for removing them from the site. A *New York Times* reporter also noted this, suggesting that the greater likelihood of identifying a firefighter's remains was because their

fire-retardant gear could better withstand the violence of the collapse and the intense flames beneath the rubble rather than being attributable to the firefighters' intentionally bypassing non-firefighters' remains. Nonetheless, this was a source of tension at the site, as evidenced by some graffiti at the site: "Hey FDNY, look for everyone, not just your own!" (LeDuff 2002b, A1).

16. In many cases, those who tried to promote alternative views of the firefighters' actions on the day of the attacks and thereafter were labeled unpatriotic heretics and subjected to vilification. William Langewiesche (2002), a journalist who was able to gain virtually unrestricted access to the WTC site for months after the attacks, later suggested that some members of the FDNY had taken advantage of their unfettered access to the WTC site to steal consumer goods (Gap jeans) from the retail stores located below the collapsed towers. While there is some question as to whether this particular theft actually occurred (the veracity of these claims is still being debated by the involved parties), the point is that this story received surprisingly little attention by much of the mass media. In fact, most of the coverage of Langewiesche's claims criticized his reporting and questioned his motives.

17. SDS leaders first tried to turn their individual celebrity into a political resource for the movement itself, but eventually they treated their celebrity as a personal resource to be individually hoarded, fought over, and invested in ways beneficial to themselves (Gitlin 1980).

18. William Langewiesche, the reporter who was granted extensive access to Ground Zero during the response-and-recovery effort and who was particularly critical of the firefighters' approach, suggested that "the image of 'heroes' seeped through their ranks like a low-grade narcotic" (2002, 158).

19. Shan Nelson-Rowe (1995) refers to this kind of symbolic activity as "collective identity bargaining."

20. Philip Blumstein has argued that the individual in search of public favor will often manipulate his performance so that it "will parallel the expectations presumably held by his audience" (1973, 348). In other words, popular figures often find that some aspects of their persona or performances resonate more strongly with audiences than others, so they may refine their style and actions to make them more in line with what audiences seemingly want in order to ensure continued success in the public realm.

21. On November 11, 2001, five firefighters from FDNY, Ladder 9, Engine 33 squad, which lost ten firefighters in the attacks, embarked on a "Thank You America" bike tour to thank Americans all over the nation for their support for the FDNY after the attacks. The tour began at Ground Zero and ended a little more than two months, and more than three thousand miles later, in Pasadena, California.

22. We can understand the firefighters' efforts in this regard using Mukerji and Schudson's notion of "performance" behaviors and/or Lofland and Fink's "symbolic protest." Mukerji and Schudson define performance as "a kind of activity that is formally staged or an aspect of everyday life in which a person is oriented to and intends to have some effect on an audience" (1986, 50). Lofland and Fink view symbolic protest as "those orderly and nondisruptive but more or less ostentatious ways in which people collectively draw attention to their grievances," usually in the form of "the procession (e.g., marches, parades), the assembly (e.g., the rally) and various kinds of public acts, including picketing" (1982, 4).

23. More than three hundred charities raised money for 9/11-related causes, making it nearly impossible to develop a precise figure of the money raised. The U.S. Government Accountability Office (GAO) estimated that $2.4 billion was raised.

24. Father Mychal Judge, the FDNY chaplain who was killed when he was struck by falling debris during the precollapse response, received numerous posthumous honors. In addition to having a street named after him, his helmet was accepted as a gift by Pope John Paul II; the French named him to the Legion of Honor; and there was even talk about his being made a saint, which is continuing today (Wakin 2002).

25. Firefighters were treated to games featuring the two New York–area football teams (Giants and Jets) and the two New York baseball teams (Mets and Yankees) at their respective home stadiums and at their games throughout the country. They were also given free tickets to countless concerts, as well as events like the circus and the annual Macy's Thanksgiving Day parade. There were free trips to upstate New York, Massachusetts, Delaware, Tennessee, Michigan, Arizona, Pennsylvania, Colorado, South Carolina, Mississippi, North Carolina, Florida, California, Hawaii, and several other states. The German government provided free two-week holidays in Germany for fifty firefighters, and the French government treated twenty-five firefighters and their families to a week in France. In addition, firefighters and their families received all-expenses-paid trips to Canada, Jamaica, Panama, the Virgin Islands, the Grand Cayman Islands, New Zealand, Austria, Spain, and dozens of other destinations throughout the world.

CHAPTER 9

1. It took some time for the FDNY and its members to recognize the extent of their new status and to capitalize on its symbolic value. This required analysis of a more expansive period of coverage than what an analysis of the first week of *Today* could offer. Thus, for this chapter I drew on reports from more than a year of *New York Times* coverage of the response-and-recovery effort at Ground Zero. As I identified themes in the first year of coverage, I followed many of them over subsequent years to better understand the dynamics and outcomes of the processes I discuss here.

2. The FDNY's official memorial service for their members who died in the attacks was finally held on October 12, 2002 (Flynn 2002b), nearly a year after its originally scheduled date.

3. Those who have closely followed Giuliani's political career no doubt immediately recognize that his handling of this dispute with the firefighters was not like his usual approach to political conflict (which was to stubbornly refuse to negotiate and to go on the offensive). Accordingly, this indicates the power of the firefighters' moral currency. A Giuliani aide noted as much in a February 27, 2002, *New York Times* article: "'Here's the key difference. With almost every other constituency he rarely backed down, and if he did, he almost always arrived at the middle. But when it came to the families [of 9/11], particularly the firefighter families, he would go to great lengths to accommodate them'" (Herszenhorn 2002b, B4).

4. Firefighters also brought their moral currency to bear in other smaller battles related to the response and recovery at Ground Zero. For instance, in January 2002, city officials tried to ban the firefighters' practice of rushing to the site to participate in the

body removal ceremony whenever a firefighter's remains were discovered (claiming that the massive influx of FDNY personnel disrupted the work at the site and compromised fire-response capabilities in other parts of the city) (Herszenhorn 2002a). The firefighters' leaders quickly sprang into action, and within days the city had relented almost entirely (the only restriction was that only firefighters from the local company to which the deceased firefighter was assigned were to be called to the site) (Lipton 2002a).

5. After years of contentious contract negotiations (in which UFA leaders argued that firefighters deserved significantly higher raises than did other municipal unions), numerous protest rallies, and several public disputes between city officials and union leaders, the UFA and city officials agreed on a contract in October 2005 (Fahim 2005).

6. In the end, Finley lost the election by a resounding margin (Ryan 2002).

7. In addition to trying to create the impression that he had the unconditional support of firefighters and other rescue groups, Pataki also tried to align himself with Mayor Giuliani (presumably to benefit from his status in some way), even though the two had long been publicly at odds with one another (McKinley 2002).

8. *New York Times's* reporter Richard Pérez-Peña seemed to somewhat glibly suggest that Pataki's tactic was tantamount to pandering: "He [Pataki] tells his audiences that they are heroes. Financial exchange workers are heroes for returning downtown. Parents are heroes for consoling children. State workers are heroes for keeping services running. All New Yorkers are heroes for being decent, resilient and tolerant" (2002, B1). Pataki was reelected in November 2002.

9. For instance, a plan to combine a pair of fire companies with a city EMS unit was implemented by city officials despite stern objections from the FDNY (Cardwell 2002).

10. Of course, the individual actor also matters. As Kane notes, "Incumbents' actions are liable either to degrade or confirm the reputation of the institution" (2001, 35).

11. This discussion of the sourcing of moral prestige underscores the value of the support that firefighters received from political leaders, cultural elites, and other social actors (discussed in chapter 8).

CHAPTER 10

1. Biden first made this comment in late October 2007 during a debate among Democrats running for president in the 2008 general election. Senator Biden was one of the Democratic candidates, and Giuliani was a candidate for the Republican Party nomination.

2. Many books offer insights into the ways that the September 11 attacks have been used by U.S. government officials, political elites, and other social actors to gain political advantage or justify domestic or international policies and actions. See Kellner 2003; Mayer 2006; Simpson 2006; or Welch 2006.

3. The other characters on the list included Andrew Card, former White House chief of staff, who whispered news of the attacks to President Bush at a Florida elementary school; Howard Lutnick, CEO of Cantor Fitzgerald, the hardest hit of all the companies in the WTC; Bernard Kerik, New York City's police commissioner; Coleen Rowley, the FBI "whistleblower" who revealed the FBI's mishandling of preattack intelligence that, if handled appropriately, might have prevented the attacks; and Ed Fine, a businessman who worked in the north tower and emerged covered in dust ("dust man") dressed in business

attire and still carrying his briefcase. This image was widely circulated in media outlets and came to signify for many the suddenness and depth of the horror of that day.

4. Consider the case of social problems' "claims makers." Their primary task is to call attention to the issue of concern to them (the accuracy or inaccuracy of the mediated representation may not always be of concern, as claims makers often look to refashion the discourse so that it best matches their interests and goals). But media attention is difficult to attain and even harder to retain, making it a valued asset in the highly competitive social problems marketplace. Since public drama is, by nature, a news production with a fairly long shelf life, it is valuable to those who want to bring attention to an issue and frame how it is to be understood. Social problems' claims makers who are able to participate in a prominent public drama can become part of its media presentations, which might translate into a broader public awareness of the issues or problems they are promoting.

5. Chancer's analysis of how high-profile cases of violent crime become celebrated social causes (what she terms "provoking assaults") illustrates the potential of a high-profile media story to gain traction in nonmediated social and political realms.

6. Throughout this study I have referred to "full-blown" public dramas that are created and nurtured in the national news cycles. Public dramas also can develop and exist for quite some time at a local or even regional level. Some of these may become the kinds of national news stories discussed here, or only a fleeting headline in the daily news cycle.

7. The story of the "Runaway Bride" remained in daily news cycles for weeks, for reasons other than those that had originally brought it to national attention. Many news reports of this case in the first few weeks of May 2005 positioned it as a cautionary tale for the media. It was argued that this story could provide a much-needed point of departure for discussions about journalistic ethics; after all, news workers had readily and fully embraced what proved to be rather sparse information and prematurely crafted it into a familiar plot structure.

8. *USA Today* reporters and staff members compiled a list of the top twenty-five news stories of the past twenty-five years. It includes a number of high-profile media stories that might be suitable for reanalyzing in a public drama framework. See Hampson 2007.

9. The focus on New Orleans also facilitated the infusion of long-standing but divisive cultural values into the media narrative. A prominent discussion point in the mainstream media, usually offered by conservative Christians appearing on prime-time cable news programs, was that the severity of the storm and the resulting havoc should be viewed as God's wrath against a city (New Orleans) that had enjoyed unchecked sin and debauchery for far too long. Although the media did not necessarily advocate this view, they did tacitly support it by featuring it so frequently. This view also allowed the disaster to be discussed and portrayed in melodramatic terms of "good versus evil."

Bibliography

Abel, Scott, Andrea Miller, and Vincent Filak. 2005. "TV Coverage of Breaking News in First Hours of Tragedy." In *Media in an American Crisis: Studies of September 11, 2001*, ed. Elinor Kelley Grusin and Sandra H. Utt, 105–15. Lanham, MD: University Press of America.

Allport, Gordon W., and Leo Postman. 1947. *The Psychology of Rumor*. New York: Henry Holt.

Altheide, David L. 1976. *Creating Reality: How TV News Distorts Events*. Beverly Hills, CA: Sage.

———. 2004. "Consuming Terrorism." *Symbolic Interaction* 27:289–308.

———. 2006. *Terrorism and the Politics of Fear*. Lanham, MD: AltaMira Press.

Altheide, David L., and Robert P. Snow. 1979. *Media Logic*. Beverly Hills, CA: Sage.

Anderson, Bonnie M. 2004. *News Flash: Journalism, Infotainment, and the Bottom-Line Business of Broadcast News*. San Francisco: Jossey-Bass.

Anker, Elisabeth. 2005. "Villains, Victims and Heroes: Melodrama, Media, and September 11." *Journal of Communication* 55:22–37.

Baker, Al. 2002. "The True Toll on Firefighters Is Still Untold." *New York Times*, March 10, sec. 1, 41.

Ball-Rokeach, Sandra J. 1973. "From Pervasive Ambiguity to a Definition of the Situation." *Sociometry* 36:378–89.

———. 1985. "The Origins of Individual Media System Dependency: A Sociological Framework." *Communication Research* 12:485–510.

Barkin, Steve M. 2003. *American Television News: The Media Marketplace and the Public Interest*. Armonk, NY: Sharpe.

Barnes, Julian E. 2001. "Media; Tough Call, Spider-Man." *New York Times*, October 8, C9.

Barrett, Wayne. 2007. "Rudy Giuliani's Five Big Lies about 9/11." *Village Voice*, July 31.

Barron, James, with Diane Cardwell and Adam Nagourney. 2002. "Boldface Names." *New York Times*, February 22, B2.

Barry, Dan, and Kevin Flynn. 2001. "A Nation Challenged: The Firefighters; Firefighters in Angry Scuffle with Police at Trade Center." *New York Times*, November 3, A1.

Barstow, David, and Diana B. Henriques. 2001. "A Nation Challenged: The Families; Gifts to Rescuers Divide Survivors." *New York Times*, December 2, A1.

———. 2002. "9/11 Tie-ins Blur Lines of Charity and Profit." *New York Times*, February 2, A1.

Bellafante, Ginia. 2001. "Front Row." *New York Times*, October 30, C24.

Berger, Matthew E. 2008. "At Ground Zero, Palin Mum on Stevens." MSNBC.com, September 25. Available at http://firstread.msnbc.msn.com/archive/2008 /09/25/1448510. aspx.

Berke, Richard L. 2001. "A Nation Challenged: The Elections; Local Candidates Every-where Focus on Terrorism." *New York Times*, November 5, B6.

Best, Joel. 1990. *Threatened Children*. Chicago: University of Chicago Press.

——. 2008. *Social Problems*. New York: Norton.

Blumstein, Philip W. 1973. "Audience, Machiavellianism, and Tactics of Identity Bargaining." *Sociometry* 36, no. 3:346–65.

Bogart, Leo. 1981. *Press and Public: Who Reads What, When, Where, and Why in American Newspapers*. Hillsdale, NJ: Erlbaum.

Bone, James. 2007. "Rudy Giuliani Accused of Exploiting 9/11 Role." *Times Online*, September 12. Available at http://www.timesonline.co.uk/tol/news/world /us_and_americas/article2428868.ece.

Boorstin, Daniel J. 1978. *The Image: A Guide to Pseudo-Events in America*. New York: Harper & Row.

Bovino, Arthur. 2002. "You're Too Kind, Firefighters Say, Truly Meaning It; Gifts Pour In, but Space for Them Grows Scarce." *New York Times*, July 24, B1.

Breithaupt, Fritz. 2003. "Rituals of Trauma: How the Media Fabricated September 11." In *Media Representations of September 11*, ed. Steven Chermak, Frankie Y. Bailey, and Michelle Brown, 67–81. Westport, CT: Praeger.

Brewer, Marcus, and Maxwell McCombs. 1996. "Setting the Community Agenda." *Journalism and Mass Communication Quarterly* 73, no. 1:7–16.

Bromberg, Minna, and Gary Alan Fine. 2002. "Resurrecting the Red: Pete Seeger & the Purification of Difficult Reputations." *Social Forces* 80, no. 4:1135–55.

Brown, Michelle, Leia Fuzesi, Kara Kitch, and Crystal Spivey. 2003. "Internet News Representations of September 11: Archival Impulse in the Age of Information." In *Media Representations of September 11*, ed. Steven Chermak, Frankie Y. Bailey, and Michelle Brown, 103–16. Westport, CT: Praeger.

Brown, Patricia Leigh. 2001. "Ideas and Trends; Heavy Lifting Required: The Return of Manly Men." *New York Times*, October 28, 4, 5.

Brown, Robert S. 2004. "Sport and the Healing of America after 9/11." In *Language, Symbols, and the Media: Communication in the Aftermath of the World Trade Center Attack*, ed. Robert E. Denton Jr., 117–28. New Brunswick, NJ: Transaction Publishers.

Brown, William, Mihai Bocarnea, and Michael Basil. 2002. "Fear, Grief, and Sympathy Responses to the Attacks." In *Communication and Terrorism: Public and Media Responses to 9/11*, ed. Bradley S. Greenberg, 245–59. Cresskill, NJ: Hampton Press.

Brown, William, James Duane, and Benson Fraser. 1997. "Media Coverage and Public Opinion of the O. J. Simpson Trial: Implications for the Criminal Justice System." *Communication Law and Policy* 2:261–87.

Bumiller, Elisabeth. 2001. "A Nation Challenged: The Visit; Bush Tries to Reassure Children and Executives." *New York Times*, October 4, B9.

Bunis, William K., Angela Yancik, and David A. Snow. 1996. "The Cultural Patterning of Sympathy toward the Homeless and Other Victims of Misfortune." *Social Problems* 43, no. 4:387–402.

Cantor, Joanne. 2002. "Fright Reactions to Mass Media." In *Media Effects: Advances in Theory and Research*, ed. Jennings Bryant and Dolf Zillmann, 287–306. Mahwah, NJ: Erlbaum.

Cardwell, Diane. 2002. "Metro Briefing New York: Queens: Council Approves Disputed Firehouse Plan." *New York Times*, May 22, B6.

Carey, John. 2003. "The Functions and Uses of Media during the September 11 Crisis and Its Aftermath." In *Crisis Communications: Lessons from September 11*, ed. A. Michael Noll, 1–16. Oxford: Rowman & Littlefield.

Carter, Bill. 2009. "A Matrix of News Winners Buoys NBC." *New York Times*, March 9, B1.

Chancer, Lynn S. 2005. *High-Profile Crimes: When Legal Cases Become Social Causes*. Chicago: University of Chicago Press.

Chaney, David. 1993. *Fictions of Collective Life: Public Drama in Late Modern Culture*. New York: Routledge.

Chermak, Steven, Frankie Y. Bailey, and Michelle Brown. 2003. Introduction to *Media Representations of September 11*, ed. Steven Chermak, Frankie Y. Bailey, and Michelle Brown, 1–13. Westport, CT: Praeger.

———, eds. 2003. *Media Representations of September 11*. Westport, CT: Praeger.

CNN.com. 1995. "The Players." CNN.com. Available at http://www.cnn.com/US/OJ/ players /index.html.

Cohen, Elisia L., Sandra J. Ball-Rokeach, Joo-Young Jung, and Yong-Chan Kim. 2003. "Civic Actions after September 11: A Communication Infrastructure Perspective." In *Crisis Communications: Lessons from September 11*, ed. A. Michael Noll, 31–43. Oxford: Rowman & Littlefield.

Confessore, Nicholas. 2005. "Mayor Says It's Best to Let Police Control Terror Scenes." *New York Times*, April 23, B3.

Cook, Fay, Tom Tyler, Edward Goetz, Margaret Gordon, David Protess, Donna Leff, and Harvey Molotch. 1983. "Media and Agenda Setting: Effects on the Public, Interest Group Leaders, Policy Makers, and Policy." *Public Opinion Quarterly* 47, no. 1:16–35.

Cooper, Michael. 2002. "The Mayoral Transition: The Last Day; on His Final Day in Office, No Slowing Down for Giuliani." *New York Times*, January 1, B1.

Cooper, Michael, and Kevin Flynn. 2002. "Budget-Cutting Struggles Sting an Already-Pained Fire Dept." *New York Times*, October 25, B1.

Dayan, Daniel, and Elihu Katz. 1992. *Media Events: The Live Broadcasting of History*. Cambridge, MA: Harvard University Press.

Dearing, James W., and Everett M. Rogers. 1996. *Agenda Setting*. Newbury Park, CA: Sage.

Debatin, Bernhard. 2002. "'Plane Wreck with Spectators': Terrorism and Media Attention." In *Communication and Terrorism: Public and Media Responses to 9/11*, ed. Bradley S. Greenberg, 163–74. Cresskill, NJ: Hampton Press.

Desfor Edles, Laura. 2002. *Cultural Sociology in Practice*. Malden, MA: Blackwell.

Dimaggio, Anthony R. 2008. *Mass Media, Mass Propaganda: Examining American News in the "War on Terror."* Lanham, MD: Lexington Books.

Downey, Kevin. 2001a. "Fall Season Kickoff Punted for a Week: ABC and CBS Join NBC in Postponing Season." *Media Life Magazine*, September 13. Available at http://www.medialifemagazine.com/news2001/sep01/sep10/5_fri/news2 friday.html.

———. 2001b. "NBC Leads in Its Disaster News Coverage: 13% Jump in TV Viewing as Tragedy Unfolded." *Media Life Magazine*, September 17. Available at http://www.medialifemagazine.com/news2001/sep01/sep17/ 1_mon/ news1monday.html.

Dunlap, David W. 2008. "The Toll from 9/11 Grows Again, to 2,751." *New York Times Online*, July 10. Available at http://cityroom.blogs.nytimes.com/2008/07/10/the-toll-from-911-grows-again/.

Dwyer, Jim, and Kevin Flynn. 2002. "A Nation Challenged: Firefighting Inquiry; before the Towers Fell, Fire Dept. Fought Chaos." *New York Times*, January 30, A1.

Dwyer, Jim, Kevin Flynn, and Ford Fessenden. 2002. "Fatal Confusion: A Troubled Emergency Response; 9/11 Exposed Deadly Flaws in Rescue Plan." *New York Times*, July 7, sec. 1, p. 1.

Edelman, Murray. 1988. *Constructing the Political Spectacle*. Chicago: University of Chicago Press.

Elliott, Deni. 1989. "Tales from the Darkside: Ethical Implications of Disaster Coverage." In *Bad Tidings: Communication and Catastrophe*, ed. Lynne M. Walters, Lee Wilkins, and Tim Walters, 161–70. Hillsdale, NJ: Erlbaum.

Elliott, Stuart. 2001. "The Media Business: Advertising; Hucksters or Patriots? You Be the Judge. It's Again Time for 20 Questions on Madison Avenue." *New York Times*, November 26, C12.

———. 2002. "The Media Business: Advertising; to Avoid Looking Exploitive, a Great Many Big Marketers Will Not Run Advertising Tomorrow." *New York Times*, September 10, C8.

Elshtain, Jean Bethke. 2003. *Just War against Terror: The Burden of American Power in a Violent World*. New York: Basic Books.

Entman, Robert M. 1993. "Framing: Towards Clarification of a Fractured Paradigm." *Journal of Communication* 43:51–58.

Fahim, Kareem. 2005. "Firefighters Reach Accord with the City." *New York Times*, October 28, B1.

Farmer, John. 2005. "Saving Our Lives and Protecting Their Turf." *New York Times* May 15, sec. 4, p. 15.

Fessenden, Ford. 2002. "9/11; after the World Gave: Where $2 Billion in Kindness Ended Up." *New York Times*, November 18, F6.

Fine, Gary Alan. 1999. "John Brown's Body: Elites, Heroic Embodiment, and the Legitimation of Political Violence." *Social Problems* 46, no. 2:225–49.

———. 2005. "The Chaining of Social Problems: Solutions and Unintended Consequences in the Age of Betrayal." Presidential address, Annual meeting of the Society for the Study of Social Problems, August 13, Philadelphia.

Fine, Gary Alan, and Ryan D. White. 2002. "Creating Collective Attention in the Public Domain: Human Interest Narratives and the Rescue of Floyd Collins." *Social Forces* 81, no. 1:57–85.

Fischer, Henry W. 1998. *Response to Disaster: Fact versus Fiction & Its Perpetuation: The Sociology of Disaster*, 2nd ed. Lanham, MD: University Press of America.

Flynn, Kevin. 2001. "2 More Firefighters Arrested in Dispute on Search for Bodies." *New York Times*, November 6, D3.

———. 2002a. "Ground Zero: A Memorial; Firefighters Block a Plan for Statue in Brooklyn." *New York Times*, January 18, B4.

———. 2002b. "Thousands Will Honor Fire Department's Dead." *New York Times*, October 9, B3.

———. 2002c. "U.S. to Pay to Clean Trade Center Fire Trucks." *New York Times*, May 21, B3.

Flynn, Kevin, and Jim Dwyer. 2002. "9/11 in Firefighters' Words: Surreal Chaos and Hazy Heroics." *New York Times*, January 31, B1.

Fox, Richard L., Robert W. Van Sickel, and Thomas L. Steiger. 2007. *Tabloid Justice: Criminal Justice in an Age of Media Frenzy*. 2nd ed. Boulder, CO: Lynne Rienner.

Gamson, Joshua. 1994. *Claims to Fame: Celebrity in Contemporary America*. Berkeley: University of California Press.

Gamson, William A. 1992. *Talking Politics*. Cambridge: Cambridge University Press.

Gamson, William A., David Croteau, William Hoynes, and Theodore Sasson. 1992. "Media Images and the Social Construction of Reality." *Annual Review of Sociology* 18:373–93.

Gamson, William A., and Andre Modigliani. 1987. "The Changing Culture of Affirmative Action." In *Research in Political Sociology*, ed. Richard G. Braungart and Margaret M. Braungart, 137–77. Greenwich, CT: JAI Press.

———. 1989. "Media Discourse and Public Opinion." *American Journal of Sociology* 95:1–37.

Gans, Herbert J. 1979. *Deciding What's News: A Study of* CBS Evening News, NBC Nightly News, Newsweek, *and* Time. New York: Vintage Books.

(GAO) U.S. Government Accountability Office. 2002. September 11: Interim Report on the Response of Charities (September). Available at http:// www.gao.gov /new.items/ d021037.pdf.

Gitlin, Todd. 1980. *The Whole World Is Watching: Mass Media in the Making and Unmaking of the New Left*. Berkeley: University of California Press.

Goffman, Erving. 1959. *The Presentation of Self in Everyday Life*. Garden City, NY: Doubleday.

———. 1969. *Strategic Interaction*. Philadelphia: University of Pennsylvania Press.

Grabe, Maria E., Shuhua Zhou, Annie Lang, and Paul D. Bolls. 2000. "Packaging Television News: The Effects of Tabloid on Information Processing and Evaluative Responses." *Journal of Broadcasting and Electronic Media* 44, no. 4:581–98.

Graham, Renee. 2004. "Verdict Is In on Peterson Media Circus." *Boston Globe*, December 14, B7.

Greenberg, Bradley S., ed. 2002. *Communication and Terrorism: Public and Media Responses to 9/11*. Cresskill, NJ: Hampton Press.

Greenberg, Bradley S., Linda Hofschire, and Ken Lachlan. 2002. "Diffusion, Media Use and Interpersonal Communication Behaviors." In *Communication and Terrorism: Public and Media Responses to 9/11*, ed. Bradley S. Greenberg, 3–16. Cresskill, NJ: Hampton Press.

Greenhouse, Steven. 2001. "A Nation Challenged: Compensation; Survivors See Inequity in Aid to Families of Guards Who Died." *New York Times*, December 16, 1B, 7.

———. 2002. "Firefighters' Union Accepts Nearly Same Deal as Police." *New York Times*, November 14, B4.

Grusin, Elinor Kelley, and Sandra H. Utt, eds. 2005. *Media in an American Crisis: Studies of September 11, 2001*. Lanham, MD: University Press of America.

Gusfield, Joseph. 1981. *The Culture of Public Problems: Drinking-Driving and the Symbolic Order*. Chicago: University of Chicago Press.

————. 1986. *Symbolic Crusade: Status Politics and the American Temperance Movement.* Urbana: University of Illinois Press.

————. 1996. *Contested Meanings: The Construction of Alcohol Problems.* Madison: University of Wisconsin Press.

Halberstam, David. 2002. *Firehouse.* New York: Hyperion.

Halbfinger, David M. 2001. "Charges That a Schundler Ad Exploits the Heroism of Rescuers." *New York Times,* October 2, D5.

Hamilton, James T. 2004. *All the News That's Fit to Sell: How the Market Transforms Information into News.* Princeton, NJ: Princeton University Press.

Hampson, Rick. 2007. "Is 9/11 Becoming Just Another Calendar Date?" *USA Today,* September 9.

Hannigan, John. 1995. *Environmental Sociology.* New York: Routledge.

Harper, Jennifer. 2001. "Terror Coverage Feeds Nationalism." *Washington Times,* September 13, 17.

Harris, Aimee. 2007. "Mayor Calls Detective Hero but Adds to the Confusion." *New York Times,* November 6, B1.

Hayt, Elizabeth. 2002. "Pulse; Designed to Leave You Wanting More." *New York Times,* June 30, sec. 9, p. 3.

HBO. 2002. "In Memoriam: New York City, 9/11/01." *Home Box Office Films.*

Herszenhorn, David M. 2002a. "Metro Briefing New York: Manhattan: Fire Dept. Sets New Rules on Recovery." *New York Times,* January 2, B8.

————. 2002b. "No More Mr. Mean." *New York Times,* February 27, B4.

Hester, Joe B. 2005. "NYTimes' Coverage Before, During, and After 9/11." In *Media in an American Crisis: Studies of September 11, 2001,* ed. Elinor Kelley Grusin and Sandra H. Utt, 40–47. Lanham, MD: University Press of America.

Heyer, Paul. 1995. *Titanic Legacy: Disaster as Media Event and Myth.* Westport, CT: Praeger.

Hilgartner, Stephen, and Charles Bosk. 1988. "The Rise and Fall of Social Problems: A Public Arenas Model." *American Journal of Sociology* 94:53–78.

Hoffner, Cynthia, Yuki Fujioka, Amal Ibrahim, and Jiali Ye. 2002. "Emotion and Coping with Terror." In *Communication and Terrorism: Public and Media Responses to 9/11,* ed. Bradley S. Greenberg, 229–44. Creskill, NJ: Hampton Press.

Horton, Donald, and R. Richard Wohl. 1956. "Mass Communication and Para-social Interaction: Observations on Intimacy at a Distance." *Psychiatry* 19:215–29.

Iyengar, Shanto. 1991. *Is Anyone Responsible? How Television Frames Political Issues.* Chicago: University of Chicago Press.

Jacobs, Ronald N. 1996. "Producing the News, Producing the Crisis: Narrativity, Television, and News Work." *Media, Culture & Society* 18:373–97.

————. 2000. *Race, Media and the Crisis of Civil Society.* Cambridge: Cambridge University Press.

James, Caryn. 2002a. "Critic's Notebook; Television's Special Day of Pain and Comfort." *New York Times,* September 6, E1.

————. 2002b. "Critic's Notebook; TV Searches for Distinction as Sept. 11 Programs Begin." *New York Times,* September 3, E1.

Jasper, James M. 1997. *The Art of Moral Protest: Culture, Biography, and Creativity in Social Movements.* Chicago: University of Chicago Press.

Jasper, James M., and Jane D. Poulsen. 1995. "Recruiting Strangers and Friends: Moral Shocks and Social Networks in Animal Rights and Anti-Nuclear Protests." *Social Problems* 42:493–512.

Jenkins, Henry. 2006. *Convergence Culture: Where Old and New Media Collide.* New York: New York University Press.

Jenkins, Philip. 1989. "Clergy Sex Abuse: The Symbolic Politics of a Social Problem." In *Images of Issues: Typifying Contemporary Social Problems,* ed. Joel Best, 105–30. New York: Aldine de Gruyter.

Johnson, Glen. 2008. "Uh, Oh . . . October Surprise! Last-Minute Scandals, News Events Have the Potential to Reshape U.S. Presidential Race." *Toronto Star,* October 3, AA2.

Jones, Jamie L. 2001. "Three Newsweeklies Putting Out Special Issues." *Media Life Magazine,* September 13. Available at http://www.medialifemagazine.com/ news2001/sep01/ sep10/4_thurs/news3thursday.html.

Jones, Steve, and Lee Rainie. 2002. "Internet Use and the Terror Attacks." In *Communication and Terrorism: Public and Media Responses to 9/11,* ed. Bradley S. Greenberg, 27–37. Cresskill, NJ: Hampton Press.

Kadushin, Charles. 1974. *The American Intellectual Elite.* Boston: Little, Brown.

Kahn, Jennifer. 2008. "A Cloud of Smoke: The Complicated Death of a 9/11 Hero." *New Yorker,* September 15, 44.

Kaminski, Robert, and Eric Jefferis. 1998. "The Effect of a Violent Televised Arrest on Public Perceptions of the Police." *Policing* 21:683–706.

Kane, John. 2001. *The Politics of Moral Capital.* Cambridge: Cambridge University Press.

Kanihan, Stacey Frank, and Kendra L. Gale. 2005. "Within 3 Hours, 97 Percent Learn about 9/11 Attacks." In *Media in an American Crisis: Studies of September 11, 2001,* ed. Elinor Kelley Grusin and Sandra H. Utt, 207–18. Lanham, MD: University Press of America.

Katz, Elihu, and Paul Lazarsfeld. 1955. *Personal Influence.* Glencoe, IL: Free Press.

Kellner, Douglas. 2003. *From 9/11 to Terror War: The Dangers of the Bush Legacy.* Lanham, MD: Rowman & Littlefield.

Kirkpatrick, David D., and Stuart Elliott. 2001. "Media Trying, with Dignity, to Stem Huge Losses in Advertising." *New York Times,* September 17, C2.

Klapp, Orrin E. 1964. *Symbolic Leaders: Public Dramas and Public Men.* Chicago: Aldine de Gruyter.

Kleinfield, N. R. 2001. "A Nation Challenged: The Ladder Company in Stopping to Save Woman, Rescuers Saved Themselves." *New York Times,* September 28, B1.

Klinenberg, Eric. 2002. *Heat Wave: A Social Autopsy of Disaster in Chicago.* Chicago: University of Chicago Press.

Kovler, Jessica. 2001. "Top of the List for Santa: Toys of Heroism and Rescue." *New York Times,* December 9, sec. 14WC, p. 7.

Kuczynski, Alex. 2001. "Gossip Holds Its Tongue." *New York Times,* September 23, sec. 9, p. 1.

Lambert, Bruce. 2002. "Hurt in Ground Zero Work, Firefighter Runs for Congress." *New York Times,* June 21, B1.

Lambeth, Edmund B. 1978. "Perceived Impact of the Press on Energy Policy Making." *Journalism Quarterly* 55:11–18, 72.

Lang, Gladys Engel, and Kurt Lang. 1986. "Some Observations of Long-Range Effects of Television." In *Media, Audience, and Social Structure*, ed. Sandra J. Ball-Rokeach and Muriel G. Cantor, 271–79. Beverly Hills, CA: Sage.

Langewiesche, William. 2002. *American Ground: Unbuilding the World Trade Center*. New York: North Point Press.

Lauro, Patricia Winters. 2002. "The Media Business: Advertising; New York Police and Firefighter Merchandise Tests the Market at the 2002 Licensing Exposition." *New York Times*, June 10, C11.

LeDuff, Charlie. 2001. "A Nation Challenged: Squad 1; amid Grief for Buddies, Unit Mourns Its Own End." *New York Times*, September 25, B11.

———. 2002a. "Last Steel Column from the Ground Zero Rubble Is Cut Down." *New York Times*, May 29, B3.

———. 2002b. "Still Digging for Lost Sons after a Million Tons of Pain." *New York Times*, January 8, A1.

LeDuff, Charlie, and Steven Greenhouse. 2002. "Far from Business as Usual: A Quick Job at Ground Zero." *New York Times*, January 21, A1.

Lee, Matthew T., and M. David Ermann. 1999. "Pinto 'Madness' as a Flawed Landmark Narrative: An Organizational and Network Analysis." *Social Problems* 46, no. 1:30–47.

Lester, Marilyn. 1980. "Generating Newsworthiness: The Interpretive Construction of Public Events." *American Sociological Review* 45:984–94.

Lew, Julie. 2001. "Comics Turning Tragedy into Tribute." *New York Times*, December 29, A28.

Li, Xigen, and Ralph Izard. 2005. "9/11 TV, Newspapers Coverage Reveals Similarities, Differences." In *Media in an American Crisis: Studies of September 11, 2001*, ed. Elinor Kelley Grusin and Sandra H. Utt, 89–103. Lanham, MD: University Press of America.

Liebes, Tamar, and Elihu Katz. 1990. *The Export of Meaning: Cross-Cultural Readings of Dallas*. New York: Oxford University Press.

Lipton, Eric. 2002a. "At Ground Zero, New Manager, New Machines, New Focus." *New York Times*, January 3, B1.

———. 2002b. "Widows Seek Wider Inquiry into Trade Center Collapse." *New York Times*, March 4, B3.

———. 2004. "New York Settles on a Number That Defines Tragedy: 2,749 Dead in Trade Center Attack." *New York Times*, January 23, B7.

Lipton, Eric, and James Glanz. 2002a. "Ground Zero: Firefighting; 9/11 Inspires Call to Review Response Plan for Crises." *New York Times*, January 23, B4.

———. 2002b. "A Nation Challenged: The Site; in the Pit, Dark Relics and Last Obstacles." *New York Times*, January 13, A1.

Lofland, John, and Michael Fink. 1982. *Symbolic Sit-ins: Protest Occupations at the California Capitol*. Washington, DC: University Press of America.

Lowney, Kathleen S., and Joel Best. 1995. "Stalking Strangers and Lovers: Changing Media Typifications of a New Crime Problem." In *Images of Issues: Typifying Contemporary Social Problems*, ed. Joel Best, 33–57. New York: Aldine de Gruyter.

Lull, James, and Stephen Hinerman. 1997. "The Search for Scandal." In *Media Scandals: Morality and Desire in the Popular Culture Marketplace*, ed. James Lull and Stephen Hinerman, 1–33. New York: Columbia University Press.

MacKuen, Michael B., and Steven L. Coombs. 1981. *More Than News: Media Power in Public Affairs*. Beverly Hills, CA: Sage.

Martin, Patrick, and Sean Phelan. 2003. "History and September 11: A Comparison of Online and Network TV Discourses." In *Crisis Communications: Lessons from September 11*, ed. A. Michael Noll, 167–84. Oxford: Rowman & Littlefield.

Mayer, Jeremy D. 2006. *9-11: Aftershocks of the Attack*. Belmont, CA: Thomson Wadsworth.

McCombs, Maxwell E., and Donald L. Shaw. 1972. "The Agenda-Setting Functions of the Mass Media." *Public Opinion Quarterly* 36:176–87.

McFadden, Robert D. 2001. "After the Attacks: The President; Bush Leads Prayer, Visits Aid Crews; Congress Backs Use of Armed Force." *New York Times*, September 15, A1.

McKinley, James C. Jr. 2002. "Pataki Vows to Limit Spending and to Avoid Delaying Tax Cuts." *New York Times*, January 10, A1.

Media Bistro. 2008. "Nancy Grace's Best Ratings Ever." Mediabistro.com (December 12). Available at http://www.mediabistro.com/tvnewser/cnn/nancy_graces_best _ratings_ ever_103301.asp.

Miller, Gale, and James A. Holstein. 1989. "On the Sociology of Social Problems." In *Perspectives on Social Problems*, ed. James A. Holstein and Gale Miller, 1–18. Greenwich, CT: JAI Press.

(MLM) *Media Life Magazine*. 2001. "New Media Shorts: CNN.com Ranks as Top News Site in Crisis." Available at http://www.medialifemagazine.com/ news2001/ sep01/ sep17/4_thurs/news8thursday.html.

Mogenson, Kirsten, Laura Lindsay, Xigen Li, Jay Perkins, and Mike Beardsley. 2002. "How TV News Covered the Crisis: The Content of CNN, CBS, ABC, NBC, and Fox." In *Communication and Terrorism: Public and Media Responses to 9/11*, ed. Bradley S. Greenberg, 101–20. Cresskill, NJ: Hampton Press.

Molotch, Harvey, and Marilyn Lester. 1974. "News as Purposive Behavior: On the Strategic Use of Routine Events, Accidents, and Scandals." *American Sociological Review* 39:101–12.

———. 1975. "Accidental News: The Great Oil Spill as Local Occurrence and National Event." *American Journal of Sociology* 81:235–60.

Monaco, James. 1978. *Celebrity*. New York: Delta.

Moore, Martha T. 2007. "Giuliani's Role in '01 Gives Him Slight Edge." *USA Today*, September 11, 2A.

MSNBC.com. 2008. "9/11: 7 Years Later; Where Are They Now?" Available at http://www. msnbc.msn.com/id/26562000/.

Mukerji, Chandra, and Michael Schudson. 1986. "Popular Culture." *Annual Review of Sociology* 12:47–66.

Nagourney, Adam. 2002a. "Bush, in New York, Affirms $20 Billion Aid Pledge." *New York Times*, February 7, A1.

———. 2002b. "The Postpartisan Governor; Defying a Democratic Tide, Pataki Seeks a Third Term." *New York Times*, April 3, B1.

Nelson-Rowe, Shan. 1995. "The Moral Drama of Multicultural Education." In *Images of Issues: Typifying Contemporary Social Problems*, 2nd ed., ed. Joel Best, 81–99. New York: Aldine de Gruyter.

Nemy, Enid. 2002. "Metropolitan Diary." *New York Times*, January 28, B2.

New York Times. 2001a. "The Mayor's Remarks: 'You're All My Heroes.'" *New York Times,* September 17, A7.

———. 2001b. "Mourning Their Loss." *New York Times,* November 5, A16.

———. 2001c. "A Nation Challenged: Excerpts from President's Speech: 'We Will Prevail' in War on Terrorism." *New York Times,* November 9, B6.

———. 2001d. "One Month Later: The Ways of Remembering." *New York Times,* October 11, A24.

———. 2001e. "Portraits of Grief: A Firefighter with Credits, a Man with Wanderlust and a Barbie Doll Collector." *New York Times,* December 8, B8.

———. 2001f. "Portraits of Grief: A Love Story, a Letter from a Firefighter, a Proud Moment in Church." *New York Times,* November 29, B10.

———. 2001g. "Portraits of Grief: Still Alive in the Hearts of Those Who Loved Them." *New York Times,* September 17, A10.

———. 2001h. "Portraits of Grief: The Twin Tower, the Full Life, the Policeman Who Spoke Swedish." *New York Times,* October 30, B11.

———. 2001i. "Stickers for 'My Daddy.'" *New York Times,* October 25, A20.

———. 2002. *Portraits: 9/11/01: The Collected "Portraits of Grief" from the* New York Times. New York: Henry Holt / Times Books.

Nichols, Lawrence T. 1997. "Social Problems as Landmark Narratives: Bank of Boston, Mass Media and 'Money Laundering.'" *Social Problems* 44, no. 3:324–41.

———. 2003. "Rethinking Constructionist Agency: Claimsmakers as Conditions, Audiences, Types and Symbols." *Studies in Symbolic Interaction* 26:125–45.

Niebuhr, Gustav. 2001. "After the Attacks: A Day of Worship; Excerpts from Sermons across the Nation." *New York Times,* September 17, A8.

Nimmo, Dan. 1984. "TV Network News Coverage of Three Mile Island: Reporting Disasters as Technological Fables." *International Journal of Mass Emergencies and Disasters* 2:115–45.

Noll, A. Michael, ed. 2003. *Crisis Communications: Lessons from September 11.* Oxford: Rowman & Littlefield.

O'Donnell, Michelle. 2001. "Shadows across the City; Just Regular Guys in the Urban Wild, until the Bell Rings." *New York Times,* September 23, sec. 14, p. 4.

———. 2005a. "Fire Chief Who Assailed Mayor's Policy Is Set to Testify." *New York Times,* May 9, B1.

———. 2005b. "New Terror Plan Angers Fire Dept." *New York Times,* April 22, A1.

Olick, Jeffrey K. 1999. "Collective Memory: The Two Cultures." *Sociological Theory* 17, no. 3:333–48.

Olick, Jeffrey K., and Joyce Robbins. 1998. "Social Memory Studies: From 'Collective Memory' to the Historical Sociology of Mnemonic Practices." *Annual Review of Sociology* 24:105–40.

Oliver, Pamela E., and Daniel J. Myers. 1999. "How Events Enter the Public Sphere: Conflict, Location, and Sponsorship in Local Newspaper Coverage of Public Events." *American Journal of Sociology* 105, no. 1:38–87.

Orth, Maureen. 2004. *The Importance of Being Famous: Behind the Scenes of the Celebrity-Industrial Complex.* New York: Henry Holt.

Patterson, Philip. 1989. "Reporting Chernobyl: Cutting the Government Fog to Cover the Nuclear Cloud." In *Bad Tidings: Communication and Catastrophe,* ed. Lynne M. Walters, Lee Wilkins, and Tim Walters, 131–47. Hillsdale, NJ: Erlbaum.

(PEJ) Project for Excellence in Journalism. 2004. "State of the News Media 2004: An Annual Report on American Journalism." Available at http://www. stateofthenewsmedia. org/2004/index.asp.

———. 2005. "State of the News Media 2005: An Annual Report on American Journalism." Available at http://www.stateofthenewsmedia.org/2005/index.asp.

———. 2007. "State of the News Media 2007: An Annual Report on American Journalism." Available at http://www.stateofthenewsmedia.org/2007.

———. 2009. "State of the News Media 2009: An Annual Report on American Journalism." Available at http://www.stateofthenewsmedia.org/2009/index.htm.

Peltu, Malcolm. 1985. "The Role of Communications Media." In *Regulating Industrial Risks: Science, Hazards, and Public Protection*, ed. Harry Otway and Malcolm Peltu, 128–48. London: Butterworth.

Pérez-Peña, Richard. 2002. "Pataki's Tours for 9/11 Silence Usual Critics; Political Thrust and Parry Is Hard." *New York Times*, September 7, B1.

Perse, Elizabeth, Nancy Signorielli, John Courtright, Wendy Samter, Scott Caplan, Jennifer Lambe, and Xiaomei Cai. 2002. "Public Perceptions of Media Functions at the Beginning of the War on Terrorism." In *Communication and Terrorism: Public and Media Responses to 9/11*, ed. Bradley S. Greenberg, 39–52. Cresskill, NJ: Hampton Press.

PEW Research Center for the People & the Press. 2001a. "Terror Coverage Boost News Media's Images: But Military Censorship Backed" (November 28). Available at http://people-press.org/reports/display.php3? ReportID=143.

———. 2001b. "Terrorism Transforms News Interest: Worries over New Attacks Decline" (December 18). Available at http://people-press.org/reports/display.php3?ReportID=146.

———. 2004. "Cable and Internet Loom Large in Fragmented Political News Universe: Perceptions of Partisan Bias Seen as Growing, Especially by Democrats" (January 11). Available at http://people-press.org/reports/ display.php3?ReportID=200.

Poindexter, Paula M., and Mike Conway. 2005. "Local, Network TV News Shows Significant Gains." In *Media in an American Crisis: Studies of September 11, 2001*, ed. Elinor Kelley Grusin and Sandra H. Utt, 175–86. Lanham, MD: University Press of America.

Polletta, Francesca. 1998. "'It Was Like a Fever . . .' Narrative and Identity in Social Protest." *Social Problems* 45, no. 2:137–59.

Postman, Neil. 1985. *Entertaining Ourselves to Death*. New York: Viking.

Raines, Howell. 2002. Foreword to *Portraits: 9/11/01: The Collected "Portraits of Grief" from the* New York Times. New York: Henry Holt / Times Books.

Rainie, Lee, and Bente Kalsnes. 2002. "The Commons of the Tragedy." Pew Internet and American Life Project, October 10. Available at http://wwwpew internet.org.

Randle, Quint, Lucinda D. Davenport, and Howard Bossen. 2005. "Newspapers Slow to Use Web Sites for 9/11 Coverage." In *Media in an American Crisis: Studies of September 11, 2001*, ed. Elinor Kelley Grusin and Sandra H. Utt, 49–60. Lanham, MD: University Press of America.

Rappoport, Paul N., and James Alleman. 2003. "The Internet and the Demand for News: Macro- and Microevidence." In *Crisis Communications: Lessons from September 11*, ed. A. Michael Noll, 149–66. Oxford: Rowman & Littlefield.

Reynolds, Amy, and Brooke Barnett. 2003. "'America under Attack': CNN's Verbal & Visual Framing of September 11." In *Media Representations of September 11*, ed. Steven Chermak, Frankie Y. Bailey, and Michelle Brown, 85–101. Westport, CT: Praeger.

Rich, Frank. 2002. "Sacrifice Is for Losers." *New York Times*, June 22, A11.

Roberts, Donald F., and Christine M. Bachen. 1981. "Mass Communication Effects." *Annual Review of Psychology* 32:307–56.

Rogers, Everett M. 2003. "Diffusion of News of the Sept 11 Terrorist Attacks." In *Crisis Communications: Lessons from September 11*, ed. A. Michael Noll, 17–30. Oxford: Rowman & Littlefield.

Rogers, Everett M., and Nancy Seidel. 2002. "Diffusion of News of the Terrorist Attacks of September 11, 2001." *Prometheus* 20:209–19.

Ruggiero, Tom, and Jack Glascock. 2002. "Tracking Media Use and Gratifications." In *Communication and Terrorism: Public and Media Responses to 9/11*, ed. Bradley S. Greenberg, 65–74. Cresskill, NJ: Hampton Press.

Ryan, Desmond. 2002. "Opinion; This Just In: More Election Results." *New York Times*, December 1, 14, 19.

Scanlon, Joseph. 1989. "The Hostage Taker, the Terrorist, the Media: Partners in Public Crime." In *Bad Tidings: Communication and Catastrophe*, ed. Lynne M. Walters, Lee Wilkins, and Tim Walters, 115–30. Hillsdale, NJ: Erlbaum.

Scheufele, Dietram, A. 1999. "Framing as a Theory of Media Effects." *Journal of Communication* 49, no. 1:103–22.

Schudson, Michael. 1986. "The Menu of Media Research." In *Media, Audience, and Social Structure*, ed. Sandra J. Ball-Rokeach and Muriel G. Cantor, 43–48. Beverly Hills, CA: Sage.

———. 1992. *Watergate in American Memory: How We Remember, Forget, and Reconstruct the Past*. New York: Basic Books.

Scott, Janny. 1998. "The President under Fire: The Media; a Media Race Enters Waters Still Uncharted." *New York Times*, February 1, sec. 1, p. 1.

Seeger, Matthew, Steven Vennette, Robert Ulmer, and Timothy Sellnow. 2002. "Media Use, Information Seeking, and Reported Needs in Post Crisis Contexts." In *Communication and Terrorism: Public and Media Responses to 9/11*, ed. Bradley S. Greenberg, 53–63. Cresskill, NJ: Hampton Press.

Shils, Edward. 1965. "Charisma, Order, and Status." *American Sociological Review* 30, no. 2:199–213.

Shoemaker, Pamela J., and Stephen D. Reese. 1991. *Mediating the Message: Theories of Influences on Mass Media Content*. New York: Longman.

Sigal, Leon V. 1973. *Reporters and Officials*. Lexington, MA: Heath.

Sigelman, Lee, Susan Welch, Timothy Bledsoe, and Michael Combs. 1997. "Police Brutality and Public Perceptions of Racial Discrimination." *Political Research Quarterly* 50:777–91.

Simpson, David. 2006. *9/11: The Culture of Commemoration*. Chicago: University of Chicago Press.

Smelser, Neil J. 2004. "September 11, 2001, as Cultural Trauma." In *Cultural Trauma and Collective Identity*, ed. Jeffrey Alexander, Ron Eyerman, Bernhard Giesen, Neil Smelser, and Piotr Sztompka, 264–82. Berkeley: University of California Press.

Smith, Dennis. 2002. *Report from Ground Zero*. New York: Viking.

———. 2004. Testimony to the U.S. Commission on Terrorism, May 19.

Snow, David, and Robert Benford. 1992. "Master Frames and Cycles of Protest." In *Frontiers in Social Movement Theory*, ed. Carol McClung Mueller and Aldon D. Morris, 133–55. New Haven, CT: Yale University Press.

Snyder, David, and William R. Kelly. 1977. "Conflict Intensity, Media Sensitivity, and the Validity of Newspaper Data." *American Sociological Review* 42:105–23.

Stallings, Robert A. 1990. "Media Discourse and the Social Construction of Risk." *Social Problems* 37, no. 1:80–94.

Steinhauer, Jennifer. 2001. "A Nation Challenged: The Mayor; Blunt Words to Describe Grim Reality at the Site." *New York Times*, November 3, B10.

———. 2002. "If Needed, City Is Ready to Cut Budget Further." *New York Times*, April 13, B1.

Stempel, Guido H. III, and Thomas Hargrove. 2002. "Media Sources of Information and Attitudes about Terrorism." In *Communication and Terrorism: Public and Media Responses to 9/11*, ed. Bradley S. Greenberg, 17–26. Cresskill, NJ: Hampton Press.

———. 2003. "Newspapers Played Major Role in Terrorism Coverage." *Newspaper Research Journal* 24:55–57.

Stempel, Guido H. III, Thomas Hargrove, and Joseph P. Bernt. 2000. "Relation of Growth of Use of the Internet to Changes in Media Use from 1995 to 1999." *Journalism and Mass Communication Quarterly* 77, no. 1:71–79.

Strom, Stephanie. 2002. "Ground Zero: Charity; a Flood of Money, Then a Deluge of Scrutiny for Those Handing It Out." *New York Times*, September 11, B5.

Swidler, Ann. 1986. "Culture in Action: Symbols and Strategies." *American Sociological Review* 51:273–86.

Thomas. W. I. 1923. *The Unadjusted Girl*. Boston: Little, Brown.

Thye, Shane R. 2000. "A Status Value Theory of Power in Exchange Relations." *American Sociological Review* 65:407–32.

Tierney, Kathleen. 1994. "Making Sense of Collective Preoccupations: Lessons from Research on the Iben Browning Earthquake Prediction." In *Self, Collective Behavior and Society: Essays Honoring the Contributions of Ralph H. Turner*, ed. Gerald Platt and Chad Gordon, 75–95. Greenwich, CT: JAI Press.

Tierney, Kathleen, Christine Bevc, and Erica Kuligowski. 2006. "Metaphors Matter: Disaster Myths, Media Frames, and Their Consequences in Hurricane Katrina." *Annals of the American Academy of Political and Social Science* 604, no. 1:57–81.

Tuch, Steven, and Ronald Weitzer. 1997. "Racial Differences in Attitudes toward the Police." *Public Opinion Quarterly* 61:642–63.

Tuchman, Gaye. 1972. "Objectivity as Strategic Ritual: An Examination of Newsmen's Notions of Objectivity." *American Journal of Sociology* 77, no. 4:660–79.

———. 1978. *Making News: A Study in the Construction of Reality*. New York: Free Press.

Turner, Ralph, and Lewis Killian. 1987. *Collective Behavior*. Englewood Cliffs, NJ: Prentice-Hall.

Van Ginneken, Jaap. 2003. *Collective Behavior and Public Opinion: Rapid Shifts in Opinion and Communication*. Hillsdale, NJ: Erlbaum.

Vengerfeldt, Pille. 2003. "The Internet as a News Medium for the Crisis News of Terrorist Attacks in the United States." In *Crisis Communications: Lessons from September 11*, ed. A. Michael Noll, 133–48. Oxford: Rowman & Littlefield.

Verhovek, Sam Howe. 2001. "Sept. 11 Casts a Shadow on S Tax-Curb Referendum." *New York Times*, November 3, A8.

Von Essen, Thomas, with Matt Murray. 2002. *Strong of Heart: Life and Death in the Fire Department of New York*. New York: HarperCollins.

Wakin, Daniel J. 2002. "Killed on 9/11, Fire Chaplain Becomes Larger Than Life." *New York Times*, September 27, A1.

Weitzer, Ronald. 2002. "Incidents of Police Misconduct and Public Opinion." *Journal of Criminal Justice* 30:397–408.

Weitzer, Ronald, and Steven A. Tuch. 2004. "Race and Perceptions of Police Misconduct." *Social Problems* 51, no. 3:305–25.

Welch, Michael. 2006. *Scapegoats of September 11: Hate Crimes and State Crimes in the War on Terror*. New Brunswick, NJ: Rutgers University Press.

White, Elizabeth. 2001. "CNN Whups Butt in Cable News Race." *Media Life Magazine*, September 21. Available at http://www.medialifemagazine.com/news2001/ sep01/ sep17/4_thurs/news1thursday.html.

White House press release. 2002. "President Bush Delivers Commencement Address at Ohio State University" (June 14). Available at http://georgewbushwhitehouse. archives. gov/news/releases/2002/06/20020614-1.html.

White House press release. 2008a. "President Bush Discusses Protect America Act" (February 13). Available at http://georgewbush-whitehouse.archives.gov/news/ releases/2008/02/20080213.html.

———. 2008b. "Vice President's Remarks to the Heritage Foundation" (January 23). Available at http://georgewbushwhitehouse.archives.gov/news/releases/2008/01/20080123-2. html.

Wyatt, Edward. 2001. "Officials Irked as Merchants Cash in on City's Heroic Logos." *New York Times*, December 14, D1.

Zald, Mayer N. 1996. "Culture, Ideology, and Strategic Framing." In *Comparative Perspectives on Social Movements: Political Opportunities, Mobilizing Structures, and Cultural Framings*, ed. Doug McAdam, John D. McCarthy, and Mayer N. Zald, 261–74. Cambridge: Cambridge University Press.

Zelizer, Barbie. 1992. *Covering the Body: The Kennedy Assassination, the Media, and the Shaping of Collective Memory*. Chicago: University of Chicago Press.

Zinser, Lynn. 2002. "Auto Racing; Earnhardt in New York, Causes S Rock-Star Stir." *New York Times*, August 9, D2.

Index

ABC television network, 55
agenda-setting, 19, 184n1, 184n2
Al-Qaeda, 135
"America: A Tribute to Heroes" telethon, 145
American Airlines Flight 11, 95
American victimization, 64, 191n17
analogizing September 11 attacks, 60–61, 78
"A Nation Challenged," 14, 64
Anthony, Caylee, 5, 29, 39–43, 188n1, 188n3;
    audience interest in, 41–42; on *Nancy
    Grace*, 40–42, 188n1, 188n6, 188n7; on
    NBC *Today*, 41, 188n4
audience consumption of September 11
    news, 11, 63–64, 131–132,184n10; Internet,
    190n4, 190n5; newspapers, 12, 63–64;
    television, 12–13, 59, 63, 70, 190n3

Beamer, Lisa, 175
Beckwith, Bob, 175
"Beltway Sniper" saga, 29, 189n15
Best, Joel, 187n27
Biden, Joe, 171, 200n1
Bin Laden, Osama, 135, 172, 175
Bloomberg, Michael, 158, 169, 175
Brokaw, Tom, 67, 77; career, 71; on Septem-
    ber 11, 89–90; *The Greatest Generation*, 71
Bush, George W., xvi, 142, 172–173, 175;
    address to the nation on September 11, 91;
    Booker Elementary School, 76–77, 83;
    State of the Union address, 161; symbi-
    otic lending, 160–161, 164; whereabouts
    on September 11, 83, 86

Cantor Fitzgerald, 126, 128, 200n3
carrying capacity, 188n8

CBS television network, 55; "9/11," 145
Challenger shuttle disaster, 59, 183n3
Chancer, Lynn, 177, 201n5
Cheney, Dick, 173
claims-makers, 187n30, 201n4
CNN, 188n2; CNN.com, 57, 190n5; Septem-
    ber 11 coverage, xiv, 65, 192n3
Columbine, 177–178
"Come Together" benefit concert, 145
"Concert for New York," 145
convergence culture, 189n10
Couric, Katie, 71
cultivating emotionality, 48–51, 121; in
    September 11 coverage, 117–18, 122–131;
    techniques, 50–51, 121

Daily Show, 173–174, 185n15
data, sources of, 9, 11–15, 70, 192n18, 193n5,
    199n1
dealing and healing frame, 64, 66–67
definition of the situation, 59, 190n7
diffusion of September 11 news, 57, 190n1,
    190n2
Disaster Research Center, xiii
dramatic amplification, 46, 96; in Sep-
    tember 11 coverage, 96–100, 102–105,
    107–109, 111–115; techniques, 47–48
Duke University lacrosse scandal, 6
Durkheim, Emile, 142
"dust man," 200n3

economic impact of attacks, 86
elements of public drama, 43–46; audience
    investment, 45–46; media attention,
    43–44; media treatment, 44–45

"missing person" fliers, 128
moral capital, 37, 200n10, 200n11
moral currency: appropriation, 164–167; cultural limits, 168; defined, 37–38, 141, 154, 168; leveraging, 154–159; structural limits, 167–168; symbiotic lending, 159–164
moral exemplars, 142, 154
moral shock, 58, 190n6, 190n7; historical examples, 59, 191n11, 191n12, 191n13; September 11 attacks as, 58
MSNBC, 70, 175, 192n2; MSNBC.com, 57, 184n9, 190n5, 192n2

Nancy Grace, 5, 40–42, 188n1, 188n2, 188n5, 188n6, 188n7
narrative simplification, 44–45, 188n9
National Football League, 145–146, 162–163, 199n25
NBC television network, 55, 70
NBC Dateline, 71, 91, 195n3
NBC Nightly News, 71; September 11, 89–90
NBC Today: as data source, 13, 15, 183n7, 184n8; history, 13, 71–72, 192n1; ratings, 16, 72; revenues, 72, 192n2
news: building blocks of, 4, 21; entertainment, 3; frames, 20–21; "franchises," 28–29; social construction of, 4, 22–23, 43; story form, 27–28
news functions: agenda-setting, 19, 184n1, 184n2; during crisis events, 17, 56, 58; framing, 20–21, 184n4
news holes, 24, 185n8; expansion of after September 11 attacks, 63
news industry: audience patterns, 25; competition in, 3; entertainment orientation, 3–4; fragmentation, 3; profit model, 3, 23–24, 176, 184n5, 184n6; shifts, xi, 18, 23–24, 176
news values, 3–4, 192n19
Newsweek, 6, 56; "Closure," 6
New York Daily News, 63
New York Mercantile Exchange, 166
New York Stock Exchange, 162

New York Times, 63, 195n3; "A Nation Challenged," 14, 63; as data source, 14–15; "Portraits of Grief," 118–121, 126, 194n1, 195n3

Obama, Barack, 174
Oklahoma City (Murrah Federal Building) bombing, 59, 78, 193n7

Palin, Sarah, 174
para-social interaction, 189n19
Pataki, George, 166, 200n7, 200n8
PBS NewsHour, 181
Pearl Harbor, 78, 196n6
Pentagon attacks, xv, 68, 77, 78, 87, 91, 95
Peterson, Laci, 5, 7, 29
Pew Research Center, 185n10, 185n15, 191n14
popular culture marketplace, 145
"Portraits of Grief," 118–121, 126, 194n1, 195n3
presidential campaigns and September 11: 2004 campaign, 172–173; 2008 campaign, 35, 171, 173–174, 200n1
Princess Diana, 7, 191n12
Project for Excellence in Journalism, 25, 27–28, 185n10, 189n14
Protect America Act, 173
public arenas, 187n30
public drama: building blocks of, 4, 6, 8; characters, 33–34, 45–46; defined xii, 4, 6, 18, 23, 182; drawbacks, 8–9; emergence, 18, 23; entertainment, 7–8, 30, 39; life cycle, 7–8; media logic, 10, 96; print media, 6; social influence, 9, 30–33; status rewards, 34–38; 186n22, 186n23, 187n24, 187n25, 187n26, 187n31; television, 5, 182

Ramsey, JonBenet, 7–8, 29
Red Cross, 151
responsibility and retaliation frame, 64–67, 191n15, 191n16
"Runaway Bride," 178, 201n7
Runnion, Erin, 187n28

Saturday Night Live, 145, 161, 185n15

About the Author

BRIAN A. MONAHAN is an assistant professor of sociology at Iowa State University.